Residential Design
for Aging in Place

Residential Design for Aging in Place

Drue Lawlor, FASID

Michael A. Thomas, FASID, CAPS

WILEY

John Wiley & Sons, Inc.

Copyright © 2008 by John Wiley & Sons. All rights reserved.

Published by John Wiley & Sons, Inc., Hoboken, New Jersey

Published simultaneously in Canada

Library of Congress Cataloging-in-Publication Data:

Lawlor, Drue.
  Residential design for aging in place / Drue Lawlor, Michael A. Thomas.
      p. cm.
  Includes bibliographical references.
  ISBN 978-0-470-05614-1 (cloth : alk. paper)
1. Barrier-free design for older people—United States.   2. Older people—Dwellings—United States.   I. Thomas, Michael A., 1953–   II. Title.
  NA2545.A3L37 2008
  720.84′6—dc22
                                                                    2008022813

Printed in the United States of America

10 9 8 7 6 5 4 3 2 1

Contents

Acknowledgments

Writing a book I have found to be like building a house. A man forms a plan and collects materials. He thinks he has enough to raise a large and stately edifice; but after he has arranged, compacted, and polished, his work turns out to be a very small performance. The author however, like the builder, knows how much labor his work has cost him; and therefore estimates it at a higher rate than other people think it deserves.

—James Boswell (1740–1795), Scottish author

I HAVE BEEN TRULY BLESSED IN MANY WAYS and by so many people. I dedicate this effort to those who have been so supportive in my professional practice and in my personal life. I am blessed through your friendship and devotion.

To Michael D. Baker, an individual who has provided unselfish support for more than three decades as friend, associate, and partner in my life and work endeavors.

To Ann Huff, ASID, CAPS, a great designer, wonderful employee, and close friend and design partner who I trust and value as family.

To the current and past members of my staff at the Design Collective Group who contributed their efforts to help me grow a responsible, professional design practice even though their fearless leader was yet on another trip to share his passion on aging in place in a workshop or traveling to another ASID meeting or event.

To Evelyn and Aaron Levy, Laura and Ron Larizza, Tina and Robert Kraft, Fraeda and Bill Kopman, and Veda and Len Decof, as cherished clients of my firm and patrons of my professional practice. I am indeed grateful to you for your support through the ages.

And to my mother, Ms. T., who always did it "her way" despite all her life challenges. In a sense, she is responsible for putting me on this "aging" path and awakening me to the challenges that lie ahead.

—MICHAEL A. THOMAS, FASID, CAPS

Total absence of humor renders life impossible.

—COLETTE CHANCE ACQUAINTANCES, French novelist (1873–1952)

I dedicate this work to my parents, Bill and Denise Lawlor, who always showed so much strength and humor in the face of adversity. They were the ones who first instilled in me the love of architecture and interiors, and who ultimately were responsible for the path that I have taken within design.

To my father, the inventor, who came up with so many creative ways of practicing universal design, before the term was ever introduced. To my mother, who so valiantly fought not to let physical challenges take over her life. And to their constant willingness to help others no matter the obstacles they themselves were facing.

I am truly blessed to be their daughter, and only hope that I can share a little of their wisdom and positive outlook on life.

—DRUE LAWLOR, FASID

The authors are indebted, grateful, and owe their combined thanks to:

The many peers, wonderful friends, and valuable alliances, assembled into a great tapestry of design, woven together as a result of our membership with and participation in the American Society of Interior Designers. Each of you has shared your knowledge, experience, vision, and expertise to collectively raise the waters for all the design community. Thank you.

John Wiley & Sons, who provided this unique opportunity in the first place so that we could tell one very important story and in our own way, make a difference in the lives of generations far down the road; John Czarnecki, Assoc. AIA, our Wiley editor, who pushed and pulled to get these words collected; and Raheli Millman, Wiley's editorial assistant, who helped us polish the manuscript.

Many thanks to the interior designers, architects, and homebuilders who shared their projects, pictures, and offered their "aged" wisdom and sage advice as the book evolved. Their projects show how far aging in place has come in a short time and where the passion will lead all of us as we all age in place.

The authors wish to acknowledge those design professionals and interior design firms whose photos of their design projects appear within these chapters. Their work showcases design expertise, experience and creativity that truly support the independency of their clients and end users.

Jeffrey Anderzhon, AIA
Omaha, Nebraska

Pat Gericke, Allied ASID
New York, NY

Carol Axford, ASID
Fayetteville, Georgia

Rita Goldstein, ASID
Marietta, Georgia

Lena Brion, ASID
Solana Beach, California

Anna Marie Hendry, Allied ASID
Peachtree City, Georgia

Lisa Brooks, Allied ASID
Cumming, Georgia

Ann Huff, ASID, CAPS
Jupiter, Florida

Margery Caruana Farr, Allied ASID
Atlanta, Georgia

Interiors Joan and Associates
Omaha, Nebraska

Susan Cozzi, Allied ASID
Boca Raton, Florida

Janet Kay, ASID
Richmond, Virginia

Design Collective Group, Inc.
Jupiter, Florida

Bonnie Kissel, Allied ASID
Fort Lee, New Jersey

Adrienne Gamba, ASID, IIDA
Tucson, Arizona

Lawrence-Mayer-Wilson Interiors
Brielle, New Jersey

Candace A. McNair, ASID
Marietta, Georgia

Keith Miller, ASID
Seattle, Washington

Susan Nilsson Interior Design
Asheville, North Carolina

Maria Nutt, Allied ASID
Marietta, Georgia

Jane Page Design Group
Houston, Texas

Holley B. Peck
Atlanta, Georgia

Bernice R. Phelps
Newnan, Georgia

Kathleen Pyrce, Allied ASID
Lawrenceville, Georgia

Jo Rabaut, ASID, IIDA
Atlanta, Georgia

Muriel Sackey, Allied ASID
Mableton, Georgia

Pamela Goldstein Sanchez,
  Allied ASID, CMKBD
Atlanta, Georgia

Shannon Schilling, Allied ASID
Roswell, Georgia

Sharon L. Sherman ASID, CKD
Wyckoff, New Jersey

Judith Sisler-Johnston, Allied ASID
Jacksonville, Florida

Abbie Sladick, CGR, CAPS
Naples, Florida

Janis B. Sundquist, ASID
Decatur, Georgia

Bernadette Upton, ASID, LEED
North Palm Beach, Florida

Andrea Vollf, Allied ASID
Schaumburg, Illinois

Patti Watson, Allied ASID
Jamestown, Rhode Island

Ann Wisniewski, ASID
Roswell, Georgia

Robert Wright, FASID
San Diego, California

To education-works, inc. for sharing products, resources, and information gathered over the years for inclusion in the appendices.

To Julie Warren who bravely met the challenge of working with first-time authors and enhanced our efforts despite everything else.

To Jennifer Wilcox and Michael Behrens, two individuals who helped to keep the knowledge, resources, and opportunities flowing in our direction. Thank you for your help over the many years.

Introduction: Growing Up and Getting Wiser

Beginning January 1, 2006, on average, a new 60 year old was celebrating a birthday every seven seconds, and these celebrations will continue for another 18 years. The impact of this demographic shift will affect every level of our social, economic, and political systems.

—White House Council on Aging, Executive Summary, 2005

AGING IN PLACE IS NOT "THAT" OLD

The concept of residential design for aging in place is simple: Create houses and homes that adapt to an elder population, segments of the society who are or will begin to endure the aging process. Pretty simple concept really but not any easy task when one considers that most typical American housing already has many sorts of physical obstacles that deter its occupants from freely moving about and remaining agile and mobile and that make it difficult for them to easily maneuver in and about the home. Add the natural effects of the aging process on the physical body, and the situation gets more complicated.

The evolution has begun to emerge in the headlines, in magazines, and on TV in much the same way as "green" or sustainable design. And at the writing of this book, the age wave is just now building.

So how did all this get started in the first place?

At the beginning of the development of this book, the authors wanted to take a look back before looking forward to tell the complete story. The birth of the baby boomer and presently the concept of aging in place began in earnest with a surge in live births in the United States between 1946 and 1964, a time when U.S. Service men and women were returning from World War II and the Korean War. They were young, anxious to get on with their young lives, secure gainful employment, get married if they weren't already, build a family, and have a home to call their own and raise their children.

The stage was set, and some five decades later the effects would begin to be realized.

The age wave began to pick up speed in the early to mid-1990s and a change in residential design was getting going. Groups of interior designers, architects, and homebuilders, somewhat independent of each other, began to seriously look at the marketplace. As the new millennium approached, they wanted to know more about potential design consumers in the new century.

What kinds of services or products would "new century" consumers desire, need, or require as they contemplated buying or building, designing, or remodeling their homes? Who are these people in that category we now call baby boomers? Would they want professional design services? What trends should be noted as it related to architecture and home building?

As surveys were commissioned, numbers compiled, and studies completed, what was clear was that a significantly large percentage of the U.S. population was now in their middle ages and, depending on circumstances, would be in need of the kind of housing that would accommodate the baby boomers through various phases of the aging process—a group that is reported to be around 76 million, give or take a few million.

> Somewhere between a third and a quarter of all people living in America today were born between 1946 and 1965, and if you think you're tired of hearing about us, you should try being one of us.
>
> —ANNA QUINDLEN, U.S. JOURNALIST, COLUMNIST, AUTHOR

This was a large enough number that others took notice. Sociologists, gerontologists, physicians, politicians, marketing and media specialists, and a slew of other related professions began to examine what effects this cultural evolution might have on government, businesses, and American society as a whole. Indeed this was not a trend but a significant change to the fabric of the American society.

Analysis by U.S. Census Bureau examined this evolution and defines it by the numbers:[1]

- At the beginning of 2000, about a third of the U.S. population were 50, and older and their numbers would likely double in the next 35 years.

- The number of people age 65 and older will increase in similar proportions.

- Those in the age 85 and older segment would represent the fastest growing segment of the population.[2]

In December, 2005, a conference sponsored by the White House Council on Aging (WHCoA), an event that occurs once a decade to develop recommendations to the President and Congress on policies related to aging, contemplated the many social, public, and private issues with so many Americans becoming senior citizens in just a few short years. Discussions included social security, healthcare, and retirement planning.[3]

In the Conference's Executive Summary, it was pointed out that tomorrow's older population will have a profile that is different than previous generations:

- Their bodies will be healthier and their pocketbooks wealthier.

- They will be better educated and desire to make contributions beyond the traditional age of retirement.

- The average age of the population will grow higher as people will live longer; this will include an increase in the number of centenarians.

But there was also a realization that to improve the life of older Americans by understanding the needs for housing would permit these large numbers of Americans to age in place.[4]

Formal resolutions outlined in the WHCoA Executive Summary called for:

- The coordination of aging-in-place programs including improvements in the delivery systems at the state and local levels.

- Encouragement of designs for livable communities that provide the structures necessary to support aging in place.

- The expansion of creative and innovative housing design for the needs of seniors.

National organizations and groups such as the American Society of Interior Designers (ASID), American Institute of Architects (AIA), the National Association of Home Builders (NAHB), and the National Kitchen and Bath Association (NKBA) developed specific councils and committees to keep their members apprised of these developments.

The American Association of Retired Persons (AARP) promotes the welfare of senior citizens and also began to dig deeper about the same time, realizing that there were too few housing options for its members, and by association for a whole senior population. NAHB also looked at the specific needs of this segment. Both groups essentially came to the same questions:

"Would there be sufficient housing inventory of a type that would easily and effectively allow someone to stay in a personal living environment no matter the abilities? And what changes would need to occur to the physical environment that would allow an older resident to remain in a private home, a place of their own choosing?"

> With so many of us old people out there, someone was bound to catch on to us before we were gonners.
>
> —Anonymous Client

ASID also spotted this large blip on their radar. In December 1999, the Society had assembled a small group of designers, researchers, and industry professionals to examine these distinct changes to the population as it relates to the profession of interior design. Their findings, compiled in a white paper study, *Aging in Place: Aging and the Impact of Interior Design,* came to many of the same conclusions that other groups had. Something of this scale needed to be addressed.[5]

The ASID study discovered in their research of the marketplace and through surveys of homeowners 35 and older that:

- Many are just beginning to think about their retirement years, while some are seriously considering how they will spend the rest of their active years;

- Generally this segment has a higher education level and more discretionary income than the generation of their parents;

- Having a choice, those surveyed expressed a desire to stay where they are, remaining independent for as long as their physical abilities permit, and in an environment that is comfortable to them, in familiar surroundings; and

- This group places a high value on the functionality and appearance of their homes, and they have a desire for their homes to be more luxurious.

SO WHY AGING IN PLACE AND WHY NOW?

Quite simply, there are significant numbers of aging Americans who have a real motivation to stay active, who will live and love longer, and who one day will realize they might not be able to do all the things they have enjoyed at one point or another in their lives. They tell the real story behind this evolution. But the story goes beyond this group. It also extends beyond the concept of universal design (UD) and the American Disabilities Act (ADA). And it goes well beyond installing grab bars and creating wider doors and halls.

Residential design for aging in place instructs design professionals about the aging process and the fear of abandonment, dependency, and depression that elder clients experience when reliance on family and friends goes from being an occasional thing to a daily requirement. It extends to the need to comprehend how the human body responds to the aging process as well as providing solutions to address the mental and social issues associated with growing older.

Aging in place encourages a special, higher quality of life in which one might from time to time highly desire to continue to live privately in a place that offers more security and protection than the status quo. Aging in place speaks to the design communities about the need and necessity to create and implement accessible and adaptable designs for home and haven, no matter the age or infirmity of the occupants.

Perhaps as important, it speaks to the desires of the American population to maintain their independence; a critical component that defines the U.S. lifestyle clearly yet is often forgotten until something occurs that threatens it.

> The aging of America is not about to stop any time soon. To understand what kind of housing an aging America will need, and then to design, build, and deliver it is really a remarkable—not to say tempting—opportunity for anyone who wants to seize it.
>
> —William D. Novelli, AARP's director and CEO

AGING IN PLACE IS ABOUT WELL BEING, THEIRS AND OURS

Residential design for aging in place encourages inclusiveness rather than exclusive living. Effective solutions discourage the fear of being alone, helpless, or a burden on family and friends. It supports the frailties of the aging process with barriers removed or reduced with continued personal comfort.

In an even larger view, residential design for aging in place is also about providing the senior population with more choices of housing, of where to "age in place," and creates a menu of design options, allowing homeowners to choose what works for them by customizing the built environment to their needs in the years ahead.

The aging baby-boomer population is a determined group, and though they are aging, they do not plan to be sedentary. They are living longer, but "younger" lives, and are willing to invest in designs that will allow them to live as they choose and where they choose for as long as possible. This segment is not willing to "settle" for anything less than a life on their terms.

SO IS THIS BOOK ABOUT UNIVERSAL DESIGN?

The authors' objectives with this book are to provide design professionals—primarily interior designers, architects, and builders working in residential settings—the basic philosophies and tools for the design of inclusive environments appropriate to age and ability. Aging in place does indeed take into account the basic principles of universal design. But this is not a book exclusively about universal design. And the words assembled in the text sincerely encourage the use and concepts of barrier-free environments, visitability, accessibility, and adaptable designs. But there are many other resources and documentation that already exist in the marketplace.

But through the words, research, drawings, and pictures gathered together, we wanted to define the big picture and unique opportunities that lie just ahead. We wanted to identify the greatest concerns of a whole marketplace of baby boomers, who have just begun to realize that getting old is really not one of those things you can fix on a permanent basis with a face lift or tummy tuck.

As the authors began this journey, the vision of what they wanted the book to accomplish became crystal clear. They wanted to:

- Provide core-level information on the aging-in-place philosophy and what it means to design professionals as they counsel this segment of the elder population, a group that is searching for answers related to quality of life and living;
- Showcase the creative work of design professionals as examples that great aging-in-place design is also design that is transparent, without an institutional appearance;
- Create a "go-to" reference guide that gets daily use rather than a book that rests on the shelf and gets dusted occasionally;
- Weave throughout the manuscript the important role "independence" plays in the heart, soul, and spirit of the American population, perhaps more so with this segment;
- Create a book that spans across interior design, architecture, and home construction to show the common partnerships that can be built within

the design communities and develop a dialogue in hopes of building a complimentary team approach; and

- Assemble a list of reference materials, resources, and products that would help the design professional develop a skill set adequate to answer the needs of the group.

The impact of all of this has yet to filter down to every segment of the business world. And this book is not intended to be the complete and final story about the aging-in-place evolution. (The headlines of that story are only now being written.) Nor does it include all the definitive answers for design for the aged.

There is so much more discovery to be done, a lot more to be documented, more products that are available off the shelf, and a lot more information still to come as many awaken to the call.

Governments and businesses haven't seen the tipping point either but will certainly know its effects in just a few short years. National aging programs and social services will struggle to accommodate all those in need. The insurance industry, health professions, and Social Security will need to consider their options in providing services as resources become stretched.

This book emphasizes the pivotal position that can be played by interior designers, architects, and homebuilders. It points out to design professionals a business opportunity that will extend for at least two decades. It is also a call to bring together the knowledge, skills, and experience of gerontologists, health professionals, and physical and occupational therapists to enhance the overall design process. And those roles holistically include a social, perhaps even a moral responsibility to design havens of all types, of all shapes, in all locations—ones that adapt and evolve.

- An opportunity for designers to create a body of work that will be so important and mean so much to so many when lives are the most challenged.
- A challenge to build the evidence that design, in and of itself, impacts quality-of-life experiences, indeed supports and defends personal independence while addressing health, safety, and welfare of the public.
- An opportunity to create designs that will span more than the baby boomer generation and into the lives of generations of families to come.

This is the beginning of a challenging time with this advocacy to change the approach to residential design, with an emphasis on the quality of life of 76.8 million American baby boomers. Exciting opportunities for the boomers, the current elder generation, and the design community lie just ahead. The clock is ticking. Catch the senior tsunami.

References

1. U.S. Census Bureau, *Projection of the Total Resident Population by 5-year Age Groups* (2000).
2. Ibid.
3. White House Conference On Aging, *The Booming Dynamics of Aging, From Awareness to Action* (2005) http://www.whcoa.gov/about/resolutions/Conference_Agenda.pdf (accessed September 16, 2007).
4. Ibid, WHCoA Executive Summary, *Report to the President and the Congress*, http://www.whcoa.gov/press/05_Report_1.pdf (accessed September 16, 2007).
5. American Society of Interior Designers, *Aging-In-Place: Aging and the Impact of Interior Design*, Washington, DC (2000).

CHAPTER 1

Designs for Independence

Psychologists say that all of us have four basic psychological needs: status, affection, independence, and security. They claim that these needs working together or in isolation dictate many of the ways we adjust to our environment.

—Herschel G. Nance, from *Contracting to Build Your Home: How to Avoid Turning the American Dream Into a Nightmare*

Courtesy of: Library of Congress/Prints and Photographs Division.

AGING IN PLACE IS ALL ABOUT INDEPENDENCY

It is often too easy to take things for granted in the United States, a country renowned for its abundance. The basic tenants defined by the United States Declaration of Independence, the U.S. Constitution, and the Bill of Rights forms the basis for these freedoms and more than 200 years after helps to shape the American society. These documents guarantee each U.S. citizen the freedoms to speak without restraint, to assemble peacefully, and to practice any religion or life philosophy we choose. And the freedoms expressed in those documents continue today in the nation's heart, mind, and spirit just as they did more than 200 years ago. As a result, the choices, options, and opportunities for U.S. citizens are nearly boundless. But personal freedom and independency doesn't stop there.

What we think and believe, what we say, and how we live our lives as adults are further shaped by our individual upbringings, parents, family and friends, the part of the country we are born in, and the type of education and life experiences we have amassed. When we combine these personal values and beliefs with our "certain unalienable Rights," they form the core essence of who we are as individual Americans. And because they are rooted so deeply in each of our lives, they are more often than not taken for granted until or unless an event or something takes away our independence.

The freedoms that we most expect can be grouped together under a single designation: self-determination. Consider freedoms such as the ability to travel throughout the country at will, to associate and make friends with those whose company we enjoy, and to choose our own spouse or partner. Through self-determination we select a profession and pursue a career determined by our individual interests and talents. Our freedom also includes whether or not to have children, how many, and where and how to raise them. Collectively, these liberties further define our independence as well as establish our quality of life.

Early in life, it's hard to imagine losing or relinquishing any of these freedoms. As the years go by, however, the aging process can rob us of some of our physical options. Despite scientific advances and breakthroughs in science and technology that permit us to resist or prevent disease and extend our lives longer,

---

CASE IN POINT

Until I had both knees replaced, I never gave much thought about how many roadblocks there were in my condo. Once I got home from the hospital, the place just seemed to be filled with obstacles that slowed me down from doing the simplest daily routine. Getting up to answer the door or going to the kitchen wasn't too difficult. It just took a lot of time. I was always afraid that I would fall trying to get there in a hurry. But trying to take a shower all by myself was just such a chore. There was the effort of getting my leg over the curb to try to turn the water on and then there was no place to sit down once I got inside. I can only imagine what more permanently disabled people must go through.

—From a client interview, 52 years young

1.2 Narrow foyers and entries can make it difficult to welcome guests into the residence, if the foyers are small or crowded with furnishings. They can be particularly challenging to negotiate for those who need to use walkers or wheelchairs. Less furnishings and open floor spaces will keep the entry welcoming.

1.3 It is easy to make a bathroom more functional for everyone just by the specification of plumbing fixtures. Lever-style faucets, taller heights on the toilet, and bright lighting are good starts.

for many of us our later years will not be without some challenges. Of course, our ability to live without physical restrictions, barriers, and encumbrances can be compromised at any age, but for once-active seniors, adjusting to physical limitations can be especially difficult.

Imagine being an active adult who is able to participate in a full array of activities at age 60, 65, and even 70. Such a person may continue to work beyond the expected retirement age, to enjoy sports, and to travel wherever he or she desires. Then imagine how such a person might react to the requisite limitations of six to eight weeks of recuperation for something like hip replacement surgery. The inability to move from the bedroom to the bathroom or the kitchen without the use of a cane, walker, or wheelchair can be psychologically devastating.

Consider the physical challenges posed by hallways too narrow to accommodate a walker, wheelchair, or scooter, by shower thresholds that must be stepped over, and by toilet seats that are so low that standing up from being seated places a lot of stress on the aged back, knees, and legs. Imagine, too, the psychological impact of such a limited environment on an individual who previously was accustomed to being fit, useful, and independent.

Or imagine someone whose hands are shaped like a boxer's fist because he or she is so crippled by the effects of arthritis that his or her fingers cannot be outstretched. If door or cabinet hardware, such as knobs or pulls, must be gripped, how then does such an individual open a door or drawer? Simple tasks like turning on the kitchen faucet or opening a utensil drawer to prepare a meal can seem insurmountable to a person with such disabilities.

Depending on the situation, a person afflicted with the later stages of a degenerative illness, such as Multiple Sclerosis (MS), Parkinson's Disease, Amyotrophic Lateral Sclerosis (Lou Gehrig's Disease), or Familial Alzheimer's Disease (FAD) may no longer have the capacity to complete their normal routine and must rely physically on others to get out of bed, bathe, dress, prepare a meal, or even simple tasks such as answer the door or the phone. Eventually, such an individual might be faced with having to live with family members, reside in a residential community, or receive more direct care in a nursing facility, relinquishing the independence once taken for granted.

To accommodate the prospect of such physical challenges, dramatic—and sometimes immediate—alterations to one's home may be necessary. Thoughtful and effective home adaptations and modifications can make any home safer and more manageable for its resident's advancing disabilities.

By making important design decisions early in their lives, residents can minimize the physical barriers and restrictions in their homes and secure access to essential rooms, such as bathrooms and kitchens, thus, maintaining their dignity and independence in the event their mobility becomes restricted.

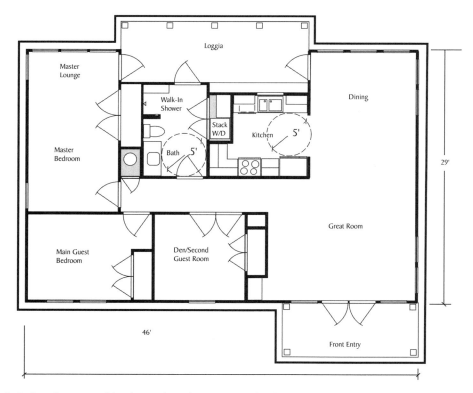

1.4 Creating accessible places doesn't mean an aging-in-place home or apartment requires additional square feet of space. Creating wider, more open spaces makes for a great foundation to any accessible plan no matter the level of abilities.

SIMPLE DESIGN PROPERLY EXECUTED
CAN MAKE A DIFFERENCE

"Aging in place," as it applies to interior and exterior design, is a philosophy as much as a concept that promotes independency and livability of all types of living environments no matter the age of the occupant or their level of abilities. Properly applied, aging-in-place principles allow an individual to remain in an environment that he or she chooses, often in a house that he or she owns and has lived in for many years in a familiar neighborhood with which he or she has established a connection. Aging-in-place principles support such vital attachments, as well as physical convenience, well being, security, and comfort.

There are many elements within the concept of aging in place. It incorporates aspects of universal and barrier-free design, adaptability, visitability, and accessibility. But it extends further. Design professionals need to understand how the aging process degrades physical and mental capabilities. Design professionals, as well as those in related occupations and the trades that support the design process, should learn how growing older impacts mobility and agility and how sight, hearing, touch, and balance diminish over time.

Aging in place also requires an understanding of other possible results of aging: denial, depression, the loss of long-standing social connections, the possibility of experiencing age prejudice, and—perhaps most important—the dread of being dependent on others.

AGING IN PLACE IS ABOUT THE NUMBERS,
BIG NUMBERS

With some 76 million Americans classified as baby boomers—those born between 1946 and 1964—approaching retirement age, the aging phenomenon in the United States is quite dramatic. According to various studies of this age evolution by groups such as the American Society of Interior Designers (ASID), the American Association of Retired Persons (AARP), the National Council on Aging (NCOA), and the National Association of Home Builders (NAHB), the sheer number of people who will face age-related decisions in the next few years is a strong indicator for those in the interior design, architecture, and building professions that aging-in-place principles need to be employed now.

Consider the following examples of what lies ahead:

- More than three-quarters (77 percent) of all Americans over the age of 45 live in single-family residences.[1]

- There are approximately 9.8 million senior homeowners with some type of disability or impairment that can make it difficult to live at home.[2]

- The first wave of baby boomers will reach the traditional age of retirement around 2011.

- By 2019, all of the 76 million baby boomers will be age 55 or older, an age at which most people are planning retirement; setting aside funds for long-term care; caring for an aging parent or other relative, spouse, or friend; or considering options in the event they themselves become physically disabled.[3]

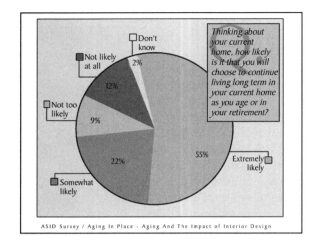

Thinking about your current home, how likely is it that you will choose to continue living long term in your current home as you age or in your retirement?

Don't know 2%
Not likely at all 12%
Not too likely 9%
Somewhat likely 22%
Extremely likely 55%

ASID Survey / Aging In Place - Aging And The Impact of Interior Design

1.5

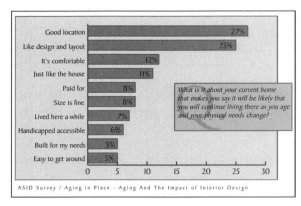

Good location	27%
Like design and layout	25%
It's comfortable	12%
Just like the house	11%
Paid for	8%
Size is fine	8%
Lived here a while	7%
Handicapped accessible	6%
Built for my needs	5%
Easy to get around	5%

What is it about your current home that makes you say it will be likely that you will continue living there as you age and your physical needs change?

ASID Survey / Aging in Place - Aging And The Impact of Interior Design

1.6

- In 2025, baby boomers will comprise about one-quarter (25 percent) of the total U.S. population.[4]
- Seventy-five percent of Americans aged 45 and older believe that they will be able to stay in their current residence for the rest of their lives.[5]
- Despite life's inevitable changes, most older Americans have not prepared to remain in their homes, yet will require home modifications to age in place.[6]

As group homes, assisted living centers, retirement villages, and extended-care facilities sometimes are usually less desirable or not affordable options, some forward-thinking members of this population segment are now considering their options. At the top of the list, of course, is just staying put, if one is able, in a home where one's family was raised, near one's place of worship, close to favorite stores and familiar recreational facilities, and in a neighborhood full of memories. Some seniors are considering alternatives like renovating and remodeling existing homes for better accessibility for themselves, family members, and visitors; creating sleeping spaces to accommodate future in-home caregivers; and, if circumstances don't permit full independence, sharing a home with family or friends.

1.7 Bathrooms can be both functional and attractive when planned with elements like cabinetry to allow someone to sit at a sink, a taller toilet with a grab bar nearby, and a shower without the traditional curb at the entry.
Design by: Thyme & Place Design.

The American Society of Interior Designers commissioned a survey of homeowners over the age of 35 who owned their own homes. With that survey as a basis, the Society created a detailed study of the marketplace, *Aging In Place: Aging and the Impact of Interior Design*, to determine the wants and needs of the baby boomer generation.[7] Their findings uncovered what this segment has been thinking about as they anticipate their needs for the future. As the survey discovered, this segment of the population will be more active, better educated, and more financially sound than previous generations, but they have a strong desire to stay where they are for as long as they are able.

THIS IS A WAKE-UP CALL FOR ALL DESIGN PROFESSIONALS

All of these factors present unique opportunities for interior designers, architects, building contractors, home remodelers, and landscape designers. These design professionals can create designs that will truly make a difference in the lives of their clients. But with a deeper and fuller understanding of the aging process and thoughtful planning, design professionals can make even small changes to create environments that are more healthy, secure, and supportive for those with age-related disabilities.

Simple, low- or no-cost design adaptations and modifications to an existing bathroom, kitchen, or entry can make an elderly person's daily routine flexible, easy to accomplish, and economical. When remodeling, the design professionals can specify taller toilet seats to reduce stress and strain on knees, hips, and legs; change the bathroom and kitchen sink fixtures from knobs to levers; provide additional interior lighting to alleviate diminishing eyesight; and install sound-absorbing finishes to reduce ambient noise to aid those with hearing loss.

During new construction, it is simple for an architect to design wider door openings and hallways, a contractor to provide a level or flush threshold at the primary or main entry into the residence, and an interior designer to specify non-slip flooring.

Design professionals can implement effective aging-in-place principles that also can make a difference in how an individual accepts the aging process. The thought of living in an institutional-looking space—with a hospital bed placed in the living room and a set of hastily installed grab bars next to the toilet or in the shower—can be unappealing to anyone, particularly seniors who may face an imminent need for such alterations to their homes. Thoughtful, long-term, design-savvy solutions—rather than short-term, immediate fixes—can be essential tools that can improve a client's outlook and encourage a sense of independence at a critical time.

1.8 Doorways that are 36 inches wide are an easy adaptation during the framing of the interior. Wider doors also create a better line of sight through hallways and into adjacent spaces.

1.9 Aging-friendly residential developments will have a strong appeal to the elder population with amenities such as wide walkways and open green park-like landscaping.

When considering the alternatives, such as an extended stay in a nursing home or an assisted living facility, the potential cost of care could soar well beyond an individual's resources, requiring government assistance from Medicare and Medicaid. A much less costly—as well as a much more desirable—alternative is to remain in one's home, especially if the living environment can be adapted for optimum use.

The needs of the growing older population call upon designers to not only consider safety and ease of access and mobility, but also to bear in mind baby boomers' strong desire for style, value, comfort, and enjoyment of their surroundings—all important components in providing effective age-related design solutions.

The concept of aging in place is neither a trend nor is it a style of the moment or the color *du jour*. Aging in place is a permanent, cultural evolution that will change how we think about homes and housing. Aging in place will impact interior design, architecture, and building and construction professionals by creating dialogues and partnerships with gerontologists, social workers, occupational and physical therapists, physicians, and caregivers.

Never has there been a more important time for design and building professionals to accept the challenge and take the initiative. The growing need for the application of aging-in-place principles provides design professionals everywhere with the unique opportunity to showcase how good design actually affects quality of life and to dispel the impression of design as only about decoration and aesthetics.

CASE IN POINT

Just after my wife came home from her cancer surgery, I realized that it was going to be difficult to take care of her. And she realized that, too. She constantly told me that she was sorry that she was such a burden on me. But it was something that this husband had to do for his wife of 40 years. It wasn't practical to put her in the master bedroom upstairs. So I had to rent this big hospital bed and place it in the middle of the family room. It was good that it was there because I was able to attend to her constantly, but it afforded her no privacy. When she needed her sleep, I had to make sure that I kept the place quiet, turning off the phone and the TV so she could rest. And I put a "Quiet, Please" sign on the entrance door. The powder bathroom wasn't too far away from the family room, but when she wanted to take a bath, we had to go back upstairs to the master bathroom. Everything seemed so difficult for her. And it was for me, too.

—From a client interview, 62 years young

It Is Time to Sharpen the Saw

This loss of independence is the thing that is most disturbing to older clients. First of all, it is hard for them to even acknowledge or discuss it. No one just calls up one day and asks for a grab bar next to the toilet unless something has occurred in their lives. They also won't readily admit they may have to rely on others at some point for their day-to-day care. But one day they realize they have to do something to keep them at home. As a designer, I provide my clients choices about their home, about their comfort, personal safety, and about their future as they age. As we discuss the plan, they come to realize all the possibilities, and it gives them hope for the future; that with a few changes to the place, they might be able to hang onto to their space filled with their personal belongings for a good while longer. Is there any better reason to do all this?

—ANN HUFF, ASID, CAPS, INTERIOR DESIGNER

Design professionals can prepare themselves to answer the broader needs of the growing elder population by exploring what products address specific physical abilities, by implementing thoughtful design solutions, and by expanding services to support this "age wave." Designers can even become the point person on behalf of the client and coordinate available aging resources by teaming together with contractors, physicians, and physical and occupational therapists. They can also share information about government or private funding, feasibility studies, and financial options to create a menu of effective independent living solutions for their clients' short- and long-term objectives.

The implications are immense for designers involved in this evolution. Aging in place will impact residential and commercial projects of all types as it creates global business opportunities for a myriad of design- and age-related goods and services that cater to the needs of an ever-growing community of baby boomers, each seeking to secure his or her future comfort.

Many developers, builders, architects, and interior designers have already changed their thinking about the design of specialized care facilities for the aging population as they realize the old concept of institutionalized, warehoused care wasn't effective or profitable and would be rejected by baby boomers who may have had to place a family member in some type of facility like a nursing home. The typical nursing home of yesterday is giving way to home-like living environments that are warm and welcoming just by their layout and arrangement.

More important, by creating such secure and safe living and working environments that offer barrier-free, universal, and inclu-

1.10 Rethinking the "traditional model" of assisted-living centers results in a functional and beautiful environment with a strong home-like appeal. For the resident, the effect is a much more comforting atmosphere that is reminiscent of a family residence with common dining spaces adjacent to food-prep areas. *Design by: Jeff Anderzhon, AIA.*

1.11 Clean lines without a lot of clutter have a strong appeal since getting in and out of a space should be easy and uncomplicated for anyone, no matter their abilities. *Design by: Muriel Sackey. Photo by: Gerlick Photography.*

sive features, designers can offer long-lasting housing options and workplace opportunities to everyone, without consideration of age, income, or physical ability.

This biggest evolution to the American society is rapidly advancing. It is time to build the skill set and catch this wave.

References

1. National Association of Home Builders (NAHB), *Study of Life Expectancy of Housing Components*, Washington, DC (2007).
2. National Council on Aging (NCOA), *Use Your Home to Stay at Home*, Press Briefing, Washington, DC (January 25, 2005).
3. American Society of Interior Designers (ASID), *Aging in Place: Aging and the Impact of Interior Design*, Washington, DC (2001).
4. U.S. Census Bureau, 2000 Census of Population and Housing (2000).
5. AARP, *These Four Walls: Americans 45+ Talk About Home and Community*, Washington, DC (2003).
6. National Association of Home Builders (NAHB), *Evaluate Your Home for Aging-in-Place*, Washington, DC (2006).
7. American Society of Interior Designers (ASID), *Aging in Place: Aging and the Impact of Interior Design*, Washington, DC (2001).

CHAPTER 2

The American Senior Tsunami

The places we live become a part of who we are. The town squares and local parks. The sidewalks and street corners and backyards. The neighbors who live right next door who watched us grow from children to parents to grandparents—and who we watched grow up too.

—Advertisement from Levitt and Sons, Home Builders

THE BIRTH OF 76 MILLION BOOMERS

A number of events in American history have had a permanent impact on the culture, beliefs, and values in the United States. Certainly the American Revolution, when a small band of determined colonists established the right to be governed as they chose, is significant. And although nearly a century later the War Between the States severely damaged the nation, a belief was built on its vestiges that every American citizen, no matter what race, should have the same freedoms afforded by the Constitution and Bill of Rights. World War I and II made it evident to Americans living then how easy it would be to loose their freedoms of thought, voice, assembly, and religion.

Another more subtle revolution began in the United States as World War II ended and soldiers returned home—a demographic change, perhaps more evolution than revolution, but one whose impact would change the face of the country a half a century later.

The baby boomer generation probably began sometime around January 1946. According to the U.S. Census Bureau, in 1940 the U.S. population was 131 million.[1] Some studies at that time projected that the country's population would begin to decline: The number of live births in 1915 was nearly 3 million, a number that fell by 600,000 twenty years later.[2] The 16 million U.S. casualties as a result of World War II compounded the forecast.

Contrary to these projections, as the fighting wound down in Europe and the Pacific, the number of live births in the United States began to increase. There were 2.8 million births in 1945, and in the following year, live birth numbers spiked. By the end of 1946, the numbers had increased to 3.4 million, an increase of 500,000 new babies over the previous year. With so many soldiers returning from their armed service in the war, building a family was the next tour of duty. And the American "baby boom" had begun in earnest.

By the end of 1950, the country's population had increased by nearly 19 million people.[3] The U.S. Census Bureau observed the number of new babies had now reached 3.6 million. A new record was established in 1954 with more than 4 million, and for the next 12 years, the numbers held steady.

Because of the record number of births in the preceding two decades, by 1960 the population of the United States had expanded to nearly 180 million people. By 1965, 40 percent of the population was under the age of 20. In a period of a mere two decades, the stage had quietly been set for the nation's next revolution.[4]

With so many youngsters making up the population, culturally and economically, the very nature of the American family changed. According to Landon Jones, author of *Great Expectations: America and the Baby Boom Generation*, the baby boom was a result of the increase in the number of women who got married and had families, rather than to the increase in the number of births to large families, which was the case in earlier decades.[5] In this evolving culture, almost all married women had at least two or three children, creating a greater economic demand for more of everything to help them grow a family: more housing, more grocery and retail stores, more schools, and more places of worship.

The Birth of the American Suburb

Developers and builders, anticipating the need to shelter all these young families, began to invest in land and develop affordable communities. Construction of new homes, apartments, and commercial property bolstered the rapid establishment of new cities and towns where a few years prior there had been open fields and farmland.

To give direction and control to this building boom—and to address existing limited and challenged structures—some thoughtful developers carefully planned communities. One case study describes how the profile of the American housing market changed during this time to meet the unprecedented demands of returning veterans and the growing population: Abraham Levitt, along with his two sons William and Alfred, purchased 4,000 acres of inconspicuous potato fields on Long Island 25 miles east of Manhattan.[6] Calling the new

2.2 With the birth of the baby boomer, more housing was required to accommodate the number of growing families. But it was also the birth of the American suburbs, beginning with developments such as Levittown, New York. *Courtesy of Levitt Homes.*

neighborhood Levittown, the Levitts built the new subdivision with an eye to construction efficiency and offered a short menu of floor plans and amenities. Everything a young couple needed to begin married life and start a family, from appliances to carpeting and wall covering, was included in the construction price.[7]

Initially, the Levitt houses were offered as rental property. As VA and FHA government home loan programs became readily available to returning veterans, the Levitt family offered the homes for sale. First-time homeowners could purchase Levittown homes as fast as Levitt could build them, often with as little as a $100 down payment. Since monthly mortgage payments were often cheaper than the cost of renting a New York City apartment, significant numbers of city folk moved to the new suburban developments.[8] Augmenting the migration, tax laws that allowed the interest paid on a mortgage to be tax deductible were enacted, encouraging the purchase of homes.

Levittown IN 1957

2.3 Levitt Homes created simple single-family residences with limited choices of architectural styles and floor plans to facilitate the building process and make the homes economical for new homebuyers. *Courtesy of Levitt Homes.*

CASE IN POINT

Aaron and I hadn't been married too long when we purchased our first home in a community that Levitt and Sons was building outside of New York City. I think it cost about $20,000, a little more than some other houses in the neighborhood because it was to be built on a third of an acre rather than the standard quarter acre lots. It came with everything we needed for a young family starting out—appliances, a carport, a couple of fruit trees, two choices for paint and wallpaper, and a mortgage. We raised kids in that little house, just like everyone else was doing on the block. And we got to know our neighbors, and sometimes even learned more than we wanted to know. But it was that idyllic American life we only read about now.

—From a client interview, 68 years young

At its completion in the early 1950s, Levittown included 17,400 homes. The new development was now a major suburban community that included 82,000 husbands and wives and their children. In a second wave of development and construction in 1951, the Levitt family created an additional Levittown community of 17,000 homes in Bucks County, Pennsylvania, near Philadelphia.[9] The suburban sprawl had begun. Families would fill them quickly.

The growing popularity and availability of automobiles also encouraged the flight to get out of big cities. The National Highway Program of 1956 built highways and interstate roads connecting rural areas to metropolitan areas, contributing to a flurry of even more suburban development.

Another event altered the economic direction of the country: After the end of World War II, the United States switched its focus from an economy that primarily supported the war effort to one that produced goods and materials to meet growing domestic use and for export to countries ravaged by war. This sustained growth period bode well for the U.S. economy, and continued despite the country's involvement in the Korean War during the early 1950s. It was indeed a healthy time for businesses of all types but especially for those that built buildings and companies that manufactured durable goods. Anyone who sought employment had more than a sufficient opportunity for work.

Additionally, low-cost federal financial aid for education became available in the 1950s, opening the door to young men and women to build better lives than those of previous generations. Record numbers of students attended colleges, universities, and trade schools, obtaining educational goals out of reach to most people in their parents' generation. Better education led to larger personal incomes for many young families, providing them with the resources to raise larger families.

All these occurrences paralleled each other—seemingly at the same speed—and created the unique opportunity for the baby boom generation to prosper beyond any previous generation, permanently altering the face of the country.

Fast Forward: Boomer Wave Begins to Make an Impact

As the first wave of the baby boomers reached the age of 50 in 1996, many became "empty nesters," a term that describes the period in boomers' lives when their children are old enough to leave home and start lives of their own and boomers' elder parents are still capable of living by themselves. At this point, boomers often live in homes much larger than those they needed when their children were at home. Extended families with several generations living under the same roof, a lifestyle still popular in other countries, became rare in the United States by the mid-twentieth century.

A close examination of this life stage reveals what many studies completed during the 1990s indicated: The baby boomers have the potential to change the economic, political, and cultural climate of the United States for the next three decades—and beyond.[10] And those involved in residential architecture, interior design, and construction will certainly experience the impact.

2.4 While baby boomers tend to be progressive thinkers, more conventional architecture will bring back memories of a time when being a part of a neighborhood was an important component to life. Entry doors near sidewalks and front porches encourage the feeling of being a part of a community.

With advancement in healthcare, lifestyle changes, environmental conditions, and technology, baby boomers will likely live longer than all previous generations. As this group ages, according to a study by the American Society of Interior Designers (ASID), there will be a dynamic need to care for, support, and house this vast population.[11]

Aging in Place also emphasizes the point that "taken together, these factors promise a major opportunity for interior designers who understand how people's needs change as they age and how to integrate features into today's designs that will benefit them for years to come."

The U.S. Census Bureau reports that the number of people aged 65 and over increased eleven-fold between the years 1900 and 1994, exceeding the growth rate of the population as a whole. As this evolution continues, by 2025, baby boomers ranging in age from 61 to 79 will comprise about 25 percent of the total population. The number of people 65 years and older will more than double to 80 million by 2050.[12]

According to the Social Security Administration, the very first of some 76 million baby boomers applied for Social Security benefits on October 15, 2007. Born one second after midnight on January 1, 1946, in Philadelphia, Kathleen Casey-Kirschling, a retired schoolteacher from Camden, New Jersey, was the very first boomer to apply for Social Security benefits. Over the next two decades, there will be 10,000 people a day who will turn 62 and become eligible to apply and receive Social Security benefits, a number that many in the U.S. government believe will overwhelm the system and possibly result in a reduced benefit package after the year 2041.[13]

According to an AARP report, as baby boomers turn 55, they will be most likely caring for an aging parent, relative, or friend while in the middle of planning their own retirement years.[14] AARP's study also found that most boomers want to age in place and are willing to make home modifications to accomplish this.

Nearly 80 percent of those homeowners surveyed in the ASID *Aging in Place* study said they are "extremely likely" or "somewhat likely" to remain in their current homes as they age, even into retirement years. Many consider planning for the future need of their home as significant as planning for financial security or healthcare. Conversely, the AARP survey also disclosed that about one-third of older Americans have not planned for future living arrangements.

The National Institute of Seniors Housing, a constituent organization of the National Council on Aging (NCOA), concluded in their research on the aging population that many of the elder population may not need a menu of support services or extended care as much as they may need housing specifically designed to adapt and accommodate them in the future.[15]

In its manual, *Retrofitting Homes for a Lifetime*, the National Association of Home Builders indicates that as their capacity to perform activities of daily living (ADLs) declines, people "must be supported by actions that enhance independent living. For many, the prospect of aging in place is preferred over costly institutional options."[16]

Ken Dychtwald, psychologist, gerontologist, and author of eight books on health and aging issues, makes it clear that the baby boomers also hold great potential. In his book *Age Wave*, this segment of the over-55 population, "hold 70 percent of the total wealth of the country . . . and own 77 percent of all financial assets in America. People over 50 earn almost 2 trillion dollars in annual income."[17] Another point the author makes is that the population over the age of 55 holds 58 percent of all discretionary dollar buying power in the United States. Further, those between the ages of 65 and 69 possess the most amount of discretionary buying power of any age segment in our population.

The ASID study offers an even more detailed view of what boomers are thinking as the traditional age of retirement grows closer: Homeowners over the age of 50 who were surveyed have already recognized they will need to address issues such as access, safety, and mobility. The group also revealed their desire for value, comfort, and enjoyment. Their priorities include living in a place that has low maintenance and is easy to navigate.

One other concern for this group is losing the ability to climb stairs. For some, this may mean giving up a home in which they have lived for years—perhaps a home with no mortgage—to move into a single-story residence. If space permits, this group may consider adding on or converting an existing ground-level space into a bedroom with an accessible full bath.

The National Safety Council (NSC) puts a different emphasis on the challenges for boomers who may be injured as a result of a fall.[18]

- Falls account for 50 percent of all injury-related deaths in the United States.
- Falls are the second leading cause of injury-related death for ages 55 to 79.
- Falls become even more prevalent for individuals over the age of 80.
- The injuries are often linked either to some obstacle in the immediate surroundings or to inadequate lighting.

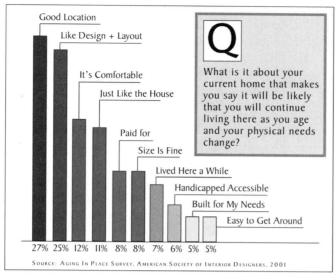

Good Location
Like Design + Layout
It's Comfortable
Just Like the House
Paid for
Size Is Fine
Lived Here a While
Handicapped Accessible
Built for My Needs
Easy to Get Around

Q

What is it about your current home that makes you say it will be likely that you will continue living there as you age and your physical needs change?

27% 25% 12% 11% 8% 8% 7% 6% 5% 5%

SOURCE: AGING IN PLACE SURVEY, AMERICAN SOCIETY OF INTERIOR DESIGNERS, 2001

2.5

Overall, baby boomers have a strong preference to remain just where they are for as long as possible even if modifications to the residence are required to accommodate their changing needs. Several studies support this concept, confirming that elderly Americans prefer home-delivered assistance of some kind over the option of nursing homes or other institutionalized care.

While they revealed these serious concerns, in the study by ASID, 40 percent of baby boomers also expressed a desire for luxury in their homes, from whirlpool spas to gourmet kitchens, even to adding or remodeling specific rooms. And with record high disposable incomes, a significant number of boomers can afford such luxuries.

PLAN FOR A LIFETIME AND DESIGN FOR A LIFE SPAN

In designers' endeavors to create sanctuaries, the mission is simple: Get to know as much as you can about your clients and how they see their future.

It is critical to the solutions for designers and other building professionals to fully understand clients' past experiences and how the aging process may affect them physically, intellectually, financially, psychologically, and spiritually. Consider the impact that even small, short-term changes to the built environment can make and how those changes allow residents to make choices about where and how they want to be as the years roll on.

Help elderly clients plan ahead: Many clients initially may reject the concept that they will ever need grab bars to get on and off the toilet, and some will find it too costly when remodeling to install wider doorways that can accommodate a walker or wheelchair. Younger boomers,

2.6 For existing bathrooms, small changes can make a space an accommodating environment. Adding a grab bar near the toilet, installing a wall-hung sink, and providing more lighting are elements easy and quick to accomplish, especially when sudden changes or events occur that might affect a client's mobility.

particularly those who have not been exposed to anyone with a physical disability, will tend to overlook the likelihood of special needs later in life.

Each part of a design solution should address the possibility and effects of future chronic conditions, such as arthritis, heart disease, hearing loss, and visual impairments. Further study of gerontology can provide designers with the skills to assess comprehensively the needs of those with disabilities, infirmities, or diminished mobility, as well as the social and psychological aspects of such limitations.

> As designers we need to acknowledge with the client that it is OK to think about these things and to plan for them. We must encourage the client to preplan and incorporate modifications that address their possible future needs into their new construction or renovation. So many selections can be made or adapted if we just keep those needs in the forefront of our design programming. We also need to be mindful of their fears and concerns. Sometimes we can make the discussion less intense just by how we "approach" it with them.
>
> —JO RABAUT, ASID, IIDA, INTERIOR DESIGNER

2.7 Larger open spaces with fewer walls and wider halls and doorways mean not only more flexible spaces but also options for the future should the needs of the client change. Later on, interiors can be segmented with walls, sliding panels, or folding doors to provide additional sleeping spaces for a family member or caregiver.

In one of the largest studies of consumers aged 50 and over, the research group Focalyst discovered what many other similar studies had found: Boomers are planning to stay right where they are at present.[19]

- Sixty percent of those surveyed expect that they will continue to live in their current residences at least during the next five years.
- Sixty-five percent of those surveyed plan to improve or do some type of remodeling to their homes.
- Seventy-seven percent of those surveyed believe that the appearance of their homes is a reflection of who they are as individuals.
- Seventy-three percent of those surveyed say they consider the kitchen the most important room in the house.

A contractor who is building or remodeling a home can easily incorporate universal design elements as a natural component of the work. Without emphasizing the reason, a contractor or designer can plan to include products, fixtures, and lighting that will accommodate everyone, regardless of their abilities.

Interior designers can plan more open areas on one level and design flexible interior spaces, such as a room that can initially be used as a den or office but that can be reconfigured as a bedroom with or near a bathroom sometime in the future. Architects can design structures that are easily adapted to changing lifestyles as residents consider the possibility of living to age 80 or 90 or beyond. Builders can create a menu of options into their next project and tap into this vital, emerging demand for accessible, adaptable housing.

In addition, as residents continue to age and part- or full-time care may become necessary to help prepare meals, do laundry, run errands, and dispense medications, the need to accommodate caregivers should be incorporated into home plans.

Interior designers can arrange furnishings to optimize the use of natural light and increase the levels of task and ambient light. Since cognitive impairments can affect memory and sense of orientation, the design of cabinetry and storage spaces should be well organized, easy to locate and identify, and be within easy reach. And in consideration of diminishing eyesight, designers can create and specify contrasting colors or patterns between floors and walls and tabletops and counters to help avoid accidents.

Thoughtful development of small to midsized, multi- and mixed-use communities provide easy access to shopping, travel, entertainment, and healthcare, which is critical to the support of an aging community. Land planners can take advantage of the natural features and terrain of properties to create walks, paths, and areas with benches scattered between parks and recreational facilities to encourage elderly residents to get out and exercise.

Cookie-cutter projects with rows of monotonous housing may create the impression of an "old-folks" place, so creating exterior and interior architectural

2.8 Good interior lighting is important in any space, but it is especially important for individuals with eye disorders. Plan for a variety of ambient, task, and accent light sources and use larger, open-style windows and window coverings to gain as much natural lighting into the room as possible. *Design by: Interiors Joan & Associates.*

2.9 In new developments, baby boomers, many now with families of their own, desire not only functional neighborhoods, close to stores and services, but they also desire diversity in the architecture and landscape, avoiding the appearance of mass-produced housing.

diversity is an important solution to the sometimes negative impression associated with senior-style housing.

From all these ideas and concepts there emerges an overall consideration—helping those who are aging to maintain their independence and freedom. Many older citizens will insist on living in places they have come to know, in communities where they have connections with friends and family, rather than being warehoused in nursing homes and other eldercare facilities. And many will have difficulty facing the realization that they no longer can independently care for themselves.

It is essential—and part of the core of American life—to formulate designs that encourage and support personal independence for residents, clients, and end users. Setting the stage for a better quality of life and creating safe, secure living environments for this wave of aging citizens should be the shared missions of the entire design team.

References

1. U.S. Census Bureau, *Historical Count of the U.S. Population* (2000).
2. The Center for Disease Control, *Live Births, Birth Rates, and Fertility Rates: United States*, 1909–99 (2000).
3. U.S. Census Bureau, *Historical Count of the U.S. Population* (2000).
4. Ibid.
5. Jones, Landon Y., *Great Expectations: America and the Baby Boom Generations*, Coward, McCann and Geoghegan: New York, NY (1980).
6. Levitt and Sons, Home Builders, Boca Raton, FL. *Levitt History: Building a Legacy*, www.levittandsons.com (accessed September 12, 2007).
7. Hanauer, David, *Suburban Sprawl in Bucks County (and Beyond)*, www.davidhanauer.com/buckscounty/sprawl (accessed August 8, 2007).
8. Ibid.
9. Ibid.
10. American Society of Interior Designers, *Aging in Place: Aging and the Impact of Interior Design*, Washington, DC (2001).
11. Ibid.
12. U.S. Census Bureau, *Historical Count of the U.S. Population* (2000).
13. "Baby Boomers and Social Security: Benefits Stampede Begins," *The Palm Beach Post*, Palm Beach, FL (October 16, 2007).
14. Novelli, William D., *AARP, Helping Aging Boomers to Age in Place*, Washington, DC (2005).
15. National Council on the Aging, *A National Survey of Health and Supportive Services in the Aging Network* (2001).
16. National Association of Home Builders, *Retrofitting Homes for a Lifetime*, NAHB Research Center, Inc., Washington, DC (1994).
17. Dychtwald, Ken and Flower, Joe, *The Age Wave: How the Most Important Trend of Our Time Can Change Your Future*, Bantam Books: New York, NY (1990).
18. National Safety Council, *Leading Causes of Unintentional-Injury Death by Age*, Washington, DC (2001).
19. "Life Events Trigger Home Updates and Remodel Projects," *The Focalyst*, New York, NY (2006).

CHAPTER 3

Laws, Codes, and Regulations

A man's house burns down. The smoking wreckage represents only a ruined home that was dear through years of use and pleasant associations. By and by, as the days and weeks go on, first he misses this, then that, then the other thing. And when he casts about for it he finds that it was in that house. ... It will be years before the tale of lost essentials is complete, and not till then can he truly know the magnitude of his disaster.

—Mark Twain

BUILDING TO KEEP US SAFE AND SECURE

The principles of residential aging in place and the philosophies that accompany the ideas in this book are generally focused on single-family, condominium, townhouse, or apartment living as opposed to continuing care, nursing homes, or assisted living facilities. But to ensure the safety and integrity of homes and houses with all other structures, building and construction codes define the standards under which the built environment is created.

With a history that dates back to the Greek and Roman eras, codes are as critical now to everyone as when the Acropolis was being constructed. Several centuries later, today's building codes, while more complex than those ancient predecessors, are based on centuries of knowledge, experience, and case studies of building professionals such as engineers and architects, builders, and contractors to ensure safeguards for all those who enter the built environment.

Many home modifications can be accomplished that provide safety and security for the occupant and end user in the home environment without falling under a specific code or governing regulation. The installations of grab

Design by: Keith Miller, ASID.

The development of building and regulatory codes goes back as early as eighteenth-century BC, to Babylonia and the *Code of Hammurabi*.[1] Laws were put in place that governed ancient society in general but extended to the responsibilities of those who designed and built the buildings of that time. As an example, the *Code of Hammurabi* held the builder accountable for the structural integrity of the houses he built. The consequences were stiff and occasionally severe. If one of the buildings fell and caused the death of someone, the builder would pay for the consequence with his life.

bars or changing passage door hardware from knobs to levers are two examples. However, it is very important to have an understanding of how codes are developed and what codes may apply to a residential project, especially when structural and mechanical modifications are required to achieve the desired results.

Model codes today are developed and routinely reviewed by a number of nonprofit service groups and organizations to create construction test methods, establish a level of acceptability of performance, form base criteria for various aspects of system or building components, and define standards of comparison between seemingly similar manufactured products.

In corroboration with government representatives, code officials, volunteers, manufacturers, and other related groups, these associations develop specific, technical guidelines that encompass the entire process of construction and assembly of buildings; structural, plumbing, electrical, and mechanical systems; fire protection and energy conservation and consumption within and around commercial and residential buildings, including homes and schools. Depending on the jurisdiction and type of construction, these codes also address life safety, accessibility, and indoor air quality.

Model guidelines are written and formulated through a process of consensus of their members, and any member may propose changes. Depending on the organization, updates to codes are usually published every one to three years. Using the model codes, state governments and county and city jurisdictions may then formulate laws, policies, codes, and standards to regulate the conduct of all licensed trades.

Following are groups considered to have established the gold standard of model building and construction codes.

International Code Council (ICC)[2]

Prior to the early 1990s, building codes were written by a number of entities, then often adopted, changed, and rewritten by local and state jurisdictions as their own regional issues dictated or required. The ICC was formed in 1994 as a nonprofit group from three other groups: the Building Officials and Code Administrators (BOCA), the International Conference of Building Officials (ICBO), and the Southern Building Code Congress International (SBCCI). It was established to create and encourage the adoption of a single set of building codes. Their objectives, then as now, are to provide code enforcement officials, architects, interior designers, engineers, and contractors with a consistent set of requirements, and as a result, a higher quality construction across boundaries of state, country, and continent. With an in-depth set of publications, the group leads the way in technical and educational information on the built environment that is used in many places across the globe.

Prior to the creation of international codes, the most used residential code was the *One and Two Family Dwelling Code*. However, it is now a part of the model codes published by the ICC and used for single-family homes and two-family structures such as duplexes and townhomes that have separate means of egress. The International Residential Code (IRC) includes codes for building structures, electrical, plumbing, and mechanical systems.

National Fire Protection Association (NFPA)[3]

This organization and its members represent 100 nations and serves as the leading advocate of fire prevention and an authoritative resource on matters of public safety in the building and design process. NFPA was created in 1896 for many of the same reasons as the ICC, to initially develop a consistent set of electrical codes that all would follow. Today, its objectives remain the same and through its members help to build a line of defense from fire, electrical, and other hazards.

The Life Safety Code (LSC) published by NFPA is not a building code but establishes the minimum requirements for fire safety by its focus on the challenges of protecting and removing individuals during a fire-related emergency. The LSC is the most widely accepted fire code throughout the country and abroad.

REGIONAL REGULATIONS ADDRESS SPECIFIC LOCAL ISSUES

While most states adopt general model codes as law, some governments may choose to write their own codes for specific applications. For example, California has stringent seismic and engineering codes to address building reinforcement and stabilization because of earthquakes, a relatively common occurrence in that state. States along the Gulf Coast impacted with seasons of hurricanes such as Texas, Alabama, Louisiana, and Mississippi have instituted regulations that require specific construction methods for structures so that they can withstand the extreme wind loads and address the flood hazards during and after such storms.

CASE IN POINT

After the tragic hotel fires in Las Vegas and San Juan, Puerto Rico, and the night club fire in Rhode Island, we can never take building and fire codes too lightly. These are examples when somebody just wasn't thinking, some group wasn't watching, and someone wasn't caring enough. It is the responsibility of the building owners, managers, contractors, designers, and especially the code officials. Everyone has got to play a part to avoid tragedies like these. How many lives would have been saved had there been a clear path of egress or appropriate use of materials and construction design? Imagine if one of these events had been in a facility like a school dorm, even a nursing home or an assisted living center. Imagine homes with no smoke detectors and security bars on the windows and doors that you know could trap elder folk inside with diminished responsive abilities. Those are very scary scenarios for fire rescue personnel every day, and as an official, it weighs very heavy.

—Anonymous Illinois code official

Florida state officials have adopted their own set of codes related to construction methods that expand on generally accepted codes of the ICC. After decades of their own destructive hurricane seasons, laws now cover issues related to indoor air quality. The presence of significant, unhealthy amounts of mold and mildew can occur after water intrusion and render the interior environment uninhabitable. Today, commercial and private properties are required to have mold inspections prior to a real estate sale and/or receiving a certificate of occupancy. In recent years, new business ventures have flourished by offering mold remediation and removal, requiring the State of Florida to implement certification of mold inspectors.

IT'S A MATTER OF HEALTH, SAFETY, AND WELFARE OF THE PUBLIC

It is important to understand that no matter what the jurisdiction, the primary reason for the existence of all building codes is consistent: the health, safety, and welfare (HSW) of the public. And design professionals—whether they are creating an accessible interior for a client's immediate need or designing an entire residence that will adapt easily over time to the changing abilities of its occupants—are mandated throughout the design and building process to adhere to state, county, and local building codes.

> It's not just unwise, but unacceptable that new homes continue to be built with basic barriers, given how easy it is to build basic access in the great majority of new homes, coupled with the harshness lack of access inflicts on so many people's lives.
>
> —ELEANOR SMITH, FOUNDER, CONCRETE CHANGE

Federal codes, regulations, rules, standards, and guidelines that address accessibility are generally not applicable to single-family residences unless a local government has included such provisions in its own set of codes. However, some sections of the codes may apply directly to new residential design and construction, particularly when specific criteria are met, for example, when a source of funding for buildings is federal money, in the design and construction of multi-family housing, in certain types of townhouse developments, or if rental property is being adapted for accessibility. When local codes conflict with national standards, either in technical specifications or scope of work, the most prudent policy is to follow the more stringent set of requirements.

What Are the Standards for Accessibility?

Much can be learned about accessibility such as designing entrances, creating ramps, and using size-wise doorways by reviewing standards and regulations and then developing a list of concepts, ideas, and options whether one is building new or renovating an existing house or apartment. The following national standards address issues of accessibility in public buildings, environments, and spaces within the United States.

Americans with Disabilities Act (ADA)[4]

The ADA was developed from significant discussion and debate at the federal level during the late twentieth century. The ADA is not a building code, but rather it is a law that protects the civil rights of individuals regardless of their abilities. Enacted into law on July 26, 1990, the four-part regulation's purpose addresses equal opportunity for individuals with disability in employment (Title I), public transportation (Title II), commercial spaces and places of accommodation (Title III), and telecommunications for the hearing and speech impaired (Title IV).

The provisions of the ADA to generally cover buildings are found in Title III, which ensures equal access in and out of commercial buildings and places of accommodation, including any facility that offers merchandise, food, or other services to the public. With a few exceptions, residential buildings generally are excluded from ADA regulations.

The ADA Accessibilities Guidelines (ADAAG)[5]

This is a document that sets forth the codes that govern the construction and alteration of buildings and environments in the public sector, i.e., state and local government buildings, and certain buildings in the private sector—commercial facilities such as offices, shopping centers, theaters, restaurants, and hotels. ADAAG also imparts standards for the design and construction of public spaces within multi-family housing whenever such housing is considered to be a place of accommodation. Other residential spaces regulated by the ADA include builders' model homes, designer show houses, and real estate sales offices that are temporarily located in single-family homes.

American National Standards Institute (ANSI)[6] and ANSI Standard Section #A117.1

The ANSI publishes the ANSI Standard Section #A117.1 guidelines, which regulate the design of accessible building elements and spaces. First published in 1986 and updated approximately every two years, their guidelines, the *American National Standard Specifications for Making Buildings and Facilities Accessi-ble to and Useable by Physically Disabled People*, is a voluntary consensus standard that is often the model code that local or state jurisdictions adopt into law. The U.S. Department of Housing and Urban Development (HUD) included

3.2 In some communities where officials have written codes and regulations that govern residential accessibility, homes are required to have easy access to common sidewalks that are adjacent to parking and the street.

these guidelines as a part of its *Fair Housing Accessibility Guidelines* (FHAG), which was published in 1991 to define the standards for multifamily housing of four or more units. In certain situations or as directed by local jurisdictions, these guidelines, which often make reference to ANSI #A117.1 may be applied to as few as two units that are not owner occupied.

The Fair Housing Act of 1968 (FHA),[7] and FHA Accessibility Guidelines (FHAG)

The Fair Housing Act of 1968, which was amended in 1988, defines the regulations for the sale, rental, and financing, as well as the physical design, of newly constructed multifamily housing. The FHA ensures equal opportunity in the housing market for all, regardless of race, color, sex, religion, family status, national origin, or disability, and regardless of whether the housing is privately or publicly funded.

The seven design requirements that apply to residential structures of four or more units as outlined in the Fair Housing Amendments Act include:

- Passage into and through the dwelling
- Easy-to-reach switches, thermostats, and electrical outlets
- Accommodating design of kitchens and bathrooms
- Accessible entrance doors
- Accessible routes to the building and to its entrance
- Walls reinforced for installation of grab bars
- Barrier-free access to public and common areas

Multifamily housing units are governed by regulations that address the "right to reasonable accommodations." Under such regulations, a property owner

The design and construction of accessible buildings, homes, and houses has truly become an international issue. In the late 1990s, Great Britain was experiencing a shortage of homes adaptable and accessible to its growing population of people with disabilities. In 1999, the British Parliament passed an amendment called Section M to British residential building regulations. Now it has in place a comprehensive building code that addresses residential accessibility.

Norway, Australia, South Africa, and Canada have regulations that support the implementation and concept of inclusive accessible design throughout the country for public buildings and in certain areas for private spaces.

In Japan, government census reports over the last decade indicated what other countries had discovered: that its own elder population was also growing in numbers as an overall percentage of the population. Laws and regulations such as the Heartful Building Law to mandate universal design and accessibility were created to answer the needs of the aging and the handicapped segments by requiring the removal of barriers around buildings and within the workplace.

must allow a disabled tenant to make adaptations to a building—within certain guidelines—to accommodate his or her individual needs. Such a tenant would be required to pay for the alterations, comply with all building codes, and agree to return the property to its original condition if asked to do so. The tenant also may be required to establish an escrow account to pay for any restoration of the property when he or she vacates. In such cases, typical modifications can include changing plumbing hardware from knobs to levers, constructing ramps to the entry, widening doorways, adding grab bars, or remodeling a shower to include a curb-less entrance.

Uniform Federal Accessibility Standards (UFAS)[8]

The Uniform Federal Accessibility Standards regulate federally funded building construction and federal housing programs, and constitute the standard referenced by the federal government for compliance with the Architectural Barriers Act of 1968 and Section 504 of the Rehabilitation Act of 1973. The Architectural Barriers Act requires all buildings constructed by or on behalf of the United States, leased by the government, or financed in some way with federal dollars, to be physically accessible to people of all abilities. Section 504 of the Rehabilitation Act of 1973 defines the federal rules that prohibit discrimination against those with disabilities in any activity that is supported by or receives federal funding. This includes new construction or renovations to a building using assistance from the government, including public housing programs.

Visitability, a Design Idea for Inclusive Environments

More recent laws enacted in some parts of the United States include codes that address "visitability," an accessible standard for residential construction that states that virtually all new homes must offer features that not only make aging in place easier for residents, but also make it possible for any guest with a mobility impairment to visit the residence. This "inclusive movement" encourages social integration for people with disabilities rather than isolating them in their own residences.

A visitable residence is a simple, easy process to achieve with little or no cost to execute during new construction. To make a residence visitable, the minimum design features must include:

- flat, one level walkway up to a no-step entrance,
- doorways with a 32-inch minimum clear width, and
- a main-floor bathroom that can ideally accommodate a wheelchair.

Additional features in a visitable home may include lever-style handles on the doors, reinforcements behind the walls of the

3.3 These new homes are accommodating in their design with an accessible path: a reserved parking space right up front, a curb cut up to the sidewalk, and short pathways leading to the front doors of each of the residences.

bathroom for the future placement of grab bars, and HVAC climate controls that are no more than 48 inches above the finished floor.

This design concept has benefits that extend to all types of people with a range of abilities. It can be especially appealing as a marketable feature to home-buyers of all types and ages, from those with significant disabilities to those baby boomers who have yet to experience any challenges with access or mobility. Visitability is also appropriate in many other ways than originally envisioned. With no-step entries and wider doors, many common tasks of daily life become easier, including entering and leaving with baby strollers, groceries, luggage, and large items such as furniture.

3.4 Once at the home, visitability requires that there will be at least one level threshold to get into the residence, either through the front door or a side entrance. Photo by: Gerlick Photography.

Visitability also provides for the homeowner who might need to quickly retro-fit his or her residence due to a temporary disability, such as after an injury or knee or hip replacement surgery. People who require some type of physical rehabilitation from an illness or after an injury or surgery may return to a "visitable" residence earlier than would otherwise be advisable. For those individuals who might require extended rehabilitation work, the accessible environment allows them to continue their rehab as outpatients, a significant benefit providing them with the comfort and safety of their own homes as well as some savings in healthcare costs.

Grassroot advocates for universal design have promoted such change in de-sign standards beginning as early as the 1970s. However, Eleanor Smith and a group she organized during the 1980s in Atlanta, Georgia, called Concrete Change[9] began the first serious push to persuade local government, builders, ar-chitects, and developers to design and construct homes for a lifetime of use. Di-agnosed with polio at three years old, and using a wheelchair for mobility for most of her life, Smith knew first-hand how difficult it was to visit someone's home.

By 1992, Smith and Concrete Change had encouraged, pushed, and prodded government officials in DeKalb and Fulton Counties, Georgia, to initiate the first visitability ordinance for subsidized, single-family residences, the first in the na-tion requiring a basic level of access for single-family homes. Since that time, a number of other cities have established their own ordinances that require some aspect of visitability including Urbana, Illinois; Pima County, Arizona; and San Antonio and Austin, Texas.

Unlike other regulations that govern accessibility, visitability does not mean full and accessible design. Rather, its purpose is to provide for more housing options, for access to a wider range of people with many abilities and needs, and for building more inclusive environments that remove barriers to maintaining independence. By making houses visitable now, homes in the future will be better able to successfully accommodate every member of society.

By having a strong working knowledge of all construction and building guidelines and ready access to codes and regulation manuals and books—in this case as it relates to residential construction—design professionals can ensure that clients and their families will live in safely built, accessible environments.

Modifications to design and construction laws as a result of advances in building methodologies, technology, and new products continue on an ongoing basis. Therefore, it is important to remain current with additions and changes to local and state building codes. Newly adopted regulations can greatly impact

---

CASE IN POINT

We moved into this custom-built three-story residence less than a year ago. My husband and I thought we had planned for absolutely everything that one would ever want in a house, including an elevator. What we didn't take into consideration was Jane, my mother. After suffering with MS for a long while, one day it just became necessary for her to use a wheelchair all the time. But because of the three steps up to the main entry, three steps down into the living and family areas, and three steps back up to the kitchen and breakfast room, she didn't have free access to get into the kitchen, a place where the rest of the family always hung out before Sunday dinners. There was always the chore of my husband and my boys picking her up in the wheelchair and carrying her into the kitchen so she could be with me when I was cooking and have dinner at the table.

When it came time for her to visit the bathroom, the powder bathroom wasn't big enough. We had to use the elevator to go up to the second floor to the main bathroom. After a while, Mom told the family it was just too difficult for her to travel any more. But I think she felt it was such a big ordeal to move her around the house. We tried to tell her that we wanted her to be with us for Sunday meals, and even possibly move in with us if she wanted. But nothing we could say would make her change her mind. To this day, I am not sure if she valued her privacy and what remained of her ability to live on her own or just did not want to feel she was burdening us with a handicapped old woman.

All through the building process, we had made endless lists of things we didn't want to forget. Once the house was built, we thought we had everything we wanted in the house... except for Mom.

—From a client interview, 45 years young

3.5 No matter the codes, rules, or type of architecture of homes in the local neighborhood, designing residences for the baby boomers will not only provide them with options for style but also a place that they choose to live that will adapt to their needs.

construction schedules and delay occupancy should inspections by local officials "red-tag" the project for noncompliance.

Building ordinances, regulations, and laws such as these are in place to protect the health, welfare, and safety of the public—those with and without a full set of abilities. And in the case of those with some form of disability, laws also ensure their civil rights and independence are protected.

Remember that guidelines, regulations, and codes are created to establish the minimum standards for building construction. There may be alternative and superior solutions to achieve the same objectives. However, having the criteria of the project well defined, understanding all client requirements, and providing the best return on the client's expenditures allows for intelligent designs that support the client in a time of need as well as throughout a life span and especially in a time of need.

References

1. King, Leonard W., *The Code of Hannurabi*, Kessinger Publishing: Whitefish, MT (2004).
2. International Code Council, www.iccsafe.org (accessed October 1, 2007).
3. National Fire Protection Association, www.nfpa.org (accessed October 1, 2007).
4. U.S. Department of Labor, *The Americans with Disabilities Act of 1990* (1990).
5. U.S. Access Board, www.access-board.gov (accessed October 1, 2007).
6. American National Standards Institute, www.ansi.org (accessed October 1, 2007).
7. U.S. Housing and Urban Development, www.hud.gov (accessed October 1, 2007).
8. U.S. Access Board, www.access-board.gov (accessed October 1, 2007).
9. Concrete Change, www.concretechange.org (accessed October 1, 2007).

CHAPTER 4

Assessing the Aging Process

*I have enjoyed greatly the second blooming ... suddenly you find—
at the age of 50, say—that a whole new life has opened before you.*

—Agatha Christie

AGING IS NOT FOR THE YOUNG

The study of the aging process and what happens to human physiology over a lifetime is complex and multifaceted. And because aging—not to mention growing older—has different implications for different cultures, aging is difficult to clearly define with one short set of words. Perhaps a definition of the physical aging process might be defined as the natural, normal, yet continuing biological changes that occur as physical and mental systems of the human cellular systems begin to deteriorate over a span of time.[1] So when does aging begin? And how fast does it happen? And is there anything that can be done to slow its progress?

There are those who believe the process of getting older begins at birth, while others believe that aging begins at the moment of conception. Others define aging as the time in life when declining health causes permanent physical changes. In some societies, people are considered old if they have lived a designated number of years or have become grandparents. Many under the age of 21 are probably inclined to believe that old age begins at 31 while some at 40 and 50 are still attempting to define just when middle age actually begins.

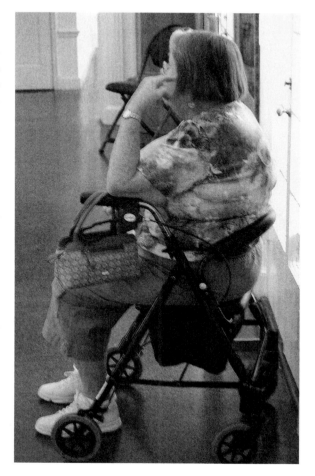

31

Those who have reached age 65—the traditional retirement age in the United States—are often considered obsolete or of little value and, more often than not, a burden on their families and/or society as a whole.

The U.S. government has established milestones that help define old age. For example, those 40 and older are protected by the U.S. Age Discrimination in Employment Act of 1967 (ADEA).[2] At age 55, low-income individuals can apply for subsidized employment and learn new work skills under Title V of the Older Americans Act.[3] For those who look forward to a time when they can retire from the daily grind of work, old age is when one qualifies to receive Social Security benefits, which can be as early as 62 or as late as 70.[4]

For certain professions, reaching a particular age has been used as the benchmark for retirement. For example, airline pilots and those in the military have occupations where high levels of mental and physical skills are required and mandatory retirement is considered justified.

Many people, old and young, famous and those not so well-known have all strung words together in the hopes of defining what age is all about. Arthur Schopenhauer, the nineteenth-century German philosopher, wrote "aging begins at the moment when we start counting backward from death rather than forward from birth." Samuel Ullman, an American poet and humanitarian, wrote, "Nobody grows old merely by living a number of years. We grow old by deserting our ideals. Years may wrinkle the skin, but to give up enthusiasm wrinkles the soul." And Satchel Paige, the American baseball player quipped, "Age is a question of mind over matter. If you don't mind, it doesn't matter."

The time when a person is unable to independently perform certain basic, personal, routine functions—referred to as "activities of daily living"—is considered by many to be the point at which that person has reached his or her elder years. Activities of daily living, or ADLs, are the fundamental activities an individual requires, such as communicating, eating, drinking, dressing, personal cleansing and grooming, bowel and bladder management, and sleeping.[5] More often than not, family members and friends are called upon first to provide assistance when a person of any age is no longer able to reasonably perform some of their ADLs. If family or friends do not have the skills or available time to assist a person with diminishing capacities, then paid staff or other healthcare professionals are often employed as circumstances advance.

CASE IN POINT

Since I am 64 years old and single, I feel I do understand the fears of our aging population. When we feel fragile or fearful, there is no place more comforting than our own home and surroundings; that is where we find sanctuary, comfort, and expression. It is frightening to think that we may not be able to function at home without assistance. We hope never to be diminished by our community when we have so much to offer. Mostly, we do not want to reverse the parent-child role with our children or become a burden to them.

—Janet Kay, ASID, interior designer

There is no consensus as to how fast aging will occur, but the process is greatly influenced by a large variety of individual elements, including diet and nutrition, race, genetics, the part of the country where one is born, access to healthcare, formal education, socio-economic status, lifestyle, and type of work the person does.

Environmental and other factors, such as exposure to air pollution or toxic work or living environments, or even political and economic events, can speed the aging process in certain individuals. Scientists have considered ways to slow the deterioration of the human cellular system by creating drugs that target diseases that particularly affect older individuals, helping to extend their life expectancy. Some even believe that a positive mental attitude during one's later years can have an effect on the aging process.

Yet there remains one irrefutable fact: No matter what steps one takes to slow, limit, or arrest the aging process, aging still happens.

MAKING ACCOMMODATIONS FOR THE AGING PROCESS

What is most relevant for professionals in the built environment is how can—and how will—residential environments accommodate and, to some degree, anticipate the physical changes of those who inhabit them? To be able to design and build functional spaces that will address the continuing needs of any client, design professionals must comprehend a range of factors about the aging process and its effects on the senses of smell, sight, touch, taste, and hearing, as well as on balance, physical strength, dexterity, and cognitive skills.

In its study on aging and the senses, The Pepper Institute on Aging and Public Policy at Florida State University determined that many Americans experience impairments to their senses as a result of the aging process:[6]

4.2 People are disabled by their physical abilities and loss of independence, but attitudes in the American culture also play a role in their disability, often-through discrimination.

- More than 38 million people aged 40 and older have significant vision-related issues, including 3.3 million who are blind. Eye disease and impairment are a significant cause of disability and lost independence.

- The loss of hearing affects 25 percent of the population between 65 and 74 years of age, and yet for 50 percent of the group 75 years and older, it remains one of the most correctable problems that often contributes to social isolation.

- After the age of 50, the sense of smell begins to decrease because of the numbers of functioning smell receptors, and by age 80, the capacity to smell is reduced by about half.

Generally, most people think of aging as a loss of dexterity or mobility, either of which can play a substantial role in limiting a person's physical independence within a built environment. The speed at which physiological changes develop and their critical nature can be amplified by several factors, including:[7]

- A gradual loss of cognitive skills, like concentration and memory, which can result in feeling isolated and estranged from family, friends, and other social connections.

- A greater susceptibility to chronic conditions, such as arthritis, osteoporosis, diabetes, and respiratory and cardiovascular ailments can limit mobility and strength.

- Injuries caused by accidents may result in devastating permanent consequences for elderly people and can sometimes lead to untimely death.

- Loss of balance, body mass, muscle strength, and flexibility can impair a person's range of motion, especially in the upper body.

- A predisposition to a genetic condition or disease can limit a person's mobility, balance, and psychological outlook.

Beyond health factors, other influences can have an impact on the social and psychological well being of older people, such as the following:

- The inability to drive or travel by public transportation due to diminishing eyesight, hearing, or mobility can limit access to routine healthcare and medication.

- Lack of affordable health insurance to cover unexpected medical issues can disrupt once-stable personal finances and limit the ability to pay for home healthcare and assistance.

- Emotional or physical abuse by a spouse, child, or other personal relationship can leave an older person feeling fearful or vulnerable.

- Changes to existing government programs that support the elderly, combined with poorly managed or underfunded social, medical, and cultural institutions, can limit services to the increasing numbers of this population segment.

- Changes to once-familiar neighborhoods may profoundly affect the safety and security of older residents, as the elderly are often targets of vandalism and other crimes.

- Age discrimination, prejudice, and stereotyping of older individuals, which may first appear in the workplace, can intimidate and limit elderly citizens' perceived options.

- Negative economics experienced at retirement when regular income is reduced and savings, if there are any, must be tapped to maintain a standard of living can cause depression and feelings of hopelessness.

- An unexpected loss of gainful employment and income due to a sudden illness, such as a stroke, surgery, or an accident, along with extended periods of recuperation, can cause or exacerbate anxiety and depression.

In his book, *Age Wave: How the Most Important Trend of Our Time Will Change Your Future*, author Ken Dychtwald[8] identifies some of the challenges faced by the older generation and defines "gerontophobia," a term that refers to the perceived hatred and hostility toward the elderly. Gerontophobia may include a fear of growing older and an attitude of self-doubt and inadequacy, and can affect the aging process. Dychtwald identifies seven points that underlie the phobia about getting older:

1. If young is good, then old is bad.
2. If the young have it all, the old are losing it.

3. If the young are creative, the old are dull.

4. If the young are beautiful, then the old are unattractive.

5. If the young are stimulating, then the old are boring.

6. If the young are full of passion, then the old are beyond caring.

7. If the children are tomorrow, the old represent yesterday.

LISTENING AND LEARNING TO CREATE BETTER DESIGN SOLUTIONS

With all the aforementioned factors as guidelines, design professionals should become familiar with the physical, psychological, and emotional limitations brought on by the aging process.

Design professionals should also be on the alert for the most significant obstacle to creating an aging-in-place environment for clients—denial. Most people will at some point in their lives reject the idea that they are getting any older. This is especially true for healthy, busy adults who have—so far—been blessed with no significant health problems.

Too often, clients contact a remodeler, contractor, or other design professional to make adjustments to a home because of an immediate need due to an accident or a stroke or because of limitations resulting from recuperation from surgery. The first goal in every short-term design endeavor, of course, is to keep the client safe and to expedite any essential and necessary changes that can increase mobility and independence. With safety as the continuing primary objective, the next goal is to create a master plan that will guide the selection of furnishings, finishes, fixtures, materials, and equipment for the long term.

Design professionals can gather insights and information about their clients and the extent of the home modifications that might be required through three simple initial steps: assessment, observation, and conversation.

These processes can initially include an informal evaluation during a walk-through of the home's living space, taking particular note of the state of repair of both the interior and exterior. A close look at the structure will reveal the potential to widen halls and doorways, build a ramp to the most commonly used entry door, or simply add strategically placed grab bars in bathrooms or other areas.

During that visit to the residence, the clients should conduct a tour of the home while the design professional observes the clients themselves. Careful attention should be paid to how the clients move from room to room; how they maneuver stairs, doorways, and thresholds; and how they manipulate existing door hardware and light switches. Do they balance with one hand against the wall? Do they open doors with an elbow or a foot or something other than their hands?

As they make their way through the rooms, ask the clients how they first came to live in this particular home, what memories they treasure about their time there, and what they enjoy most about living in the house now. Have a candid discussion with your clients about their sincere desire to remain in the

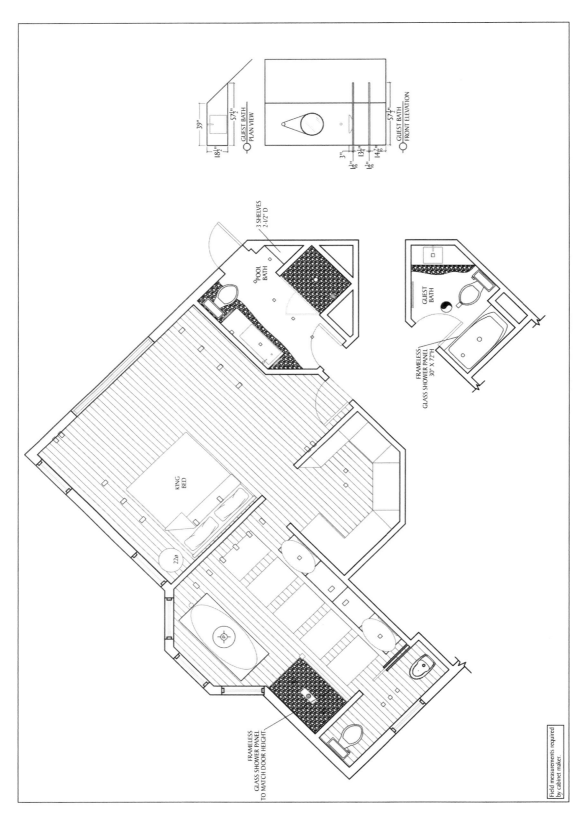

Field measurements required by cabinet maker.

GUEST BATH
PLAN VIEW

39"
57½"
18½"

GUEST BATH
FRONT ELEVATION

3"
1⁷⁄₁₆"
13¼"
1⁷⁄₁₆"
14⁷⁄₁₆"
57⁷⁄₈"

3 SHELVES
2-1/2" D

POOL
BATH

GUEST
BATH

FRAMELESS
GLASS SHOWER PANEL
30" X 72"H

KING
BED

22∅

FRAMELESS
GLASS SHOWER PANEL
TO MATCH DOOR HEIGHT

4.3 Whether remodeling or new construction, avoid designs that result in obstacles. In this plan, clear spaces without a lot of doorways between the bedroom, bathroom, and closet create easy access. *Design by: Susan Cozi. AutoCad Drawing Credit: Scott Feinstein.*

CASE IN POINT

After some two weeks in the hospital and six weeks in a nursing facility, I was finally looking forward to going back home after suffering a stroke to the right side of my body. As I made plans to return to the house, it became most apparent to me (and my doctor) that getting around inside, making a meal, or taking a shower were not going to occur without help and assistance. Always being a fairly independent cuss, the whole concept of having to hire some-one to stay with me during my rehab at home was the least of my worries. I soon began to have anxieties and concerns about how I would be able to make it on my own once a care-giver was no longer needed on a regular basis. My first thought was to put up a grab bar in the bathroom in case I fell in the shower. Maybe before too long I hoped to be independent enough through all the rehabilitation that I could cook for myself again. But what would hap-pen if I burned myself on the stove? And what would I do if I had another stroke? Would I be able to get to a phone so I could call for help? I was envisioning my life as a disabled person for the first time. I couldn't seem to find the comfort and security in the house like before I had the stroke.

—From a client interview, 61 years young

home, and what changes they believe are needed to allow them to live there indefinitely. Ask them in which rooms they currently spend most of their time and how they fill their days. Are your clients able to travel unassisted to the grocery store, do other necessary shopping, or attend religious services and social events?

Pay close attention to your clients' requests for more general ambient and task light, as this might be a sign of diminishing eyesight. Ask your clients to turn on their favorite radio or television program while you're there. A louder-than-normal volume can indicate a previously undiagnosed hearing loss. Check thermostat settings and ask if your clients are comfortable with current temper-ature settings. A high setting on the thermostat might be an indication of loss of body mass and body fat that can result in feeling chilled.

Begin to build a more thorough assessment of the current client needs, eval-uating the condition of the exterior and interior and continue to glean critical criteria by asking more probing questions.

Some examples of questions that help to create a bigger picture are:

- At what point did you decide that staying in the current residence was the right answer or at least an option for consideration?

- Are there any current or chronic health issues that need to be addressed as a part of the development of any plans or work?

- When you think about making changes so that you can fully enjoy your residence, what comes to mind that seems to be a big issue now?

- Are there any other people, consultants, family members, or friends that should be a part of the design development?

- Building a team is often a key element to a successful project from the beginning. Are you working with anyone or a group, which might include other design-related or healthcare professionals?

- Is there a certain time frame that would be important in pulling together a concept for the project and getting work accomplished?

- What are some of the things you like best about living here in the residence or in the neighborhood?

- What are the things you don't like about the house or the area surrounding the property?

- Have you ever undertaken any work like what you are now considering before, and if so, what were your experiences?

- If there is one thing you want to make sure your new plans include, what would that be?

Note that in these questions, there is a careful and purposeful avoidance of the use of terms such as age, aging in place, barrier-free, universal design, or accessibility. With a number of people who have some level of age denial, why bring up the obvious? Everyone ages. Everyone talks about it. Everyone wants to avoid answering the question of how old one is. Everyone wants to deny that though they have lived without help so far, some type of assistance (or assistive devices) down the road might be a necessity, not an option. The objective is to get the client to bring to the table their comments, concerns, and objectives. The objective of the design professional is to continue to ask questions of the client and all other related persons until a full scope has been defined and nothing has been left out of the equation.

Once a project is under contract, a complete assessment should include acquiring existing architectural plans, putting together as-built drawings, taking pictures, creating a list of current furnishing and fixtures inventory, and more in-depth information about any special equipment that may be required such as oxygen tanks or heart monitors.

IT MAY TAKE STRAIGHT TALK FROM YOU

Although it might be difficult for some design professionals, there comes a time to have a frank and more open conversation with clients to understand their specific medical needs and conditions. Ask them if they are consulting with any particular medical professionals, such as physical, occupational, or respiratory therapists, as part of a treatment for a specific medical condition.

For a more detailed assessment in certain unique cases, include in your conversation your clients' close family members, as well as any medical or rehabilitation professionals, such as caregivers, home healthcare representatives, elder care advocates, geriatric specialists, gerontologists, and physical and occupational therapists, or others with whom the clients consult on a regular basis.

Responses from such dialogues can be instrumental in making critical decisions that will influence their design plan.

> The biggest thing that people with disabilities worry about is not being able to manage things at home themselves and becoming dependent on others. Universally, people are worried about being placed in a nursing home. They are concerned that they will not be well cared for in a nursing home so [they] want to do everything they can to avoid placement.
>
> If designers approach each project with aging in place in mind, their clients will feel more comfortable about their lost abilities, or those abilities they fear losing, as they will know that there are features in their homes that will allow them to stay there even as their functions decline. An occupational therapist is an important part of the design team when it comes to creating optimally safe environments that facilitate aging in place.
>
> —STEPHANIE SAHANOW, OTR/L, OCCUPATIONAL THERAPIST

Don't be surprised to find that close family members or friends will have their own opinions about how to best take care of their loved ones. Part of what they may be going through is their acceptance of responsibility and the future role they may be called upon to play in the lives of your client. They can be resistive to changing or adapting the interior because of hidden agendas, something that might be related to finances. Others may simply be facing some element of denial themselves, that a mom or dad, aunt or uncle, friend or mentor is actually old enough to have a limiting medical condition.

A design professional listens carefully and clearly recognizes client's unique needs and special requirements and demonstrates that he or she will place the client's best interests at the core of the design. Then by acknowledging clients' desires as well as capabilities, a designer can build the high level of trust that is required to make the sometimes-difficult decisions for either simple changes or dramatically altering an interior or exterior space. Sometimes those decisions can mean including future living space for a family member or caregiver if live-in assistance or companionship should ever be required.

By working together as a team from the outset of the design process, designers and other building professionals can successfully meet the goal of keeping the clients safe from injury while they function as easily as possible within the boundaries of their current environment.

References

1. Smyer, Michael A. and Honn Qualls, Sarah, *Aging and Mental Health*, Blackwell Publishing: Malden, MA (1999).
2. U.S. Equal Employment Opportunity Commission, www.eeoc.gov/types/age.html (accessed October 1, 2007).
3. U.S. Department of Health and Human Services, Administration on Aging, Washington, DC.

4. U.S. Social Security Administration, Washington, DC.

5. U.S. Center for Disease Control, Washington, DC.

6. Pepper Institute on Aging and Public Policy, Florida State University, *Facts of Aging, Aging & the Senses* (June 2007), www.pepperinstitute.org/Facts/FoA_v3-3_Senses.pdf (accessed on October 1, 2007).

7. Spirduso, Waneen W.; Francis, Karen L.; and MacRae, Priscilla G., *Physical Dimensions of Aging, 2nd edition*, Human Kinetics, Champaign, IL (2005).

8. Dychtwald, Ken and Flower, Joe, *The Age Wave: How the Most Important Trend of Our Time Can Change Your Future*, Bantam Books: New York, NY (1990).

CHAPTER 5

Exterior Freedoms

When God made the oyster, he guaranteed his absolute economic and social security. He built the oyster a house, his shell, to shelter and protect him from his enemies. . . . But when God made the eagle, He declared, "The blue sky is the limit—build your own house!"

—Author unknown

HI, HONEY. I'M HOME!

The place where we live, raise a family, and prosper through our elder years goes by many names—house, home, and haven. And though the names may have different meanings depending on culture and location, it is that singular, private, and personal spot on the planet where lives are focused and grounded, centered and protected from the world outside.

- The house as structure is the shelter that frames lives, provides protection, and in a sense defines our sense of self by its style.
- The home as sanctuary is the environment that fosters the family unit and supports us as we mature.
- The haven as harbor is the retreat that affords privacy, gives comfort, and offers safety and security as a place of refuge from the world beyond.

Whether house, home, or haven, the exterior of the building is the first element to present its form, presence, and personality to the world. The lines define it, design shapes it, and function gives it purpose. Be it small or large, condominium or townhouse, single family or villa, the façade is responsible for that important first impression. The remaining components, the roof, walls, windows, and doors, continue the story line.

The exterior appearance, upkeep, color, and arrangement combined with location reinforce its individual quality and value, and by default, echo the qualities and values of those who own the structure to those who pass by. With thoughtful and careful execution, the exterior can open its doors and welcome home all who live within its walls or friends and family who come to visit. But without easy accessibility, the exterior creates a fortress of the home that restricts movements, limits independence, and rejects family and friends alike.

5.2 Wide entrance doors into and out of the home are both graceful and functional for many people and purposes. This mahogany wood door creates a four-foot wide passage into the home, while the double doors give easy access to the courtyard.

It is interesting that a significant amount of attention is often paid to remodeling the interior such as installing new bathroom and kitchen cabinetry, new floor and wall coverings, and for accessibility, widening hallways and doorways. But what if there is no accessible way into the home itself? Small things such as steps to enter a home or an undersized main entry door can quickly become very large problems when a fall or injury occurs. Other potential barriers include a steep sloping driveway with little or no landing pad, no covered walkway or overhanging roof at the door, a sidewalk surface that is uneven, poor or uneven outdoor lighting, and a main entry door that is too narrow.

No matter its age, its cost to construct, or its style, a home that progressively becomes more challenging to enter and leave eventually loses its safe home and haven status. But all is not lost. With basic changes to structure and layout, the exterior of a house can offer the ability for family and friends to easily arrive, independently enter, and freely exit from the home.

ACCESSIBLE EXTERIORS CREATE INDEPENDENCE

The basic process required to create a minimum of exterior accessibility is short.[1]

1. First, plan the most direct route possible—a pathway that leads from where the car is parked on the street, in the drive, or from a garage or carport directly to the entrance. An entrance can be either a main, formal entry to the home, a secondary door at the side, or a rear entrance. (Keep in mind that having a "secondary entry" that is well appointed and welcoming as a formal entry keeps family and guests from feeling like "second-class citizens.")

2. Walks and pathways leading to the front door and/or main entry should be flat and have the necessary changes to grade and elevation, ideally without steps.

3. At the doorway, there needs to be a porch or landing large enough for a sufficiently wide door to open fully and allow the individual to gain entry, ideally while remaining under cover.

Choices of exterior lighting fixtures and specification of low-maintenance materials in the hard and soft landscape contribute to well-designed and finished installations that will adapt easily to changing conditions, as needed. It also needs to be aesthetically pleasing—not just for the sake of aesthetics alone. Design an environment that is pleasing to the senses and also promotes the feeling that one has arrived not only to a safe environment, but also an environment that is secure, comforting, and inviting. And from there, the sky's the limit.

CASE IN POINT

My mother and I moved into a recently completed multi-level condominium in a retirement community. Everything was appointed so well that we knew we could easily live here for a long time to come. Unfortunately, Mom fell and broke her lower leg one day as she went down the three entrance steps going to the mailbox. After her return home from the hospital, getting her down the steps on crutches to the car for the doctors' appointments was really stressful. Even going grocery shopping, toting the bags from the car up three steps and into the house, was now an even bigger deal for the two of us. I guess we never gave any thought when we bought the place that just three stairs was going to be such a roadblock. It was like Mom had become somewhat of a prisoner in her own home because she just wanted to stay put. Even a couple of lifelong friends stopped coming to visit Mom because access for them was becoming just as challenging. I think they were fearful that they would break a leg at our house on those steps. Who plans for three steps at an entry in a retirement community anyway?

—From a client interview, 57 years young

Creating Curb Appeal and Accessibility

Most visitors to a home will park on the street or possibly be dropped off at the closest walkway to the home, which might be from the driveway. There are several key issues to keep in mind when planning the initial access.[2]

- If the driveway has a slope, allow enough flat surface area at the top of the drive or create some level plateau that has adjacent access to the walk so cars are not parking on a slope.

- Landscape berms built from ground soil and filled over with plant material, mulch, or beds of rock materials disguise the change in elevation and gradual slope of pathways. This is a good way to soften the visual impact of added ramps should they be required at the front or side of the property.

- In a climate where there is snow or ice, the grade of the property might make the entire residence inaccessible. Snowmelt tubing installed in the driveway surface or in the framing of the front porch and steps can be a valuable investment in a client's future as well as an immediate convenience. The tubing may be expensive to purchase, but it is usually less than the cost of medical bills that may result after a nasty fall.

- If there are needed or desired transitions in the hard landscape plan between areas such as the drive and walkways or, depending on the type of materials being used, there should be no more than a quarter-inch from one level to the next, if there is any level change at all.

- Avoid the use of trees or plants that may drop flowers, seeds, or fruit as they can cause a slipping hazard when they get wet or decompose.

- A covered walk from the drive to the accessible entrance is preferable to provide protection from wind and rain.

- In driveway areas, plan to allow for a 60-inch diameter for maneuvering a wheelchair when a passenger is dropped off so no one is limited from visiting the residence.

- A clear line of sight from the front entrance to the street will make finding the entrance easier and diminish the potential for criminal activity. And if someone should fall at the front entry, they will be more likely to be seen from the street.

Planning the Exterior Paths

Start your layout by ensuring there is plenty of space for the walkways to the desired entrance of the residence. The primary walkway from the curb or driveway to the accessible door should be a minimum of 36 inches wide (preferably 48 inches wide). Make a gradual approach to the entrance (less than 5 percent incline), even if it means that a longer route must be drawn out to overcome the unique contours or slope in the property.

For new construction projects, a typical landscape plan includes specifications for re-grading of paths to ensure proper irrigation and site drainage. This phase of work provides the design professional with the ideal opportunity to create a hardscape plan for both accessible drives and walkways, each working together to provide level drop-off points and landing pads and to reduce the height difference between the street, the drive, and the primary entrance door.

For an existing residence, re-grading may also be a good place to begin planning of pathways. But changes to the grading work alone are not always cost effective if there are no other significant changes or if the grading is not part of an overall remodeling plan, because the work might also then need to include the rearrangement of irrigation systems, the reposition of large trees or plants, or the moving of underground electrical, water, and sewer systems.

When planning the paths, there are a few basic guidelines to follow: eliminate all curbs (or provide cuts in curbs), avoid steps when possible in the route of the path, and specify textured non-slip, low-maintenance materials for any paths, ramps, and stair treads that carry out the design intent.[3]

5.3 In this 1955 residence by architect Paul Rupolph, FAIA, architectural features include great barrier-free access with its wide driveway and sidewalk leading up to the level threshold at the entrance door.

Building More Accessible Options into Your Plans

When the need arises to accommodate those residents or guests requiring the use of wheelchairs or crutches, the shortest line between two points is still an ideal solution. To achieve that, the situation may require the installation of a ramp to pro-

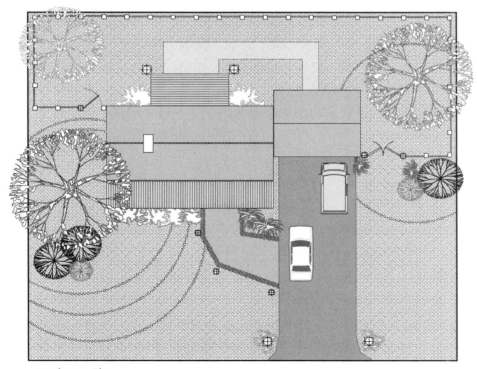

5.4 Plan the hard and soft landscape with accessibility as part of the plan. Create level common paths from the street and driveway to the entrance using low maintenance, textured materials accented with plantings, and lighting that clearly define the pathways.

Landscape Plan

5.5 This ramped access to the front door of a townhouse reflects the linear style of the balcony railing and shutters while clearly defining the accessible entrance to the residence.

vide access to the entrance to the house because of natural or manmade grades and contours of the property. Ramps may be permanent additions to the landscape or temporary, as would be the case for someone returning home after hip surgery or with a broken leg and in a wheelchair.[4]

Specifications and configurations for ramps and handrails are generally based on the Uniform Building Code (UBC) but are subject to local or community building codes. The minimum suggested width of any ramp is 36 inches wide. Wider widths of 48 inches are preferred and can more easily accommodate those in an electric wheelchair, scooter, or those with an assistive animal by their side.

Short-run ramps may be practical alternatives if the height difference between the property grade and the entrance floor is 18 inches or less. But as the height difference increases, ramps must be lengthened to maintain a proper easy-to-roll, accessible slope.

Side rails along ramps should be enclosed in some way. Horizontal bands, balusters, handrails, and/or pickets keep individuals within the ramp and path. Multiple, closely spaced pickets can be an option in place of the secondary horizontal rails provided the space between the pickets does not exceed 4 inches.

5.6 When substantial changes to elevation require the use of ramps, they should be integrated into the landscape and blend into the overall architectural statement of the residence, property, and neighborhood.

5.7 Design ramps with access from the drive to the home's entry with a slope that slowly increases in height. Ideally, there should be no more than a 1 foot rise in 12 feet of ramp length.

Handrails on the interior side of the ramp should be made up of continuous runs of railing and should extend 12 inches beyond the end of the ramp at 30 to 32 inches above the ramp floor. The rails should be between $1\,^1/_2$ and $1\,^3/_4$ inches in diameter and should be shaped so that a hand can comfortably, easily grip it. Mount handrails so that they are no more than $1\,^1/_2$ inches away from the sides to prevent an injury to an arm from sliding between the side and rail.[5]

The pitch, rise, or slope of a ramp should range between a ratio of 1:12 to 1:20 or, in other terms, no more than 1 foot rise in 12 feet of length of ramp. Slopes at 1:20 are considered suitable for walking ramps and generally don't require handrails or curbs. From beginning to end, the slope of continuous runs of ramp must always remain the same.

Bends, switchbacks, curves, and turns in the ramps due to property size limitations or ramp locations need to accommodate turns of a wheelchair. Keep the path design simple and as straightforward as possible to avoid difficulties in travel. Long circuitous ramps can be problematic for many wheelchair users because of the strength and stamina necessary to ascend a long distance. Curves of nearly all sizes, radiuses, and shapes present their own issues. Wheelchair users usually have one side of the body that is weaker than the other, which may make negotiating curves in the ramping structure difficult.

Ramps can provide the best accessible route, but they are usually difficult to conceal. Landscaping can do a lot to mask the utilitarian nature of

5.8 With small lots and building codes that require certain setbacks in construction, side ramps with switchbacks are one solution to accessibility.

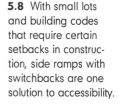

5.9 Specify materials that can stand the test of time, but the design should include visual changes between paths, ramps, and driveways such as preserved or man-made wood products, stone, brick, and/or brick pavers.

5.10 and 5.11 Metal components and railings such as powder-coated aluminum are readily available and can be installed quickly and economically when unexpected events or sudden changes require quick adaptations needed by the client.

ramps. When ramps are to become a permanent addition to the property, specify complementary construction materials like pressure-treated lumber or manmade/wood composite materials to help them blend into the backgrounds.

The ramp materials should include a type and style that provide a weatherproof, non-slip, or textured surface. Wood flooring materials may be preserved from the effects of weather and finished using deck stain or paint with small-grain sand. New concrete surfaces, before dry, can be brushed to define grains and textures. Manmade or composite deck lumber products are long lasting and have a texture and color integrated into the materials.

Brick or stone has an aesthetic appeal but should be used sparingly because it does not lend itself to being very level. Manmade tile materials with a textured finish might also be an alternative with limited applications as long as small-sized tiles are specified and installed with slightly larger grout lines. But each of these options can be used in concert with other materials, perhaps as a visual border for decorative effect and as a visual cue to the curb, at the beginning or end of a ramp section, or at a change of ramp direction.

Metal ramps, often portable, are basically acceptable, functional alternatives when other choices of materials or permanent modifications are not possible. These ramps may not contribute much in the way of aesthetic appeal or visual value, unless custom designed, but they can be a necessity, particularly if an immediate need arises due to sudden impairment. The initial higher and life-cycle costs usually do not justify their use in residential projects.

Carpeting does not provide an ideal finish material. It may become slick when wet, and continued moisture trapped between the carpeting material and the substructure below can cause concrete material to crack and sprawl and wood material to rot and decay, thus limiting the ramp's useful life.

When laying out the plans and selecting the most harmonious materials, considerations for style, type, and construction should all be made based on who will provide the maintenance, when, and how often.

For entryways where the height difference between the property's grade level and the entry floor is substantial or the property lot is small, ramps may not provide the best solution. In such cases, a motorized lift can be installed. Lifts can be integrated into the home's architectural design and should be covered with a roof structure that protects both the occupant and the mechanism from inclement weather.

For individuals who use walkers, canes, or crutches, ramps may not be the ideal choice to get to the entrance from the street, drive, or curb. It can be very challenging to walk on wood slats with gaps in between, keep balanced on even a small slope, or maintain a steady gait. In such cases, steps between grade elevations may actually provide better solutions, as long as stair risers are kept to minimum dimensions and handrails are provided (even if for only one step and one riser).[6]

House numbers are seldom at the top of the list of accessible considerations. Commonly thought of more as a decorative element, they are a part of the design of the front elevation. However, numerals that are easy to read and strategically positioned for best visibility are a must.

There are many creative ways of dealing with house numbers, but keep safety and security at the top of the list when choosing location and lighting. Here are four guidelines to follow:

1. Locate the numbers in a higher position above or along side of any architectural feature in an easily visible location that can be readily seen from the street.

5.12 On-street accessible parking in the front of this series of homes creates visitability to each individual residence, while providing access for friends and family members who may have disabilities.

5.13 and 5.14 House numbers should be of a size that is easy to read from the street and in a location that is easy to find by service people, caregivers, or emergency personnel.

2. Choose numbers that contrast well with the background.

3. Numbers should be very well lit, making the house easy to find at night by visitors and emergency and rescue personnel.

4. Remember also that generally numbers are read horizontally, from left to right, rather than vertically.

Design professionals and their clients can often get clever with signage and graphic layout, but clever is not appreciated when one is searching up and down a street for the right house when it is dark and the neighborhood is unfamiliar. It should be easy to spot the house numbers, especially when time may be of the essence.

The Americans with Disabilities Act (ADA) provides the design professional with guidelines for public and commercial property. However, local building codes and property and homeowners associations may have their own specific rules and regulations that cover exterior changes or modifications. Any structural additions must be submitted to these groups for their prior written approval.

Lighting up the Exterior

The front areas of the house should ideally have multiple sources of lighting, especially at the most-used entry areas.[7] Choose fixture styles that filter, glaze, or soften and avoid those that might create harsh glare from bare or exposed bulbs.

Illuminating the primary walkway is important for wayfinding at night. But it should be noted that paths be designed not only for access but also for the safety and security of the individual as they make their approach to the entrance of the residence. Placement of the fixtures should visually indicate the beginning of the route and the end of the path. Position the fixtures in such a way

5.15 Plan to use a variety of exterior light sources to create a safe and secure path, including accent lighting around plants that define a path, security lights that flood the landscape, and fixtures at or near the entrance.

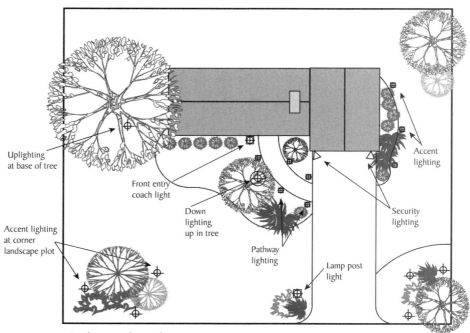

Uplighting at base of tree

Front entry coach light

Down lighting up in tree

Accent lighting at corner landscape plot

Pathway lighting

Lamp post light

Accent lighting

Security lighting

Landscape Lighting Plan

that the natural growth and spreading of plant material will not block the light, thereby creating an ongoing maintenance chore. Motion-activated lights, with sensors that turn lights on automatically when someone approaches an entrance, offer added convenience. Landscape features near the walkway such as dense bushes, tall trees, or tall fences should be well lit to eliminate shadows where potential trouble might hide.

Low-level landscape lighting typically used around plant beds, trees, and architectural elements is an economical solution to define the junctions between walkways and illuminate stairs and steps. Additional options may include photocell lighting controlled by the ambient light that will automatically go on at dusk and turn off at dawn. While many common outdoor lighting systems use low-voltage power sources with wiring that is safe and easy to install, solar-powered lighting provides the option to change, add, or move the lighting as the need arises. In either case, choose ones where replacing the lamp is an easy task.

5.16 Dual wall sconces or carriage lighting give this entrance to the courtyard of this home an aesthetic appeal, but having two fixtures means that there would be one lamp working should the other lamp burn out.

Flood lighting can provide general area illumination, but a major consideration with this type of lighting is to avoid putting the person at an entry in a bright spotlight, thereby illuminating them but possibly hiding an intruder. Install fixtures where there might be a potential obstacle as a result of the topography or grade that cannot be eliminated or moved altogether. While it may be dramatic in certain applications for decorative effect, it is best to avoid bright beams of direct light as they can be temporarily blinding.

If there must be steps or stairs, then it is important that they be properly illuminated so that the stairs and handrails are easy to locate in the dark. Lighting at the side of a stair riser is preferable to lighting under the edge of the stair tread, as a slightly extended tread nose can become an obstacle. Handrails should also be illuminated in some way, preferably from under the rail itself.

5.17 Plan that a doorbell is well lit and positioned so that it will be easy to locate and within access for someone in a wheelchair.

Adding wall sconces or carriage-style lighting to the sides of the door entrance keeps the face of a guest illuminated better than overhead lighting alone, which can create deep, dark shadows.

Specifying a two-bulb light fixture helps ensure that at least one will be working. Using extended-life light bulbs are highly desirable because maintenance might not be easily obtained or light fixtures not easily changed. Long-life, compact fluorescent bulbs are a good choice, as they are not only efficient in their energy savings, but also they will not need to be changed as often, thereby saving another form of energy.

Doorbells are another element to be considered when planning the exterior from both outside and inside the home. On the exterior, installing illuminated doorbell buttons allows them to be quickly spotted in dimly lit areas. They should be installed at a height easily reached by those in wheelchairs. For those with slight hearing loss, install several chimes throughout the home, particularly in a large home. For the more seriously hearing-impaired, an electrical-relay system will activate flashing lights when the doorbell rings. For others, a bed-rocker mechanism may be used to alert a person who may be resting or sleeping.

5.18 Combination doorbells and intercoms, when connected to a whole-house monitoring system or to the telephone, allow the resident to speak with whomever is at the door without an unnecessary trip to the entrance itself.

Having an intercom doorbell that works through the phone system is a highly desirable option. With a speaker outside the front door, certain voice-alert systems can be connected to the phone system so that when someone rings the doorbell, it activates a distinct ring to every phone in the house. Wherever the homeowner is on the property, they can answer the phone, decide whether or not to disconnect the security system, and let the person into the home without having to come all the way up to the door. This allows someone who is on another level of the home, mobility impaired, or just happens to be sick in bed that day to learn in advance who is at the door and allow the visitor to enter. Some models include mini-cameras that permit homeowners to view on television screens or monitors who is at the front door.

Creating an Accessible Entrance and Door

At the entrance to the residence, designs should include a flat, level landing or platform that is large enough for someone using a mobility device to maneuver in and around during entry-door operation. The minimum dimension should be a footprint of 5 feet by 5 feet, but larger spaces should be included whenever space permits.

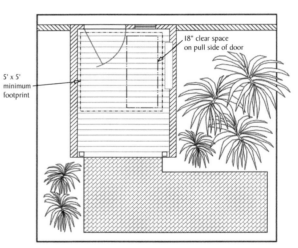

18" clear space on pull side of door

5' x 5' minimum footprint

Exterior Entry Plan View

5.19 A flat level landing pad just outside the entrance door should be provided with a minimum footprint of 5 square feet, but larger spaces give additional room for packages, luggage, and groceries.

Local and state building codes that address emergency egress may require that entry doors push out, so it may be ideal to plan for an even larger entrance footprint or landing pad to accommodate the out-swing of the door. Include a minimum of 18 inches of wall space on the pull side of the door to allow the movement of the door, allowing the individual the space to step or maneuver over and out of the path of the door swing.[8]

Space permitting, provide for seating accommodations such as a sturdy bench or add a built-in shelf that provides a place to drop packages while locating keys. Building a roof, extending a cover, or installing an awning that sufficiently covers the main entry footprint will provide shelter to residents as they unlock the door and protect guests while they wait for the door to be answered.

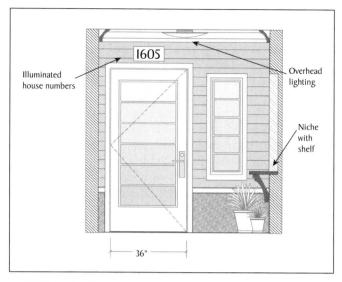

Illuminated house numbers

Overhead lighting

Niche with shelf

1605

36"

Front Entry Elevation

5.20 A recessed niche, wall-mounted shelf, or bench gives the client a spot to temporarily place items such as packages, an umbrella, or a cane while locating keys and unlocking the doors.

Specify an entry door that is at least 36 inches wide but preferably 42 to 48 inches. Another option is a set of 5- to 6-foot-wide double doors that would provide a convenient, safe entry. An extra-wide entry door will not only allow for mobility aids but also will permit a caregiver to enter alongside an adult, a person laden with packages to easily maneuver through the door, and furniture to be moved into and out of the residence.

CASE IN POINT

My entire family loves to snow ski, and it's one of the things that pulls the extended family together. During the last get-together in Park City, Utah, I was hot-dogging it down the slope when my ski pole broke in two and I tumbled down the slope, breaking my shoulder and arm and spraining my left leg. My son didn't see me fall, and both his skis ran over me. My injuries required surgery, but even after a long recuperation, I was still using a walker, sometimes crutches. As a teacher at the local community college, I wanted to get back to work. I could get around fairly well with the help of students and faculty occasionally carrying my laptop and books. Nice wide doors, sidewalks without steps, and so forth.

But once at home, going through the small side door from the garage, arms full and propped up on crutches, was just no easy task. I would have gone through the front doors, a nice wide set of double doors, doors that no one really uses except to retrieve the mail and newspaper, but with the steps up from the sidewalk to the porch, I didn't consider that the best option either. It makes me think about when I am old and gray, maybe in a wheelchair or walker. How the heck will I ever get through any of the doors?

—From a client interview, 64 years young

Extra-wide doors that can be installed to pivot offer an option to more easily open what might otherwise be a door too heavy to operate. Exterior pivot doors are not as easy to be made weather-tight as a traditional door, doorjamb, and frame, particularly in colder and/or rainy climates, but the installation of vinyl door sweeps along the bottom edge provides some protection from the elements.

Power-door operators are truly a hands-free product as far as the door itself goes, and they have become more attuned to residential use in sizing down the hardware itself. Most units still require a remote to be carried or a button to be pushed to actually open the door, but they will eliminate the need to pull or push the door itself. Your client may not be quite ready to install a power door in their front entry, but they might think about it for the door that they personally access as the primary entrance for everyday use—which is often not the main entry, but one that leads directly in from where they park their car.

5.21 Entrances to the interior should have flat door thresholds that minimize any physical barrier between the interior and exterior that might create a hazard for someone with a walker or chair.

Thresholds at doors and entrances are a required building component to help prevent water and wind intrusion, but they can become obstacles for those in wheelchairs or walkers when they are above the level of the adjacent floors.

But a threshold that may seem like such a small "bump" in the road to a fully able person can be a "mountain" to the person who is prevented from reaching the other side. If those obstacles are eliminated from the beginning of any design work, then, if at any point in their lives the client should have an accident or become less agile, complete and independent access is provided into the home.

When a fully flush and level threshold is not possible or practical, guidelines dictate that thresholds be no taller than

5.22 This entrance features a textured stone material that extends from the front entry into the residence. Weather stripping or door sweeps on the door itself combined with a roof overhang allow this entry to be covered from the elements, except for the strongest of rain and windstorms.

a $^1/_2$ inch and have bevels on each side with a ratio of 1:2.[9] If extreme weather conditions are a concern, a slotted floor drain butting up against the exterior side of the door threshold can provide additional protection from the elements.

Glass panels or sidelights next to the entry door permit natural light to be introduced into an interior entry. This is an excellent addition for homes with small, dark, and narrow foyers. The bottom of the glass should be at levels where various family members, whether they are tall or short, seated or standing, would be able to view who is at the door before opening it.

When selecting the door hardware for the entry, think in terms of aesthetics, of course, but also in terms of ease of use and operation, maintenance, and security. Passage hardware should feature lever-style handles and, along with deadbolts or locks, be installed no higher than 36 inches above the finished floor (AFF). Door-assist mechanisms and ball bearing hinges make heavy wood, solid core, or metal doors easier to open for individuals with limited body strength. Screen doors that move to the side or roll out of the way make getting in and out easier for everyone.

5.23 Choose door handles with levers rather than thumb-style latches that would be difficult for someone with arthritis or other ailments to easily use. Slightly oversized ones work well with larger doors aesthetically, but require a bit less pressure of the hand, fist, or arm to operate.

DESIGNING SECURITY FOR YOUR CLIENTS

Security measures, especially for the elder population who can be more vulnerable to attacks and home invasions, need to be included during the design process. Door manufacturers offer additional protection from break-ins with products made of steel on the exterior and wood-grained vinyl, laminates, or real wood veneers on the interior side. Additional choices include fiberglass doors because of their strength, dent resistance, ability to imitate the visual warmth of wood, and low maintenance; and French doors that have impact-resistant glass openings.

There are multiple options to keep clients and their family members safe, such as hard-wired and wireless alarms, intercoms, and phone systems. A key security product that provides convenience now but will be truly appreciated if your client is ever in a wheelchair is an intercom with a portable telephone link located near or next to the doorway. These can be linked to the telephone so that when someone is at the door, there is a special ring on the phone and then no matter where your client is on the property, they can answer, find out who is at the door, and, if they choose, input a special code into the phone and unlock the door.

Another choice might be the installation of a communications center that uses a monitor to safely screen visitors. Several products now on the market are designed to interface with each other to expand the abilities of their products. A twenty-first-century doorbell system can be installed at each exterior entrance as well as a front gate that is integrated with a camera or cameras so that the client is able to view who is at the door, hold a conversation, and then, if they wish, proceed to unlatch the door, all from a remote location.

The superior man, when resting in safety, does not forget that danger may come. When in a state of security, he does not forget the possibility of ruin. When all is orderly, he does not forget that disorder may come. Thus, his person is not endangered, and his States and all their clans are preserved.

—CONFUCIUS

Recent advances in electronic technology have made security protection both affordable and easy to install for new construction as well as for the retrofit of existing homes. Readily available systems that use existing electrical and phone wiring provide remodelers with options for voice and data controls that do not require tearing up the ceilings and walls to install cabling.

All of these systems give those with limited mobility the freedom to move about their homes and still be able to answer their doors easily. Of course, they are just as convenient for any homeowner who might be at the opposite end of the home, out in the backyard, or otherwise not able to hear someone at the front door.

Besides, there are a number of easy ways to add security without a lot of cost, such as increasing light levels at all doorways and entrances; motion-activated flood lighting around the perimeter of the residence; the use of timers to turn on and off lights, TV, and radios to create the appearance of home activity in multiple rooms; and trimming of trees and shrubs around the property that can otherwise provide hiding places for prowlers.

Additional ways to add security to a client's home include the following:

- Installation of two peepholes in each of the exterior doors at different heights to allow visibility through to any uninvited guests who may be crouching at the doorstep.

- Replacement or addition of a wall switch to activate a special flashing emergency light outside of the home. This can become an important visual cue to direct police, fire, or security directly to the home in the case of an emergency.

- Installation of deadbolts on garage and back doors in addition to the main entry. Doors into the garage and from a backyard provide more cover to would-be burglars.

- Addition of blocking devices to sliding glass doors that prevent such doors from being lifted or forced horizontally.

- Placement of highly visible decals on the glass windows and doors adjacent to the window locks that indicate that the house has an alarm system, whether or not it actually does.

- Upon completion of the project, photographs of the residence should be taken. This will create a photographic inventory of the interior and exterior, if anything is lost as a result of fire or storm, or stolen. Instruct the client to keep the pictures along with any important documents or other personal, valuable property in a fireproof safe (preferably in a location other than the master bedroom or master closet because those are areas more likely to be searched by a burglar).

Security and safety can also extend to include making sure that at least one smoke detector runs on line voltage rather than batteries; setting aside a place to install a fire extinguisher that is easy to get to in case of a fire; and installing a carbon monoxide detector in at least every sleeping room of the house. Many deaths have occurred when individuals failed to turn off their vehicle in an enclosed garage and the deadly gas works its way into the HVAC system into the interior.

Small wired and wireless video cameras, motion-sensitive announcement systems located near the drive or main walkways, fingerprint-activated door-locking systems, and individual personal alarms tied in with overall security systems are good additions to a plan to keep everyone safe and secure.

Button-operated keyless and fingerprint keypad locks are two of the possibilities that address not only security but also convenience. The need to use a traditional key to open a door is eliminated, along with the problem of finding misplaced keys.

Button-operated keyless entry systems provide easy access as long as the buttons are large, have clearly marked numbers, and require little pressure to push. However, for someone with memory loss, forgetting the number to gain entry can result in getting locked out of the house.

When installing keyless locks, different combinations can be created for additional people to whom clients would normally give keys, such as cleaning personnel, temporary workers, or visitors, thereby limiting admittance into the home. One of the main advantages to using a fingerprint-scan entry system is the elimination of either a key or a key code.

Some models also have a special timed "lockout feature" that allows the client three levels of access options. The feature allows access 24/7 for the homeowner and family members, while giving temporary access to housesitters or caregivers and time-restricted access for babysitters or housekeepers.

The work to create an accessible residence begins at the curb. It extends via paths, past the plants, up the ramps, to the entry, and across to the entry door. But the goal in all these endeavors is to provide a house, a home, and a haven that secures and comforts those who come to its doorstep.

5.24 Accessibility up to and into a home does not mean that the result will be an institutional appearance. Good-looking doors, hardware, and lighting, all well designed and installed, will ensure the safety and security of the homeowner and welcome all who knock. *Design by: Susan Cozzi. Photo by: Michiko Kurisu.*

References

1. Davies, Thomas D., Jr. and Peredo Lopez, Carol, *Accessible Home Design: Architectural Solutions for the Wheelchair User*, Paralyzed Veterans of America: Washington, DC (2006).
2. Ibid.
3. Ibid.

4. Mace, Ronald L., Barrier Free Environments, Inc., *The Accessible Housing Design File*, John Wiley & Sons: New York, NY (1991).
5. Ibid.
6. Ibid.
7. Davies, Thomas D., Jr. and Peredo Lopez, Carol, *Accessible Home Design, Architectural Solutions for the Wheelchair User*, Paralyzed Veterans of America: Washington, DC (2006).
8. Harmon, Sharon Koomen and Kennon, Katherine E., *The Codes Guidebook for Interiors*, John Wiley & Sons: New York, NY (2001).
9. Ibid.

CHAPTER 6

Creating Living Spaces

Home is a shelter from storms—all sorts of storms.

—William J. Bennett

PLEASE ENTER

As we trace American architectural styles through more than three centuries of homebuilding, they follow a recurring evolution of style. Starting with the simple and functional, moving next to a period of embellishment with the addition of structural enrichment and increased size, then adding still more ornamentation and square footage to the point of decadence, and finally reaching the last stage, which is transitional and will lead back to a more simplistic design, launching the process once again.

Historically, when studying these residences, it does not appear that aging in place was a major consideration in their design and construction. This lack of focus is not so surprising, though, considering the factors that have changed over time. People had shorter life spans; families were larger, thereby providing more possible caregivers; at least one adult child often remained in the home to care for their aging parents; if not living together, many family members remained in close proximity, thereby enabling the care for aging relatives, and there were often servants living in the home to administer any necessary care.[1]

Size, arrangement, social importance, and juxtaposition of rooms have been influenced over the years by builders, architects, topography, climate, and, to a large degree, family makeup and homeowners' personal preferences for specific architectural styles, whether they be desert adobe, New England Cape Cod, or sleek contemporary. One thing that has remained consistent in home building and design, however, is a lack of foresight as to how to eliminate barriers within houses that impede the personal freedom of residents. It is time for professionals in the built environment to make houses safe for all residents, even those who may experience physical limitations once they reach a certain age.

Often when the possibility of physical limitations are mentioned people tend to think of those who need to use wheelchairs. We need to remember that designing for those with physical limitations is not just about wheelchair users. It's about people who use walkers or who can't use steps because of stiffness or poor balance. It's about those with Post-Polio Syndrome or Parkinson's disease—or it might be about an older client who breaks a leg skiing.

When creating homes for aging-in-place, designers need not sacrifice aesthetics for accessibility. Often the changes that increase the accessibility within a home, also create other positive advantages, whether it be ease in moving furniture or even the visual sense of spaciousness that is felt.

Entries and Thresholds

Planning a home for a lifetime of accessibility—whether it is a grand Southern mansion, a New York City loft, a prairie-style residence, a Miami Beach condo, or a Craftsman-style bungalow—begins with designing at the home's entry. An entry should be large enough for those of various ages and abilities to maneuver easily to welcome guests without feeling cramped or crowded. The entry door should be as wide as possible with at least 18 inches of clear floor space on the pull side of the door for the user to move out of the way of the door when opening it to greet visitors.

The entry space should also be generous enough for guests to enter and remove jackets or outerwear, should include a bench or small chair for those who cannot stand for long periods, and should have a surface to "catch" keys, sunglasses, mail, or other hand-carried items. A coat closet or a coat tree or rack is also a valuable feature somewhere close to the front entry, regardless of the geographical location of the home. Even in climates that are warm year round, residents and their guests will always have an occasional need for sweaters, jackets, or rain gear.

The entry floor should be level and preferably without thick, high-pile area rugs (or better yet, no rugs at the entry doors at all). Another safer option—and one that keeps

6.2 Whether a single-family residence, town home, or apartment, the entry sets the tone of what lies beyond. Effective entry spaces for aging in place might include a small bench, great lighting, and a place to drop the mail while struggling with coats, shoes, or boots. *Design by: Bonnie Kissel. Photography by: Scott Levy Photography.*

6.3 Entry floors should be level with the main living spaces of the residence, and any rugs or carpets should have non-skid padding or the edges of the rugs taped down to the floor to prevent skidding around. *Design by: Interiors Joan & Associates.*

floor materials level—is to inset carpet in a recessed portion of the floor. To maintain visual interest yet provide a slip resistant surface, install textured flooring materials, such as tile or wood with a prominent grain, or specify that flooring materials be installed in patterns such as smaller tiles with well defined grout lines. But if clients prefer having an area rug in the entry, then designers should "anchor" the rug at the corners and outer edges either with furniture, if the space is large enough, or by securing the rug to the floor with tape to prevent possible tripping hazards.

Wide doorways and flush thresholds should be included throughout the home as well as at the entrance, and long hallways, which can be inconvenient at any stage of life, should be eliminated wherever possible. If it isn't feasible to actually shorten a hallway, then visually shorten it by expanding its width. A hallway that has a 42- to 48-inch minimum width not only imparts a feeling of spaciousness but also allows space for a caregiver to provide assistance, if needed, and leaves plenty of space for moving furniture from room to room. In any exceptionally large home, add a recessed niche large enough for a bench or chair in a long hallway where residents can rest along their way.

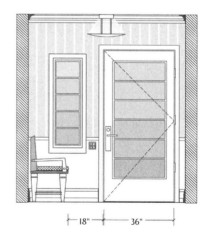

6.4 Entry spaces should have lots of light, especially when so many main entrances are often small, dark environments. Natural light through sidelight windows and overhead ceiling fixtures will illuminate spaces effectively.

Doors—What to Do In a Jamb

Doors are necessities, of course. Not only are they a form of entry and egress, but they also protect the privacy of those inside and keep out the elements, as well as intruders. A door can be an obstacle to overcome, however, for anyone—

particularly those people who require mobility aids—who is entering or exiting a house while carrying items. It is difficult enough to maneuver around an open door while carrying packages or a small child, so imagine getting in or out of the house while seated in a wheelchair: First you have to open the door, then you must hold it open with one hand while propelling the chair through with the other hand. And all of this action assumes that you have two good hands free—no packages, briefcase, suitcase and, especially, no arthritis or disability in your hands.

There are options to installing traditional hinged doors. Certainly, when doors are not required for privacy or climate control on the home's interior, then do not put them in. Because they can be a barrier and take up valuable wall space, unnecessary interior doors should be removed when creating an aging-in-place interior. Pocket doors are another option. With quality door kits and proper planning, pocket doors not only allow better ease of opening and closing, but also when they are open, they are out of sight and do not take up valuable wall space. Most pocket doors must be installed during framing; therefore, they should not be a last-minute decision. Surface-mounted pocket doors, which have a barn-door look, are popular in many loft-style buildings and are another option when retrofitting a home where there is enough wall space available.

Since pocket-door units include a track that surrounds the hanger, specify pocket-door hardware that is rated for doors weighing from 125 to 150 pounds so the wheels will not jump off the track. When hardware is grasped to pull the door open or closed, a major consideration is how much force is needed to move the door. Before specifying the model to be used, check manufacturers' guidelines. Ball-bearing units can reduce the required force from about 7 pounds to about 3 pounds. To make the pocket door especially easy to use, include D- or C-pull handles or fixed-lever handles mounted on each side of the door rather than the standard recessed finger pulls. Make the door opening wider so that the pocket door can extend into the opening approximately 2 inches to allow for the handles.

LIVING IT UP IN WIDE-OPEN SPACES

Designers and their clients should first assess the structural elements of the main living areas—or shared areas—in a home because these are rooms that are the most difficult to alter at a moment's notice to allow residents to age in place. Preventing falls should be a primary concern, and because one or two steps can easily go unnoticed and cause a fall, level changes, such as those in sunken living rooms or steps up from entries, should be avoided. Such design elements, often used by architects and builders to define large spaces and divide living areas, can also limit the entry of guests and residents who depend on mobility aids. Changes in ceiling levels can be just as effective, as are changes in wall color and texture of flooring material, among other design "tricks of the trade."

The flooring material in the main living area, as in all rooms of the home, is another important element to consider, and there are some tradeoffs among choices. It is much easier for someone who must use a walker or a wheelchair to move across hard-surface floor coverings, especially those that are non-glare and flush to the finished floor. However, very thick, plush carpeting or highly

6.5 Provide generous interior pathways around and into furniture arrangements and conversational groupings during the space planning by limiting the amount and number of upholstered and case goods. Rugs and carpets that define the groupings should be as smooth and flat as possible. *Design by: Anna Marie Hendry, Allied ASID. Photo by: Gerlick Photography.*

textured materials can have a cushioning effect if someone should fall. Flat, low-pile, wall-to-wall carpeting can be a good alternative flooring choice when warmth or sound absorption is necessary. And area rugs can be used to define spaces or add warmth or visual interest to a room so long as they are thoughtfully placed and firmly anchored to avoid being a tripping hazard.

Textural changes in flooring can delineate spaces and serve as a form of wayfinding for those who are visually impaired, just as changes in color and contrast

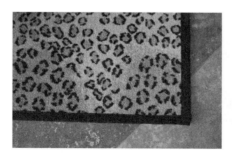

6.6, 6.7, and 6.8 Define changes in flooring materials with plenty of contrast between materials, while continuing to maintain a fairly flat surface to prevent someone from stumbling because of poor eyesight.

define spaces for others. Designers should keep in mind, however, that the impact of aging can affect clients' sight, including their perception of colors. Beginning in their 40s to 50s, most people's eyes begin to lose focus; the lens of the older eye also becomes increasingly dense and more yellow with age, which makes it more difficult to distinguish between the object itself and the background; the pupil becomes smaller in size as the eye ages and, therefore, requires more light to see clearly.[2] And according to some psychological research, strongly patterned flooring may be confusing or can even cause a sense of movement, such as vertigo, for those who are elderly or sight impaired.[3]

CREATING SUCCESSFUL ARRANGEMENTS

6.9 No matter the size of living, dining, or entertainment space, interior spaces should have furniture arrangements that not only provide accessibility but also encourage conversation between family and friends that allow for normal levels of speech.

The appeal and advantages of open floor plans is universal and certainly not limited to aging-in-place interiors. A spacious, inviting area, though, more easily accommodates those who need and use wheelchairs, walkers, canes, and other mobility aids. Since most people are uncomfortable with last-minute furniture rearrangements just so they can maneuver into a gathering, designers should position furniture in living areas to assure easy access for someone in a wheelchair, so he or she feels welcome anytime to join conversations and seated groups.

Furniture should also be arranged for those who are hearing impaired. To avoid frustration for those who might feel cut off because they can only hear parts of the conversation, designers should eliminate annoying background noises by separating conversation areas from TV and entertainment areas, if they will be used simultaneously. In addition, incorporating soft surfaces such as upholstery, soft window treatments, or acoustical flooring such as cork will help absorb noise, particularly when there are a number of hard surfaces in the room that can reflect sound. Also, include at least some seating that is arranged at 90-degree angles or face-to-face.

Have a Seat

Designers should select chairs and sofas with arms that extend to the front edge of the seat cushion and are high enough to provide stability for someone who is either standing or sitting. Chair and sofa bases designed with legs allow the person who is seated to put his or her feet back a little under the seat for stability as he or she begins to stand up. Designers should avoid specifying low, deep chairs and sofas that require someone who is seated to request assistance to get up. The best seating for aging-in-place environments are chairs in fabrics and styles that blend with other furnishings in the room and that have hydraulic or electronic "push-up" devices. With the touch of a button, the cushion and/or seat of the chair rises, then tips forward and gently lifts the seated user to an almost standing position, while the chair itself remains steady. A word of caution: Avoid recliners that are operated with levers, which require upper body strength and an ability to grip firmly or require leg strength to push the footrest down. To prevent users with limited mobility or strength from ending up as prisoners in their own chairs, specify seating that is operated with remote controls, particularly those connected to the chair via a cord or attached with Velcro® strips. Avoid selecting chairs with levers hidden between the cushion and arm of the chair.

Just as some clients have preconceived ideas of what the "standard" recliner looks like, a few people in the design industry have a mistaken idea—and not at all an aesthetically pleasing one—of what "lift chairs" look like. Remember that design professionals are problem solvers and should not be content to specify only products found "in the marketplace." Designers should locate and consult with a reputable custom furniture manufacturer or upholsterer who can guide

Design professionals should always consult with medical professionals when creating aging-in-place interiors to better understand the physical needs of their clients as they age.

According to the Urology Center of Florida, more than 13 million Americans—most of whom are women—suffer from some form of incontinence.[4] And although this condition can occur at any age, 25 percent of women and 15 percent of men over the age of 65 suffer from incontinence.[5]

Healthcare professionals usually classify incontinence either by its symptoms or by the circumstances in which it occurs. Urge-urinary incontinence, also referred to as "over active bladder" (OAB), is what happens when a person has a strong urge to urinate but cannot reach the bathroom quickly enough. According to the National Association for Continence, medical conditions such as stroke, dementia, Alzheimer's Disease, and Multiple Sclerosis (MS) can all cause urge incontinence.[6] "Typical symptoms of overactive bladder include: urinating more than eight times in a 24-hour period (urinary frequency), a strong and sudden desire to urinate (urinary urgency), and, if the urge cannot be controlled, urge urinary incontinence."[7] Sometimes outside influences will "trigger" urine leakage, such as hearing running water.[8]

Although there are treatments that can help some people with urge incontinence, challenges such as limited mobility, the inability to get out of a chair quickly, as well as distance to the nearest bathroom, can add to the problem.

Functional incontinence, which is not an inevitable consequence of aging, but rather a symptom of an underlying disorder that can be controlled or managed, is usually a situation in which a continent elderly person is unable or unwilling to urinate normally due to impaired mobility, use of sedative medication, or a psychological disturbance.[9] Although design professionals are not qualified to treat medical conditions, they can address the environmental factors, such as poor lighting, furniture that is difficult to get out of or maneuver around, long distances to bathrooms or toilets that are difficult to access—all of which are often considered contributors to this type of incontinence. And furniture specification, as well as space planning and design, can play a vital role in how well functional incontinence is managed by healthcare professionals.

the selection of an attractive chair design that is compatible with either electronic or hydraulic lift mechanisms. The function of such custom-built seating can be hidden within an attractive design of choice, a perfect blend of function and form. The installation of remote-controlled hydraulic lifts in your clients' chairs can make an immediate change in their lives, especially those who suffer with some forms of incontinence, as it will help them to get out of the chair more quickly, thereby allowing them to possibly reach the bathroom in time.

Upholstered furniture from commercial manufacturers usually has firmer seating, and most seating units are not as deep as many residential pieces, so they can be better choices for older clients. They will not get stuck in the seating and have to be pulled out.

Commercial furniture lines often use "dry construction" methods in which rather than the traditional joinery of screws and glue, pieces are attached mechanically through screws and other methods. Dry construction allows for the replacement of damaged parts without replacing the entire piece; thus, items can more easily resist wear and tear if furniture is being used to help with physical challenges such as loss of balance.

Accent pillows can serve as more than decorative accessories on a sofa or upholstered chair. They allow anyone using seating to have as much or as little back and arm support as they wish, and for someone who is shorter than average, accent pillows can make the seat shorter and, in some instances, can provide an extra "arm" to help leverage out of a chair. By the same token, a taller person can be comfortable sitting in a slightly deeper seat merely by removing a throw pillow or two.

While designers should consider individual clients' preferences when selecting cushion filling for upholstered furniture, they should also keep in mind that softer fillings that were once comfortable may become cumbersome as clients age. To make getting up and down from furniture easier and more graceful for almost everyone, designers can have seat heights of upholstered pieces raised. All-down cushions can be made more supportive by adding a central core of springs or foam. Low-slung furniture may need to become "accessory" pieces that are reserved for the use of only the most agile visitors.

Designers charged with selecting upholstered furniture should also consider the following:

6.10 While it may be decorative, pillows at the backs of chairs or on a sofa not only provide good back support but also make the seat depth shorter. The volume of interior spaces often requires the use of deep-seated upholstered items that are scaled to meet the space. *Design by: Interiors Joan & Associates.*

- Since the contrast from light to dark can help to identify the edge of a seat or a table, select furniture colors that contrast with floors and walls to compensate for visual challenges caused by aging. The recommendation is to vary the value of colors (the lightness or darkness) by at least two levels on a ten-level gray scale. This should enable most people to differentiate between the colors.

- When selecting fabrics and colors, keep in mind that color perception can be impacted by how much or how little natural light comes into a room, as well as by the type of light bulbs used.

- Details, like tassels, fringes, covered buttons, welting, and threaded trim, can become "crumb catchers" and may become maintenance issues for some clients.

6.11 Choose arms on chairs and sofas that extend to the front edge of the seat. This will make it easier for an individual to pull up to the end of the seat cushion and push up with the arms at the front of the chair. *Design by: Carol Axford, ASID, CDA Design Group. Photo by: Gerlick Photography.*

- An upholstery fabric that has even some of the following properties can be a plus: water resistance; stain resistance; antimicrobial, antifungal, and antibacterial threads; durability, and breathability.

- Specify fabric with at least 30,000 double rubs for heavy-use areas. (A double rub is a testing method using a special machine that rubs a testing pad back and forth over the fabric until it is worn out. Each back and forth stroke is known as a double rub. Commercial-grade fabrics usually wear out after 100,000 to 250,000 double rubs. Domestic fabrics are usually rated at 25,000 double rubs. You cannot tell how well fabric will hold up until it has been tested.)[10]

- Look for seat heights of 18 to 20 inches to make it easier to get in and out of chairs and sofas. Remember, however, that if the seat cushion is very soft, the "measured" height of the seat will not be accurate once someone is sitting in it.

- Strong back legs on seating, as well as stretchers, give more stability to the piece.

- The proper pitch to the seat allows people to sit comfortably with their feet on the floor and gives additional stability when sitting as well as when rising.

- Smooth edges and rounded corners help to avoid bruises or tears to thin skin.

These recommendations can be applied to projects for clients of all abilities and all ages. After all, isn't that what good design is all about?

Other Furniture and Fixtures

It is always good practice for designers of all projects—not just aging-in-place projects—to provide surfaces on which to place a drink, a plate, a book, or a lamp within easy reach of every seated person in a room. Since someone walking by may reach out to steady him or herself on a bookcase or lamp table, it is important for case pieces next to seating and close to traffic areas to be sturdy. Place delicate, purely decorative pieces in out-of-the-way corners. Assess the amount of glare reflected off of surfaces. Even when the lights are off during the day, a great deal of natural light streaming into the room may cause enough glare to be an issue.

6.12 Older clients will often have a beautiful collection of art and accessories collected through the years that help to tell their personal life story. Place those more precious items in cabinets, consoles, or other locations out of the main traffic patterns so that one can avoid running into delicate items and breaking them. *Design by: Susan Nilsson.*

Furniture corners are potential hazards not only for small children but also for adults. Square, unframed, glass-topped tables become invisible to many, resulting in bruised and battered shins and—possibly—more serious accidents. Slightly rounded corners are always more forgiving. Specify occasional table heights at levels higher than the usual 15 to 16 inches in front of a sofa or loveseat so someone who is seated can reach straight out, rather than reaching down to the table top. A table that is 20 inches high can mean less bending, particularly if the seating is firmer and higher than average. Even reaching straight out can be difficult for those whose movements are limited by arthritis, and also difficult for those with tremors caused by Parkinson's Disease, Essential Tremor Syndrome, or Multiple Sclerosis.

ILLUMINATING SPACES ADD LIGHT TO ACCESSIBILITY

In her article, "Using Color as a Therapeutic Tool," Margaret P. Calkins, Ph.D., says that as people age they not only become more sensitive to glare, but they also require three times the amount of light to see as well as those who are younger.[11] An internationally recognized leader in the field of environments for the elderly, Calkins says that the aging cornea thickens and yellows, causing the elderly to view their world through a thin yellow film, which she equates to the color of ginger ale. As the eye yellows, it tends to absorb up to 75 percent of the blue light that enters the eye. Since green is a blend of blue and yellow, this change makes it more difficult for older people to differentiate between green and blue.[12]

6.13 Good lighting in a space from a number of different light and lamp sources balances the overall light levels in a space. When choosing fixtures and lamps, keep in mind that the amount of glare from shiny surfaces makes it more difficult to see. *Design by: Maria Nutt. Photo by: Gerlick Photography.*

Calkins also points out that when complementary colors—such as green and red or other opposites on the color wheel—are used together, they will appear particularly muddy to those for whom the lens has yellowed. And according to the Center of Design for an Aging Society, because older eyes adapt more slowly to changes in light conditions, older people need more light beyond the need just for vision and safety.[13] As we age, the pupils of our eyes become less elastic and less adaptable to changes in light. An older person entering or leaving a darkened room needs more time than a younger person to adjust to changes in light levels. Abrupt changes in lighting can be hazardous and cause falls or other accidents.[14] Armed with this knowledge, good designers recognize how important it is to provide not only sufficient light but also the appropriate type of lighting because colors can be distorted by different types of light bulbs and fixtures.

When specifying ambient lighting, be sure that the fixtures are designed to conceal the bulb or the tube from direct sight to lessen the glare. Indirect lighting such as a torchiere, a wall-wash light fixture, or cove lighting will direct light toward the ceiling and walls creating ambient lighting without glare if the light source is concealed. Using dimmer switches will not only greatly extend the life of the bulb, offering less maintenance because they will

6.14 Creative lighting from overhead, indirect, and accent lighting can be dramatic, but plan to include adjustable dimmers to help balance the lighting levels while still achieving the desired type of drama. Reduced, diffused, and dimmed lighting will soften the inherent shiny nature of glass tabletops and polished marble walls but not eliminate it. *Design by: Lawrence-Mayer-Wilson Design Team. Photo by: Rosemary Carroll.*

not need to be changed as often, but it will also allow for variety in the light levels within a room. Fluorescent bulbs or tubes have a long life and, hence, require less maintenance. They also do not produce high heat, which can be a safety feature because many people lose some sense of touch as they age and could burn themselves without realizing it.[15]

To help prevent accidents, in addition to providing adequate lighting, there should be enough contrast between the color of the walls and the colors of the furniture and flooring to help those with diminished vision discern the difference. Amplify lightness contrast between foreground and background colors, and avoid using colors of similar lightness next to one another, even if they differ in saturation or hue. Select dark colors with hues from the bottom half of the color wheel against light colors from the top half of the color wheel.[16] These recommendations will help the aging eye more easily distinguish the furniture in the room, thereby helping to avoid falls.

Portable lamps not only provide flexibility but also can add to the atmosphere of the room. One of the problems, though, for some older clients may be reaching the control for the lamps or operating the switch. Several available products make it possible for residents to operate the lighting in their homes more easily. There are large adaptable switches, easier to handle for those with limited ability to grip, that can be installed over existing lamp switches to make them easier to turn, as well as non-wired, remote controls that can be plugged into a lamp itself to eliminate the need to stretch to reach the switch.

Remote controls for fixtures or appliances are always convenient for aging-in-place environments, as well as for "couch potatoes" who don't want to get up to adjust the lighting. Voice-activated units, many of which have improved in quality from previous over-sensitive models that would turn on or off inconveniently at the slightest sound, are also options for those with diminishing motor skills. Of course, everyone should be able to operate wall switches, and using rocker switches improves accessibility, as does the use of a remote. In addition, some systems can be set on an astronomical time clock that will automatically generate events at specific times of the day or times relative to sunrise or sunset. They even adjust for seasonal changes for areas where daylight savings is observed. Multiple schedules can be programmed to allow for varying settings from weekdays to weekends or holidays.

Whole-house remote control systems, whether hardwired or wireless, can manage interior and exterior lighting and security, smoke and fire alarms, as well as various modes of entertainment—computers, televisions, home theater, and radio and other audio—with a single remote touchpad. Most wired whole-house control systems are more easily installed during remodeling or new construction, but there are wireless systems that don't require special wiring to install, which is ideal for existing homes. Such systems, which operate via radio frequency technology, allow clients to enjoy many remote control features that were previously only available with hard-wired systems.

The view from an aging-in-place home can be as significant to residents as natural light, not only for the view

6.15 Wall sconces can provide the warmth not easily achieved with overhead lighting alone. Specify those that do not project out from the wall more than 4 inches and place them at 80 inches above the finished floor to avoid someone from stumbling into the fixture.

itself but also for the psychological effect that greenery has on those who experience it. According to studies led by Roger S. Ulrich, Ph.D., director of the Center for Health Systems and Design at Texas A&M University, looking at greenery can be instantly soothing, reducing fear and anger and lowering blood pressure, heart rate, and muscle tension in as little as three minutes.[17]

In homes designed with windows that are too high, outdoor views can only be enjoyed by those who are standing. To get the best garden or outdoor views from inside a home, be sure that the sill height of view windows is a maximum of 36 inches from the finished floor so that even those who are seated can enjoy seeing outdoors. This recommendation is not an aging-in-place issue, but it allows the view to be enjoyed each time the clients sit anywhere in the home.

Wall and Window Coverings

Glare and how it might reflect off of surfaces in a room is arguably the most important element to keep in mind when specifying wall treatments for common areas in the home. Glare can be affected by the time of day; the type of window coverings, flooring, and furnishings in a space; as well as by the window treatment itself. And although an abundance of natural light can be a positive factor in aging-in-place interiors, large amounts of glass can result in extraordinary glare that should be controlled.

For the hearing impaired, background noise can be just as frustrating as glare, and homes that include hard or resilient-surface flooring can be a red flag for future acoustical adjustments. Although hard-surface floors and open floorplans are easier to navigate for those who must use mobility devices, design professionals should apply their expertise to control acoustic issues that these functional necessities present. Remember that the use of fabrics and upholstered furniture can go a long way toward helping to absorb the sound bouncing off the hard surfaces in a room.

The fabric used on window treatments and upholstered pieces within a room can act as an acoustical buffer, as will area rugs. (Remember to employ methods described earlier to prevent rugs from becoming tripping hazards.) Upholstered walls, or segments of walls, and large textile wall hangings not only add to the decor of the room but can also go a long way toward absorbing background noise. Such design features can be especially beneficial in contemporary homes where less upholstery might be used.

In the dining room, runners, placemats, tablecloths, and other decorative table linens can absorb ambient sound so diners don't have to strain to hear conversations. The arrangement of

6.16 The use of fabrics for the window coverings and on the upholstered items will help to buffer the effects of sound bouncing off a large footprint of tile or wood, which is even more likely to occur if the ceilings are tall. *Design by: Lawrence-Mayer-Wilson Design Team. Photo by: Rosemary Carroll.*

furniture can also help the hearing impaired. Design the spaces so that the hearing impaired can sit without noise coming from behind them. It may be easier for them to have a conversation sitting next to a person, rather than across from them. Designers should consider this when space planning for those who are hard of hearing.[18]

It is important that residents be able to adjust window treatments and, in so doing, the amount of light admitted to a room without relying on someone else. It may seem like a small thing to those who can do so easily and without thinking, yet it can mean a lot to a disabled person when he or she doesn't have to ask for assistance to open or close the curtains or the blinds and then wait for someone else to perform the task. With the size and number of windows in larger homes today—and multiple windows per room—motorized shades are becoming popular.

6.17 These sets of solar blinds span both wide and tall windows and would otherwise be difficult to operate if they were not motorized.

There are several economical remote control options for window treatments, particularly for blinds, that can provide clients with more opportunities to maintain their independence. Motorized units are available that can operate heavier products, such as draperies, shades, shutters, windows, and many custom products—just about anything designers can create. Systems are also available that can be programmed to smoothly and quietly open and close multiple window treatments at preset times and within a fraction of an inch of coordinated preset positions—an additional advantage to the aging-in-place client. These systems answer that need for ease of use and less maintenance. Whole-house systems that integrate preset window treatment control with lighting, security, and heating and cooling throughout the home not only offer more independence and control to the residents, but can also help save on energy consumption costs as well.

WHEN IT'S TIME TO EAT

Dining rooms, the traditional gathering areas for meals, celebrations, conversation, and camaraderie, should be accessible so clients can entertain groups of family and friends without challenges to either guests' or residents' comfort or ability to maneuver. A round table lends itself to these requirements best, as demonstrated by the group that famously gathered around the Algonquin Round Table in the Roaring Twenties and came to define American wit. The group, who called themselves "The Vicious Circle," began meeting informally in 1919 for lunch at the Algonquin Hotel in New York City. They discovered that the round table worked best for involving everyone in conversation.[19]

A round table tends to lose its effectiveness in this regard, however, as the size of gatherings increases. Room size and shape also limits the use of a round table. When designers have the opportunity to configure or reconfigure a dining area, however, it is worth planning a space that will hold a round table, particularly when conversation and repartee are important factors in clients' social lives. Allow plenty of space around the table for traffic to move easily and for easy access for those who use mobility aids. Because it lacks legs at the edge that interfere with wheelchairs and other mobility devices, a pedestal table is a good choice for an aging-in-place client. To avoid tipping hazards if someone leans on the edge of the table for support, however, specify only pedestal tables that are extremely stable and well designed so the table will remain firmly in place. Another important factor in selecting a table is the depth of the table apron: An apron that is too deep can make it uncomfortable—or even impossible—for someone seated in a wheelchair or even for someone with large thighs.

6.18 In some areas of the country, compartmentalized formal dining spaces have fallen out of style in new home construction in favor of great room spaces. But dining tables still hold a heart in the American culture as a place to gather, dine as a family, and share memories. Consider tables with legs that expand to permit the client to open up the table for those special holiday events that encourage family gatherings. Avoid tables with small single pedestals that might tilt when someone places their hands at the table's edge and uses it for leverage when standing up from a chair. *Design by: Bernadette Upton ASID, LEED.*

Chairs around the dining table, as those in the living area, should have sturdy arms that come to the edge of the seat front to support the user as he or she sits or stands. Colors or materials of chairs should contrast with surrounding materials, particularly the floor and the tabletop so that the chair seat is clearly defined and easy to see. Compare, too, the depth of the table apron and the height of the chair seat and arms. The chair arm height could prevent someone who is seated from moving close enough to the table.

GATHERING SPACES FOR ONE AND ALL

With the wide use of residential custom technology and electronics, home theaters and media rooms have become very popular. Designers creating such rooms should apply the same aging-in-place principles as those applied to other living areas: No steps up or down, no sunken seating areas, flooring that accommodates mobility devices while still serving as a sound buffer, natural and artificial lighting that is easily adjusted, stable furniture that gives support, and seating that is comfortable—appropriately firm and of the correct depth—and easy to get into and out of. Specialty furniture pieces, including recliners, particularly those with built-in cup holders, are designed specifically for media rooms. Again, motorized seating operated via an easy-to-access remote control can benefit aging-in-place clients, and cup holders may mean the person seated doesn't have to reach far to set a drink on a nearby table surface.

New homes that include state-of-the-art wiring and cabling allow residents to meet their current audio/video, security, and other technology requirements, as well

6.19 Home theater systems are not only popular but also within easy access and affordable for many of aging baby boomers. Whether a dedicated space for home entertainment or not, the same principles hold true for open spaces that are easy to get around in with comfortable, flexible, and supportive sofas and chairs.
Design by: Judith Sisler Johnson.

as to anticipate future high-tech advancements. Although wireless systems are available that are options for retrofitting older homes—easily and inexpensively—for current and future technology needs, CAT5 or structured cabling for whole-house audio and video can be one of the best investments to include in a new home today. A wired home usually operates more effectively than wireless systems, particularly if there is a chance that the home will contain several other wireless signals that would cause radio interference. And even as some home buyers have come to expect high-tech infrastructures in new homes, such wiring is an extremely important feature in a home designed for aging in place.

When a high-tech infrastructure is incorporated into the design at the outset, even if not all of the equipment has been purchased right away, the system is in place and can be added to and upgraded in the future. Structured wiring systems can provide current and future multiple plug-and-play access points for computer networking, multimedia, phone, and high-speed Internet access. Technology is a key factor in home safety through the constantly upgraded security systems that are available, including safety camera systems that offer the ability to keep an eye on the outside world.

According to a 2004 survey conducted by the California market research firm, American Lives, nearly two-thirds (64 percent) of home buyers are interested in "integrated 'smart house' systems."[20] For such systems to gain widespread use, however, "a product or system has to offer a solution to a problem," says Brooke Warrick, president of American Lives.[21] This research and others like it—including findings published in *The Robb Report*[22]—also indicate that consumers, particularly baby boomers, are willing to pay more for simplicity and convenience, an attitude that will be amplified as the older population increases and aging clients become less tolerant of learning how to use new systems and equipment.[23] The old adage "keep it simple" is good advice for designers who are seeking technology that can facilitate their clients' ability to age in place.

6.20 With the proliferation of flat panel and high-definition televisions, programmable lighting systems, and motion-sensitive alarms, getting the wiring in the right location is an important first part of a successful design plan, as no one wants to tear open a finished wall to bury a wire or two.

CASE IN POINT

My wife and I both enjoy the home theater we put in last fall. We enjoy watching Gary Cooper and John Wayne movies over and over again. My only complaint is with the use of the equipment. My designer hooked me up with this electronics guy who really knows his stuff, except when it comes to dealing with people who can't see in the dark to work those tiny little remote control buttons to operate the TV and cable. Remotes need to be bigger with bigger buttons that you can actually feel with your fingers and see with aging eyes.

—From a client interview, 78 years young

6.21 Dedicated home theater spaces and media rooms are desirable to many in the aging population as it gives them the opportunity to watch favorite movies in big screen format when they might not otherwise be able to go to the movie theater due to health reasons or physical disabilities.
Design by: Margery Caruana Farr, Allied ASID. Photo by: Gerlick Photography.

At the outset of any project, designers might include specialists to assist in the planning. A CEDIA (Custom Electronic Design and Installation Association) certified professional on the design team can assist, plan, and install the home theater equipment, multiroom audio, and home automation systems. These professionals can ensure that home designs will ultimately be flexible enough to meet clients'—and their caregivers'—evolving needs. Small details such as running the wiring behind removable baseboards or crown moldings for easy access can make later adjustments much easier.

One frustration of many clients, as well as designers, is how to deal with the unsightly cords and wires that connect all the electronic equipment. Readymade solutions are available that can hide the wiring and make it appear as decorative wall paneling. These modular systems cover all or part of the wall with panels that hide cords and wires. Some systems allow easy access behind the modules when needed, and other systems include secure hiding places for small valuables within locked modules that can be accessed only with an instrument similar to a key that the owner can store separately.

With improvements in residential technology and electronics, it is likely that the communications or "command" center for a home will be either the home office or the media room—or both. And whether or not a specific room in the home is specified as a media room, with the increasing popularity of flat screen televisions, room design has become more flexible. A flat screen television does not "intrude" into the room as obviously, both visually as well as physically. Flat screen TVs have eliminated the need to hide that ugly picture tube that pushes the screen farther into the room. It also eliminates the need to find a deep enough cabinet to encase the entire TV, hiding the picture tube. Some screens today can be hidden with art. With the push of a button on a remote, the art is raised and the screen appears, or with the push of a button a projection screen comes down out of the ceiling.

Most homes include a television in nearly every room, and if the home is truly "connected," then the ability to communicate exists throughout the home. New ideas for truly connected homes can be found regularly in *Electronic House* magazine, particularly when they announce their annual awards for Homes of the Year. One example of a home designed for the future was the 2006 Gold Award winner. Each of the winners of the *Electronic House* magazine 2006 Home of the Year awards highlighted how electronics in well-planned homes can contribute to the independence and security that residents value throughout their lives.[24] The Gold Award winner was an outstanding example of this.

When any family member living in the residence enters this 4,500-square-foot home, he or she is greeted by name by Cleopatra, an "avatar," or electronic personality, who appears on a 42-inch plasma screen that faces the front door. Cleopatra then announces any event of interest that might have occurred during the family member's absence, such as visitors, phone calls, voice mails, e-mail messages, and deliveries. Next to Cleopatra on the screen is a summary of additional information, including who else is in the house, photos of recent visitors to the front door, household activity and alerts, local weather forecast, stock market changes, and even the national security level.

A whole-house control system, an audio distribution system, a security system, and a home lighting system, as well as a home theater and some video distribution, were included in the house at the time of construction, and much of the wiring was run behind removable baseboards for easy access. The home control system operates over the home's Internet Protocol Network, which is similar to a computer network in offices.

6.22 Entertainment systems, when combined with home office or adjacent workspaces, allow baby boomers to multitask, something they have grown up doing very well, such as emailing friends while keeping an eye on the stock reports ticker along the bottom line of the TV screen and listening to their favorite news reporter. *Design by: Patti Watson.*

Through motion sensors, Cleopatra "knows" when someone approaches the front door or enters a room. And by scanning tiny radio frequency identification (RFID) chips on key fobs or other personal items, Cleopatra can even detect which family member is entering or leaving as he or she passes through the door. Just imagine how much more secure a client can feel—particularly if he or she lives alone—with a system that can alert the resident when someone is approaching the front entry.

Ease of use was one of the most important considerations in designing the Cleopatra system. Similarly, ease of maintenance and ease of use are at the top of the wish lists of important features requested by baby boomers and members of other generations. Bells and whistles are impressive only if they can be put to use.

The magazine's winner demonstrates the advantages of technology when combined with simplicity of use. Imagine the freedom—whether it's freedom from being interrupted in the midst of writing, resting, or sunning by the pool, or the freedom to maneuver quickly around the property—and independence of a resident who can, from his or her home computer—or bedside or poolside—access a home control system from various points in the home, check who is at the door, alarm the door, adjust interior and exterior lighting, and modify the watering schedule. Systems can detect who is in bed, turn off lights, lower the shades, turn off the music, and set the night alarm. There are, of course, a number of separate systems on the market that handle some of these tasks, but the ideal situation is to package them all into one system and then to be able to control them throughout the home.

What we are talking about is installing a "brain" in a client's home, a system that monitors room occupancy and intelligently switches the lights, music, heating, and cooling on and off when appropriate. A system specifically designed to meet their needs can save clients' energy costs, as well as set the home for vacation mode, which can adjust lighting, television, or radio to give the impression that the homeowners are still at home.

Imagine a house that will wake up residents at requested times and provide them with weather forecasts and reminders of important appointments or events that day. Then, to make it even more inviting, when residents wake up on a cold winter morning, there already is a fire in the fireplace. These are not homes of the future, but homes that can be designed with current technology.

Security is also at the top of the list of features important to homeowners. And a home alarm system should be easy to use from anywhere—and by anyone—in the house, yet ease of use is often overlooked until the system is installed. Rather than dealing with what is installed or retrofitting systems, homeowners may not use their systems as often as they should, which makes it more of a liability. Most alarm systems must be set in one part of the home before a resident leaves the house, which requires at least one free hand and correct entry of the code. Either of these steps can be a challenge for someone with arthritis or another condition that limits small motor abilities. If a resident is carrying packages or can't move quickly because of a physical disability, then getting out of the house before the system is armed is another difficulty. When the process of getting in and out of the house

6.23 Alarm and alert system key control pads should be carefully selected. Specify those that have larger numerical displays and buttons that are easy to find and push. Consider a location from the floor that would be easy to reach should someone need to activate the system from a wheelchair.

6.24 Many baby boomers that have taken care of an ailing parent, elderly friend, or needy relative already know what lies ahead for them. That kind of life experience certainly does not stop them from desiring highly detailed interiors, full of the newest and greatest technology, finishes, furnishings, and art that can accommodate any physical challenges down the road. *Design by: Susan Cozzi. Photo by: Michiko Kurisu.*

becomes too arduous, then the system frequently is not used at all. An alarm that is linked to the whole-house control system provides the client with an easier approach by just swiping his or her key fob if they are the last one to leave the house, and then the system is automatically armed.

Baby boomers have high expectations, love bells and whistles, and want everything yesterday, so working with an expert to design a brain for a client's home, whether wireless or wired, can be an excellent investment and probably not a hard sell. A luxury? Yes, possibly. But ask someone who is recuperating from a hip replacement or who is sight or hearing impaired, suffers from arthritis, or is confined to a wheelchair, and he or she may not have the same opinion. To such a client, it might just spell that magical word "independence," and to his or her family it could mean less stress and less worry.

References

1. Mintz, Steven and Kellogg, Susan, *Domestic Revolutions: A Social History of American Family Life*, The Free Press: New York, NY (1988).
2. Lighthouse International, *The Aging Eye: Normal Changes in the Aging Eye*, www.lighthouse.org/medical/the-aging-eye (accessed June 10, 2006).
3. Landefeld, C. Seth; Palmer, Robert M.; Johnson, Mary Anne; Johnston, C. Bree; Lyons, William L., *Current Geriatric Diagnosis & Treatment*, Chapter 12, p. 82, McGraw-Hill: New York, NY (2004).
4. Urology Center of Florida, *Urinary Incontinence*, www.ucof.com/education/incontinence.php (accessed March 5, 2007).
5. Ibid.
6. National Association for Continence, *The Four Basic Types of Urinary Incontinence*, www.nafc.org/about_incontinence/types.htm (accessed June 25, 2006).
7. National Association for Continence, *Urge Incontinence*, www.nafc.org/index.asp?PageName=UrgeExpandedTreatment (accessed June 25, 2006).
8. Ibid.
9. Australian Government, Department of Health and Ageing, *Continence: Functional Incontinence*, www.healthconnect.gov.au/internet/wcms/publishing.nsf/Content/continence-what-functional.htm (last updated October 20, 2004).

10. Association for Contract Textiles, *ACT Voluntary Performance Guidelines: Test Method Descriptions*, www.contracttextiles.org/pdf/abrasion.pdf (accessed May 2, 2006).
11. Calkins, Margaret P., Ph.D., *Using Color as a Therapeutic Tool*, www.ideasinstitute.org/article_021103_b.asp (accessed May 2, 2006).
12. Ibid.
13. Center of Design for an Aging Society, *Lighting Your Way to Better Vision*, 2006.
14. Schmall, Vicki L., *Sensory Changes in Later Life*, www.extension.oregonstate.edu/catalog/html/pnw/pnw196/ (accessed May 2, 2007).
15. Pennsylvania Department of Public Welfare, *Gerontology and Normal Aging*, "Personal Care Home Direct Care Staff Person Training," www.dpw.state.pa.us/pch_comptest/module6.html (accessed June 25, 2007).
16. Arditi, Aries, Ph.D., *Effective Color Contrast: Designing for People with Partial Sight and Color Deficiencies*, Lighthouse International, www.lighthouse.org/accessibility/effective-color-contrast (accessed August 5, 2006).
17. Ulrich, Roger, "Effect of Interior Design on Wellness: Theory and Recent Scientific Research," *Journal of Healthcare Design*, The Center for Health Design: Concord, CA, Vol. 3. pp. 97–109 (1991).
18. Hound Dog Hearing, *Part 3: Better Hearing: Communication Tips and Strategies*, www.hdhearing.com/Learning/Part3.htm (accessed September 28, 2007).
19. James A. Michener Art Museum, Bucks County Artists, *Dorothy Parker: Algonquin Round Table*, www.michenermuseum.org/bucksartists/artist.php?artist=177&page=729 (accessed February 28, 2007).
20. Bevier, Charles, "High Tech Homes Are Here," *NAHB's Sales + Marketing Magazine*, Washington, DC (2004).
21. Ibid.
22. Nation's Building News Online, *Rapid Changes Foreseen for Home of the Future*, www.nbnnews.com/NBN/issues/2007-02-26/Front+Page/index.html (accessed August 25, 2007).
23. Ibid.
24. EH Staff, "*Electronic House Magazine* 2006 Home of the Year Awards: An Avatar Is Born," *Electronic House Magazine Online*, www.electronichouse.com/article/an_avatar_is_born/C203/index.php/?cr=on (accessed February 10, 2007).

CHAPTER 7

Creating Private Places

A good laugh and a long sleep are the best cures in the doctor's book.

—Irish proverb

Design by: Stephanie Driscoll.

TUCKED AWAY

There are numerous homes in existence today—including many that were built during and after the 1960s—that lack a ground floor master suite, an important component of any resident's ability to age in place. In those houses that do include a bedroom and bath on the ground floor or main level, these rooms are often small, cramped, and uninviting—originally intended as auxiliary guestrooms or offices. Bigger, of course, is not always better, and through effective professional planning these "extra" rooms don't have to be wasted space.

In designing for aging in place, designers should keep in mind that it may not be the clients themselves who need this space for long-term use. Many baby boomers are planning and renovating spaces to make life more comfortable for their parents. But whether the space is to be used now for older relatives or in the future by current residents, a thoughtful design can produce an inviting retreat.

7.2 The private places in a home, particularly the bedrooms, give everyone a quiet place to retreat to sleep, restore, and relax. Ensure that clients and those they live with have places with good storage and comfortable beds and are easy to maintain, and with space permitting, have good supportive upholstered seating for your clients to read or catch a cat nap away from the bustle of the rest of the home. *Design by: Judith Sisler Johnston.*

The job of design professionals is to share knowledge and expertise to help educate clients so that they can plan for the future, no matter what health challenges lay ahead. Younger residents who are busy with work or raising a family may be able to tolerate certain poorly designed characteristics of their home, but once those residents have a chance to spend more time at home, such as someone who is recently retired, minor inconveniences can become major frustrations.

The location and arrangement of private spaces within a home can take on increased importance for someone who is recuperating from an illness or injury, caring for a disabled or aging relative, or learning to cope with his or her own diminishing physical abilities. And as stress and lack of sleep can exacerbate a variety of health issues, a relaxing, well-designed bedroom retreat can play a major role in alleviating or preventing these difficulties.

THE CHALLENGES OF SLEEPING SPACES

Although more homes are being built with ground-floor bedrooms, too often these rooms that might have had potential as master bedrooms were originally built as afterthoughts—with inadequate square footage and insulation, not enough electrical outlets and light fixtures, and few windows for natural light and cross ventilation.

Sleep patterns may change over time, of course. As people age, the amount of sleep they can expect at one time decreases. Some people wake up several times a night, while others sleep only a few hours each night and then enjoy an afternoon nap. Whatever sleep patterns clients may experience, however, according to the National Institute on Aging, regular sleep disturbances and habitually waking up tired are not considered normal, but rather may be symptoms of a physical or emotional disorder.[1] And although designers are not medical practitioners, they can give their clients "prescriptions" for improving sleep by asking questions and basing interior design solutions on the resultant answers.

Waking up during the night is often triggered by the need for a trip to the bathroom, and a client's home should not make his or her life more difficult. Designers should design spaces and arrange furniture so the bed is close enough to a bathroom for the client to get there and back quickly and without encountering obstacles, such as furniture or extra doorways, or without having to trek especially long distances. In addition, there is the need for adequate lighting to help them find their way. For people who require mobility devices, such as walkers, canes, and wheelchairs, every piece of furniture along the way and every corner that must be turned adds another obstacle to the trip to the bathroom and back, particularly at night. Keep in mind that the term "accessible" can take on many meanings: Too many barriers or challenges to the nighttime trip to the bathroom may be the reason behind the occasional "accident" that may cause, at the very least, embarrassment or, in worse cases, emotional and physical complications later on.

7.3 Clean and uncluttered spaces make a space feel larger, but this is not always accomplishable in smaller homes. But it's an important element for someone who might need clear floor space to maneuver in and around the bed with a walker or wheelchair or to and from the bathroom at night. *Design by: Bernadette Upton, ASID, LEED.*

All agree that homes are places of refuge, and certainly the "private spaces" within any home should offer tranquility and relaxation for its residents. Too often the private and public spaces have little division, and short of closing the bedroom door, there is little sense of privacy. Even some separation from each other within the private areas of a home should be a consideration. Most people at some time or another would appreciate a space within which they can withdraw with some sense of privacy without necessarily closing a door.

Although natural daylight is an important element in alleviating diminishing eyesight—a common result of aging—older eyes are more likely to be irritated by glare. The large expanse of natural light, which is such an advantage, also poses the challenge of additional glare, and yet the option of cutting the glare by completely blocking that light is not usually the first choice, nor should it be. The artificial light that is added also becomes even more important as the client ages and may require brighter lighting as well as easier access to the lighting controls.

Convenient location of electrical outlets in bedrooms to provide for flexibility of furniture arrangement is often not effectively planned ahead and particularly if at a later stage in life medical equipment needs to be included in the room. What a shame it would be to be forced into an awkward arrangement just to accommodate the location of the outlets. This problem just adds to the sense of loss when already faced with the health challenges that require the introduction of the medical equipment.

Older homes often have a lack of storage in the bedroom areas, but even in newer homes where the storage space may have been increased, it is not necessarily easily accessible. Think of the number of times a client may go in and out of their bedroom closet for various pieces of clothing during the day. Too much effort will mean they will not find satisfaction in the layout of the space. And for those whose reach is limited and whose mobility is restricted, bigger does not always mean better. Again, accessibility is the key.

Mobility in the Master Bedroom

If a house already has a bedroom on the main floor, residents can usually be assured they won't need to consider moving to a new residence should they become disabled or experience physical limitations because of age, accident, or temporary medical issues. Even with a second master suite on an upper level of the house, a ground-floor master suite is definitely a worthwhile investment.

Ideally, a ground-floor master suite should be large enough to provide the same amenities as those in the upper-level master suite, including generous closet space and/or a dressing area and a comfortable bathroom. Any master bedroom, no matter what level of the home, should also include visual access to a pleasant outdoor view. Unlike the upper-level master suite, however, one advantage a ground-floor suite can offer is access to an outdoor garden or patio, which may

7.4 For some couples, having a separate master bedroom is a fact of life, especially if one member tends to snore or be active in bed while sleeping. Having a separate sleeping space also means that during any illness, each can get the type of rest required.

mean making structural changes like expanding square footage or adding an exterior door. Clients who are considering remodeling ground-floor rooms should be advised that planning for and living through such a renovation takes time, and they should be encouraged to make structural changes or to remodel before they are forced by a medical emergency to make those changes.

According to the MetLife Mature Market Institute, the average annual cost for an assisted living unit, identified as one private room with a private bath, was nearly $36,000 in 2006[2]—and there is no way to predict how many years an individual should expect to pay such fees. A one-time remodeling investment looks quite economical when compared to such accruing costs, which will inevitably increase. Remodeling a home so that it will appeal to buyers of all ages and abilities is also a smart investment that will increase its value.

As one ages and losses compound, the more significant the effect of environmental impact. When we successfully realize how to deliver quality of life for today and tomorrow, and can effectively communicate this to clients, their ages and abilities can be transcended by the pleasure of living with appropriate design in whatever their current present. Only the commitment level toward excelling the person-environment fit limits a design professional's success in this specialty.

—Rebecca Stahr, ASID, CAPS, Interior Designer

Design professionals are problem solvers, and their challenge is often to provide not only what they, as designers, envision, but also to provide for all their clients' wants and needs. During the programming phase of any design project, designers should talk frankly with clients about where and how they want to spend their later years. Even if clients do not plan to age in place in their existing homes, any changes they make to their homes that would allow for that choice makes their homes attractive to potential buyers. By meeting all the criteria, design professionals exemplify another value added when the client works with a professional who understands the aging market and their needs.

Since privacy can be particularly important in the bedroom areas of a home, the view into bedrooms and bathrooms should be protected from visitors at the front door or anyone who is in more communal living areas of the household. Someone who is recuperating from surgery or an injury, or whose movements are limited for other reasons, needs extra time or assistance to put on a bathrobe or adjust bedclothes for privacy or dignity.

When planning a remodeling project, specify hallways to and in the master suite at a minimum of 42 inches wide. Some forward-thinking designers specify more generous hallway widths to prevent losing valuable clearance through the area in the event that grab rails should need to be installed in the future. Minimum doorway allowances into and within the suite should be a minimum of 32 inches wide. It is important to consider that the 32-inch clearance is measured when the door is open. These dimensions are not only practical for easier navigation of people and furniture but are also more visually appealing.

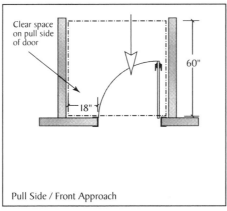

Clear space on pull side of door

60"

18"

Pull Side / Front Approach

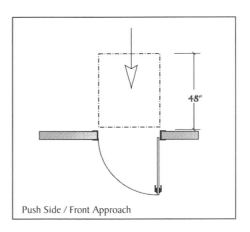

48"

Push Side / Front Approach

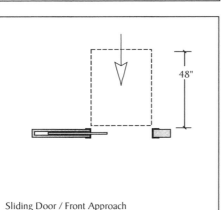

48"

Sliding Door / Front Approach

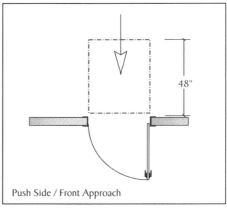

48"

Push Side / Front Approach

7.5 and 7.6 Doors, doorways, and halls should be sufficiently large enough to accommodate anyone with any disability whether he or she needs a walker, wheelchair, or someone to physically assist him or her. There needs to be a minimum of 32 inches clear space between doorjambs and ideally 36 inches. Hallways should be a minimum of 42 inches but more ideally at 48 inches to 54 inches in width.

Traffic patterns through the master bedroom suite are largely determined by the location of doors, closets, and furniture, and preventing accidents is dependant on ample clear space and easy pathways. Ideally, a room should be large enough to allow 36 inches of clear space on either side of the bed so sheets and bedclothes can be easily changed, as well as to allow space for someone who uses a wheelchair or walker to get in and out of the bed.

When planning for this space, keep in mind that a larger bed size might be used in the future. The space around the bed area can also incorporate the space needed in front of a dresser or closet, which should be adequate for someone—whether seated in a wheelchair or using a walker or other mobility aide—to fully open drawers and

7.7 To create as much independence as possible, storage in cabinets and dressers need to have the required floor space in the front and around the drawers. Taller dressers, those as much as 39 inches or 42 inches in height, will mean less bending down to locate something in a lower drawer.

doors to access the contents. There also should be a 60-by-60-inch space to maneuver within the room once the furniture is placed.

Such clearances do more than meet the needs of those who require mobility devices or who are sight impaired. More open space in a room gives the appearance of less clutter, which contributes to a more relaxing environment—a particularly important objective for any bedroom. By eliminating the distractions that come with clutter, including the TV and work or exercise areas within view of the bed, designers contribute to a stress-free space that invites restful sleep.

Windows on the World

Windows play many roles—beyond those that are obvious—in the design of a home. Yes, windows provide all-important natural light, an especially important component for those with diminishing eyesight. Windows and doors also provide fresh air and, as most design professionals know and should pass on to clients, exterior doors and windows give rooms visual extension without having to add actual square footage.

Windows offer those with limited access to the outdoors or those who are confined to bed a "window on the world"—a view of a lovely garden, a soothing waterfall, or an expansive view of nature. It is as important to include such views in the private areas of a home as it is to include them in more communal rooms. According to studies led by Roger S. Ulrich, Ph.D., director of the Center for Health Systems and Design at Texas A&M University, simply looking at greenery is instantly soothing.[3] A view from a bedroom window can start a person's day off on a positive note

7.8 Plan the bedroom window treatments that provide for a lot of natural light during the day but give a good measure of privacy at night or at times when it is necessary to sleep in a darkened environment. *Design by: Kathleen Pyrce. Photo by: Gerlick Photography.*

7.9 When doors are provided that lead to the exterior from a bedroom area, access to the outside is encouraged but especially important in the event of an emergency, rather than attempting to exit the residence via a long or winding path through the house.

7.10 Windows in any bedroom provide for natural light, fresh air into the space, and a connection to the outdoors. But pairs or multiple sets of windows on opposite or adjacent walls give the interior much more air circulation and cross ventilation. *Design by: Susan Nilsson.*

and may contribute to a more relaxing evening as well. And taking in a green scene or garden view can reduce fear and anger and lower blood pressure, heart rate, and muscle tension in as little as three minutes—with no negative side effects![4]

Exterior master bedroom doors and windows offer an additional advantage: direct emergency access, which is particularly critical when any other egress from the house is difficult to navigate or is an especially long distance from the bedroom. Because the seat height of most wheelchairs is 18 to 20 inches, a windowsill at the same height offers a comfortable exit for most wheelchair users. Although a 30-inch sill height is acceptable for enjoying the view out a window, that height would be more of a challenge as an egress for seated users. Of course, windows that are intended as emergency exits must meet code requirements and be wide enough for a person to sit on and swing his or her legs over the sill. Although codes often stipulate 24 inches as adequate space for this range of motion, a width of 30 inches provides the most desirable allowance. The sill also needs to be sturdy enough to support the weight of an average person and be free of sharp edges or any other possible dangerous projections.

If there is adequate wall space, allow for a minimum of two windows positioned on adjacent walls to generate cross ventilation when the entrance door is closed. Set windowsills at 30 inches above the finished floor, a height that will not interfere with the sight line of a person seated either in a bed, a chair, or even a wheelchair.

An exterior door is the easiest and quickest method of egress from a master bedroom suite in an emergency. Beyond the safety issue, however, an exterior door also can provide access to an adjoining patio or garden. This connection

7.11 When planning the window treatments for the bedroom, consider ones that will be easy to operate with little physical effort and frame the view to the exterior. Make windows low enough to be able to have a clear line of sight from the bed or from a chair. *Design by: Ann Wisniewski. Photo by: Gerlick Photography.*

becomes particularly important in ground-floor master bed-rooms or areas that might be used as master or in-law suites in the future. And, of course, any access through these doors should be curb-less and barrier free and make the transition from interior to exterior as level as possible.

To control air circulation and light within the bedroom, designers should provide easy-to-operate controls not only for windows or exterior doors but also for the treatments—draperies, shades, shutters, or blinds—that cover them. Crank-operated casement windows or lightweight sliding windows are the easiest to operate manually.

7.12 Motorized window treatments controlled with a wireless remote control make the blind and drapery operation easy. Consider providing two remotes programmed to the same sets of windows in case one becomes lost.

Automatic draperies and window openers are no longer considered a luxury, but are rather another means of providing independence for those with physical limitations. If at least one of the windows in the room is intended as an emergency exit, then it is important to leave clear space—no furniture, no plants, no obstructions of any kind—in front of the window so it can be accessed for that purpose.

From the wide assortment of available options, designers should be able to specify adequate window coverings that supply sufficient privacy, are easily adjusted to filter daylight or eliminate it altogether when needed, and can reduce glare yet still reveal an inviting view. To make such windows and treatments more accessible and easy to operate, consider specifying remote controls for both components. Don't forget that furniture arrangement can block access, and climbing over furniture is not only cumbersome but also less appealing as we age, no matter how agile.

7.13 and 7.14 When possible, keep furnishings away from the windows, especially if the bed backs up to the only window in the residence. However, when it's the best place for the bed, a window provides the client with great natural light for reading and as long as additional light at night can be provided. *Designs by: Bonnie Kissel (left) and Bernadette Upton ASID, LEED (bottom). Photo by: Scott Levy Photography (left).*

The time to plan where in a room to locate windows and doors is, of course, when the room—or even the house—is still on the drawing board. And where specific pieces of furniture are placed is not as important as allowing for flexibility when planning the space. For instance, when a door is located in a corner of the room, there is more floor and wall space available for furniture placement and more privacy for the individuals in the room when the door is open or ajar, and it is less of an obstacle when the door itself is open. Such considerations are more critical in smaller rooms and are particularly important when several generations are living together in order to preserve privacy without having to close a door.

There Is Never Enough Storage

Closets that are accessed several times a day are a significant part of the design and should work for everyone. Walk-in closets can be beneficial, but only if the entrance door is at least 32 inches wide, the center aisle is a minimum of 36 inches wide, and the modular storage systems within are easy to reach and adjusted for the specific needs of the client. Include closet rods that have an adjustable height of 30 to 66 inches above the floor, or install a clothes rod that pulls down and out to allow full access to the upper rod as well as the lower—a configuration that doubles accessible storage and provides a means for storing full-length clothes. When there isn't quite enough room for a full walk-in closet, consider installing a carousel closet system similar to the rotation systems used in dry cleaning shops. Not only do these systems increase the available storage area, but they also bring the clothing directly to the user. Both shelves and rods can be attached to the unit, and clothing can be easily organized.

7.15 Hanging and folded clothes storage can be provided both inside and outside of the closet, but there needs to be access at the appropriate height for the user, including shelves and open spaces appropriate to folding clothes. Glass doors give a good idea of what lies behind. *Design by: Lena Brion, ASID/Brion Design Group.*

For any type of closet, consider sliding pocket doors, which move easily and completely out of the way of the user and take up no wall space when open. Regardless of the type of doors designers specify, they all should include lever, or D-shaped, handles on both sides of the doors. Extra width may be required in the doorway to accommodate doors that don't completely disappear into the pocket opening.

Loop, D-shaped, or other easy-to-use handles are good choices for all cabinets and drawers throughout the master bedroom and dressing room areas. Always replace existing furniture handles with those that are easier to operate. It's easy to find well-designed and readily available decorative replacement hardware.

For non-walk-in wall closets, consider using bypass sliding doors, double pocket doors, double-swing doors, or bi-fold doors. Select traditional bypass sliding doors that are suspended from above so there is no track on the floor to trip over or create a barrier for a wheelchair. Double-swing doors need more space to open out of the way, whereas bi-fold doors require little space for opening. Pocket doors take no wall space within the room once they are installed and do not require maneuvering of mobility aids to open and access the interior of the closet.

With the advent of modular storage units of various shapes, sizes, and styles—and from a variety of manufacturers—closet organization has never been easier. Not only do clients now have the ability to quickly view their clothing choices, but also to access their selections without opening cabinets or drawers. An additional advantage in larger closets and dressing areas are surfaces that can be easily reached to lay out clothing for the day or to pack for a trip. Being able to have a place to lay out clothing to be packed is a convenience appreciated by clients of all ages and abilities, and the packing and unpacking for travel is another advantage to having a first-floor bedroom. Wheeled suitcases are a great convenience, but they lose their effectiveness when users face the stairs.

One of the most accessible methods of bedroom storage is the dressing room, which can be designed in a number of configurations depending on the available space and the clients' dressing habits. Design an area or room for clothing storage and dressing that is separate from the sleeping and sitting areas, and you create an opportunity for organizing clothing and personal items without cabinet doors or drawers.

Whether clients request a specific room for dressing, or choose to store their clothing in a more traditional closet, designers should provide a firm bench or seat in or near the dressing area where clients can sit while dressing.

7.16 When combined, dressing spaces and closets are no doubt a luxury for some, but they can provide spaces to pack and store luggage, and with enough floor space, a massage table can be set up on an as-needed basis.

Connections and Convenience

A well-wired home is an advantage now and into the future. Adequate wiring is particularly relevant when planning master bedrooms, in-law suites, or those rooms that might be converted to either in the future. Specify extra outlets on walls where a bed might be in preparation for medical equipment or other unforeseen needs.

Clients should have the ability to regulate the light in master and in-law suites without having to get out of bed, so designers should place lighting controls within easy reach of the bed. By incorporating remote controls for windows, window treatments, lighting, and whole-home

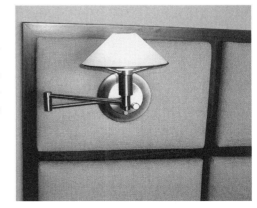

7.17 Lighting close around the bed, as in this example of a small scale wall-mount lamp, provides easy access to the dimmer control as well as the ability to move the light source around for more task-oriented needs. *Design by: Ann Huff, ASID, CAPS.*

security into one simple-to-use master remote system that is operable from the bed, designers offer independence, as well as safety and convenience, to clients with limited mobility as well as to those who are able bodied.

Floor Coverings and Finishes

When ambient temperatures are too hot or too cold, older people have more difficulty maintaining a normal 98.6-degree body temperature. Studies show that some "elderly patients are unable to regulate their body temperatures to the same degree as young adults because their responses to changes in body temperature are altered."[5] Those who are over the age of 80 are the most likely to experience this physiological phenomenon.[6]

Because a carpeted floor is visually warmer than other finishes, it can trigger a sense of warmth even when the actual ambient temperature remains the same as in rooms that have other types of floor finishes. Flooring in the bedroom and dressing room, then, can differ from the communal areas of the home. Specify low-pile carpet to assure easy passage and a steadier gait, particularly for elderly residents.

When specifying hard-surface flooring, such as hardwood, laminate, or tile, select a glare-free product for the flooring material as well as the baseboard and quarter-round trim.

There are also finishes that can be applied to stone, tile, and other hard-surface flooring to increase the coefficient of friction on these floors. It is not a coating that

7.18 Wall-to-wall carpeting provides a layer of insulation to the room while making the space feel larger. For greater ease in mobility, choose carpeting that has a somewhat flat pile and avoid carpet padding that is too soft. Commercial padding is often a great alternative and will stand up to using wheelchairs better than some residential-type padding. *Design by: Jane Page Design Group.*

7.19 To ensure there won't be problems with someone stumbling over the edge or end of carpeting at a transition, it may be necessary to raise and slope the sub floor to meet the finished height of carpeting to be level with adjacent material such as wood or tile.

can wear off, but rather a process that creates a tread design on the mineral surface itself, with no discernible change in appearance. The benefits of this process allow a client to keep their existing flooring with less worry about the dangers of falls. It also expands the available choices for new construction or remodeling.

To achieve the positive acoustical benefits, as well as the warmth that carpet can provide, you might think about some of the top quality carpet tiles on the market. They are designed to be installed as wall-to-wall carpet or area rugs, but have the advantage of much easier maintenance than traditional carpet—particularly in a sick room. When a spill or accident occurs, they can be pulled up individually, washed off, dried, and then put back down. This flexibility can be a definite advantage when trying to add warmth, in addition to acting as a sound barrier, and still keep the maintenance worry-free.

To prevent slipping or tripping hazards, secure area rugs with either furniture or carpet tape. And remember that visual contrast between area rugs and the surface under them can signal an upcoming floor level change to those who are visually challenged.

Selecting the Right Mattress

To ensure a good night's sleep for clients and guests alike, an essential item in any bedroom is a good mattress. When selecting a mattress for any client, particularly those who plan to age in place, consider the combined height of the mattress, box spring, and bed frame and the flexibility of the bed and mattress.

A number of mattresses on the market today give users the ability to adjust the softness or firmness with the push of a button. This feature also allows couples who share a bed to select a different setting for each of their needs or preferences, settling the age-old dispute of "too soft or too firm."

Now available in noninstitutional-looking styles that lend themselves well to universal design, adjustable beds offer more comfort and independence to those with limited mobility and flexibility. A number of adjustable beds also are available with cordless remote controls, individual controls for either side of the bed, and some are available with an optional dual massage feature.

7.20 Many believe that an electric or a hospital bed will have an institutional appearance. However, an upholstered bed surround, made in three sections to slide around the bed frame itself, will provide the needed aesthetic desired.

When comparing adjustable beds, remember that all things are not created equal. Some beds adjust to only a few positions, while others offer a number of adjustment options. It is important for designers to be aware of these options and their clients' physical needs and limitations when selecting a bed. Where one person may need to raise his or her feet above the heart for a certain amount of time per day, another person may need to have his or her upper torso elevated at all times.

Some clients may be interested in an adjustable bed merely for their own personal comfort. Raising the head and foot of a bed can relieve chronic lower back pain, and certainly raising the head or the

foot of a bed can provide a more comfortable position in which to read, eat, relax, or watch television. Others, however, cannot lie flat for a variety of physiological reasons. Jeffrey K. Bergin, D.C., dean at the National University of Health Sciences in Lombard, Illinois, says, "Patients I know who use [adjustable beds] have conditions like hypertension, circulation problems, decubitus ulcers, or congestive heart failure, and they find it difficult to sleep on a flat bed." And according to Charles Cefalu, M.D., spokesman for the American Geriatrics Society, "people with asthma, acid reflux disorder, heart failure or chronic lung disease usually do need to elevate the heads of their beds." Cefalu adds that "if a special bed does allow elevation, that would be one scientific reason to recommend it."[7]

Although Cefalu recommends that designers consult with their clients' physicians before selecting a bed, he is not aware of any specific statistics that demonstrate the benefits of special beds and believes that regular beds can be sufficiently modified with pillows and bolsters to work just as well as a mechanical bed. Bergin also adds, "You can mimic the features of an adjustable bed by bolstering it with pillows. It's just easier to push a button."[8] What is important for design professionals to keep in mind, however, is that for many residents the push of a button is not a luxury, but rather a necessity for maintaining control over their own comfort.

The ability to transfer into and out of bed is also important to clients. A few manufacturers have designed beds that can be lowered so that the top of the mattress is a mere 15 inches from the floor. For some users, this height facilitates unaided transfer to and from a wheelchair. These beds can be raised or lowered as needed—even to a height sufficient for users to enjoy views out windows that have a 30-inch sill height.

Most manufacturers offer adjustable beds in the usual range of sizes, including twin, full, queen, or dual king. Some companies will customize beds to designers' specifications. There is also a product on the market that can transform a client's existing bed into an adjustable bed, and, with the push of a button, assist the user with getting in and out of it. Not only is this device compact, lightweight, and portable, but it also fits any size bed, thereby providing maximum flexibility.

A word of caution, however, when considering an adjustable bed that is incorporated into an upholstered base: An upholstered base can limit how close a wheelchair can get to the mattress, making a transfer into and out of bed often more challenging for wheelchair users with such beds. By the same token, some wheelchair users find those upholstered bases that are built with a "landing" platform around the mattress helpful, particularly when the base is on the same height level as the mattress. The firm upholstered base then becomes a transfer area from the wheelchair to the softer mattress.

Bedroom Seating

Bedrooms that include seating other than on the bed become private retreats, rather than just a place to sleep. A sitting area in the bedroom can offer a welcome alternative for any client who may not have the strength or mobility to maneuver to the more communal areas of the home. Even for clients who live alone, a comfortable seating area with a lovely view and good lighting for reading or viewing the latest movie adds to the intimate atmosphere of the master bedroom suite. Seating in the bedroom—chairs, chaises, ottomans, benches, and stools—can also be an essential consideration for achieving better quality sleep. This "sleeping aid" is achieved by placing the television in the sitting area and separating the sitting area from the sleeping space—at least visually—whenever possible.

Thank goodness that we all are unique individuals, which also means that one chair size does not necessarily fit everyone. Flexibility is essential. Arms on chairs offer comfort and safety getting in and out, and throw pillows give extra support as needed and allow the user to adjust a chair's depth. Users might want to curl up in a chair sometimes and, at other times, sit up in a more formal, straight pose. Again, designers should allow enough clear space around chairs for accessibility to the seating itself as well as easy circulation in the room. Side tables are more useful than a table centered in the space: Not only is the placement of side tables more conducive to open space and clear paths through the room, but also a side table is a good place to set a reading lamp, television remote, beverage, book, or telephone. Ottomans, which are often mobile and easily rolled out of the way, can be used not only as a footrest but also as an occasional spot to set a food tray.

Bedroom seating also provides a place for residents to sit while dressing and can be a resting place for custom bedcovering at night. Seating in the form of a stool or bench is often a necessary companion to the vanity table, which might be located in the bedroom or dressing area, rather than in the adjoining bathroom. In each of these scenarios, chair arms are important for support as well as comfort and make getting in and out of the chair much easier for the person using it.

If a lack of space demands minimal furniture in the room, designers should select pieces that can do double duty. If there is no room for a bench or chair to use while dressing, then select a bench that might slide under another piece of furniture.

7.21 Choose bedroom seating the way upholstered furnishings are considered for any other part of the residence, with taller seat heights and arms that extend to the front edge of the piece. Select fabrics that will be easy to care for and low maintenance. *Design by: Lena Brion, ASID/Brion Design Group.*

Bedside Tables

Everyone needs some type of bedside surface, but not everyone has the same needs for storage next to the bed. Over-the-bed tables, much like those used in hospitals and other medical facilities, often can be very handy for residential use, particularly when a traditional bedside table or nightstand is more of a hindrance than a help for someone who regularly requires a wheelchair. Not only can a stationary table or nightstand get in the way of the user's access to the wheelchair—at least on the side of the bed where he or she gets in and out—but also a bedside table takes up space needed to store and maneuver the wheelchair. Bedside tables and nightstands can also take up space needed for an oxygen tank, compressor, or other required in-home medical equipment. When a client is faced with such limitations, his or her designer should consider creating an attractive, custom-designed, mobile over-the-bed table that meets the client's particular storage needs.

Even when there is no extraneous equipment, such as a wheelchair, oxygen tank, or other piece of medical equipment, the bedside surface doesn't have to be a traditional nightstand. A vanity table or small dresser can be an attractive and effective alternative. Whatever furniture is being considered, however, the height and accessibility of the bedside table are the most critical factors. The surface height must be easily reached from the bed and placement of the piece should be within easy reach of someone seated or reclining in the bed.

The client's bedside storage needs should also dictate furniture selection. Not everyone wants to have every item he or she might use sitting on the surface itself, so designers should pay close attention to how easy it is to access the drawers and cabinet portions of the table. Typical items that a client might want on or in a nightstand or bedside table are a telephone; a lamp; books and magazines; glasses; medication; a drinking glass; facial tissues; a clock; a remote for any electronics in the room, including lighting and window coverings; and possibly a music system, such as a radio or CD player; and a master control for security. And though some of these items, such as lighting, can be wall mounted or accessible in other ways, often the surface next to the bed is most easily reached.

7.22 Tables beside the bed that will accommodate all the necessary elements such as lighting, a telephone, and a clock should also be big enough for reading material and storage of medicine. Plan to include drawers when possible, rather than door-style cabinets. Keep the area next to the bed open and clear of furniture.

7.23 Plan for easy access to electrical switches, outlets, and alarms by locating them at the door, with additional switches close by the bedside so that the fixtures and systems can be operated while remaining in bed. Keep in mind the position on the wall relative to those who might use the controls most of the time.

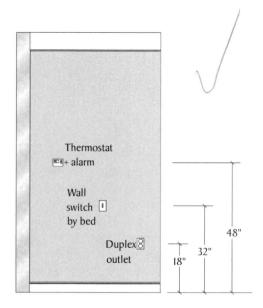

Thermostat + alarm

Wall switch by bed

Duplex outlet

48"

32"

18"

A pull-out surface designed to be accessed only when needed also can be an advantage, particularly when a client is confined to bed for an extended but temporary period, such as when recuperating from surgery. An important point to consider when selecting several pieces of furniture for a master bedroom: Pay particular attention to the juxtaposition of the bedside surface to the head of an adjustable bed when it is raised or the position of a client when propped up in bed with pillows. The client's reach may be more challenging, requiring somewhat of a backward stretch, if the bedside table is too shallow or positioned too close to the wall.

Lighting the Way

Without light, the rest of the design does not really matter, as it will not be seen! Effective lighting and the location of convenient outlets are often missing in homes, particularly in older structures. The lighting needs to be effective enough to not only provide mood and atmosphere but also to help clients avoid falls and increase the amount of light available as they age. In addition to providing a well-planned lighting design, it is particularly important to consider how easily the client can access and adjust the lighting from bed. Whether it is to light the way to the bathroom, or to check strange noises at night, safety is a major reason to be able to quickly turn on a light next to the bed. Any prolonged time spent recuperating from an accident or illness will also highlight the value of having a whole-house control system next to the bed.

There are numerous whole-house systems available, some of which are installed with minimal wiring and are controlled by radio frequencies that are easier to retrofit in older homes. These systems manage and monitor house lighting for convenience, security, and energy savings, and some offer convenient one-touch controls that also include home theater and landscape lighting. Not only is this level of control convenient, but it also contributes to the homeowner's independence. With one master control, a client can adjust the lighting anywhere in the house from one location—the master bedroom. In an emergency situation, think of the value of hitting one switch by the bed and not only turning on the lights in the house but also locking them so an intruder is unable to turn them off, and sending a signal to the outdoor lights so that they begin flashing, making it much easier for emergency help to identify the house. Add to this the ability to adjust ventilation, heat, air conditioning, window treatments, and security without having to ask for assistance, and the client's sense of independence increases exponentially.

When planning aging-in-place solutions to a residence, particularly in bedrooms, specify extra electrical outlets and amps for additional future lighting and to provide for any potential need for in-home medical equipment.

As in other rooms in an aging-in-place renovation, specify lower light switches (42 to 48 inches AFF) and higher electrical outlets (18 to 22 inches AFF) in bedrooms for universal ease of use for all ages and abilities. Eliminate cords from traffic areas and specify rocker or luminous switches so clients can easily find them at night. As added safety features, consider using lighting controls, as well as small areas of paint, flooring, or wall coverings that are phosphorescent. These products, which absorb light during the day and glow at night, can effectively provide a safe passage at night or during a power outage.

COMPLIMENTARY AND COMPANION SPACES

According to the 2000 U.S. Census Bureau findings, 3.9 million American homes have three or more generations living together, and 78,000 households contain as many as four generations.[9] These groups appear to be divided into three major segments: baby boomers who are caring for aging parents; young families who are living with their able-bodied parents to pool financial resources in order to afford a nice home; and empty nesters whose children are temporarily living at home again to save money, go back to school, or get through a financial or personal setback. An added bonus for the second segment is that the grandparents tend to be more involved in their grandchildren's lives.

To address this evolution in the composition of the American family, some builders are constructing homes with two master suites or at least with larger bedrooms and several bathrooms. These floor plans offer each generation within these families its own large bedroom/sitting area along with amenities like a walk-in closet and attached bathrooms, and sometimes even in-room kitchenettes or adjacent exercise rooms. Although such arrangements seem indulgent, when several generations live together, these extra rooms and suites often reduce frayed nerves and familial friction.

Nearly two-thirds (62 percent) of designers, architects, and other industry experts who were surveyed recently by the National Association of Home Builders (NAHB) predicted that the demand for two master suites—often referred to as owner's suites—in high-end new homes over 4,000 square feet will increase by 2015.[10] In spite of this increased demand for master suites, the overall square footage of American homes is not necessarily growing proportionately. According to a recent survey by the American Institute of Architects (AIA), although the square footage of newly built homes has more than doubled in the past

7.24 Create other bedroom spaces that provide for more sleeping accommodations should a relative, friend, or caregiver need to bunk with a member of the household during a particular period when the client needs live-in help. *Design by: Bernice Phelps. Photo by: Gerlick Photography.*

7.25, 7.26 and 7.27
Make spaces perform multiple duties by including a fold down bed in a space like these styles of the traditional "Murphy-style" bed, many of which provide decent sleeping accommodations with innerspring mattresses. *Designs by: Pat Gericke (middle and right).*

50 years,[11] for the first time, respondents reported that they are downsizing their homes, or in some instances "different-sizing," as there is an increase in multiple master suites. These multiple master suites are being used to provide a more comfortable sleeping arrangement for married couples as well as multigenerational living, or singles sharing the purchase of a home.

Homes designed with two or more master suites can make multigeneration living arrangements less stressful for everyone. And, if local building codes allow such construction, in-law suites, with separate quarters provided for multigenerations living together, can contribute to an ideal living situation. Although some municipalities continue to prohibit more than one full kitchen in single-family homes, and others eschew separate entrances for in-law suites, variances are possible with proof that such construction is needed.

In-law suites in multistoried homes are typically located on the ground floor for maximum accessibility. In-law suites are easily converted to master suites, and upstairs master suites are just as easily assigned to a future caregiver. If the communal living area is on an upper level, as in split foyer and split-level houses, lower-level spaces can be transformed into in-law suites with elevator access up to the main level. Lower-level or below-grade master suites may also have direct access to an outdoor area and can be converted to a family room at some future time.

As a design professional working with an aging population, I've created a "4F" rule: Flexibility, Functionality, and Friendliness extend an individual's independence without Fear. Creating environments and using materials that are multifunctional, low maintenance, and user friendly are key elements. A sofa bed in a home office can accommodate a guest today but can be a lifesaver for a nurses' aide should a medical situation arise. Putting ourselves in the thought process puts us in their shoes and [provides] better ideas [for] our designs.

—PAT GERICKE, ASID, INTERIOR DESIGNER

To ensure maximum privacy, an in-law suite in a one-story house should be separate from the other bedrooms. With this design, the in-law suite might eventually be converted to a caregiver's suite for aging in place or might be used as the master suite with a caregiver located in the main bedroom wing of the home.

No matter where in the house an in-law suite is located, however, a separate entrance provides the convenience of private access for deliveries, caregivers, and visitors without interrupting residents in the main part of the house. Additional insulation or an acoustical wall covering on the interior can absorb sound and provide extra privacy. When an in-law suite is no longer needed as such, it can be easily converted to a home office or guest suite. And any flexible design that offers a variety of uses can increase a home's resale value.

Unless they have already been remodeled or renovated, older homes usually do not include ground-floor master or in-law suites. When considering adding a master suite to an existing house, examine the floor plan carefully to determine if and how the house can be adapted. Two small ground-floor rooms can be combined into one larger bedroom with an adjacent bathroom, and stacked closets or other spaces that are adjacent above and below can be converted to an elevator shaft. As prices for installation continue to decline, elevators are enjoying popularity with buyers of all ages. Elevators are an added convenience—an easier way to move laundry, luggage, groceries, baby equipment, and furniture, especially in multilevel homes such as townhouses—for everyone, as well as a necessity for some residents with limited mobility.

Up and Down Accessibility

A possible option for easier accessibility in a multistoried home is to install a stair chair lift. Stair chair lifts are designed to follow the path of a staircase and are commonly battery operated. Not only are they less costly than an elevator, but they can also be set up as soon as they are purchased and can be easily removed at a later date. There are a number of types of lifts from which to select, depending on the client's needs. The most common type used residentially is the seated variety and can work well for the client who is mobile but has trouble climbing stairs. A key consideration is to check how the unit folds up when not in use. Be sure to check that the arms or other parts of the unit will not stick out and actually be the cause of an able-bodied person falling.

The second type is a standing lift that fits well into narrow staircases and works for someone who may have trouble bending their legs to climb the stairs but could ride up and down while standing. A third type has a small seat for the user to lean against while riding up and down. The fourth variety is the wheelchair lift, which transports someone in a wheelchair up and down the stairs. Although this type takes the most space, it does fold up when not in use and provides independence within a multistoried home for a wheelchair user. Many of the products on the market are designed to follow curved or angled staircases so there are few limitations.

Even with an elevator or chair lift, the day-to-day accessibility of a ground-floor master suite may still be the best scenario. Ground-floor master suites are always more convenient for all: It is much easier to grab a sweater, change shoes, or do any number of other things that might require a trip to the master suite during a 24-hour period.

7.28 and 7.29 The costs involved in installing a small elevator in a residence have come down with advancements and competition; however, the majority of the costs might be for changes to interior framing of an existing residence. In new construction, closet spaces can be stacked on the second floor above first floor closet spaces, making the addition of an elevator much easier when need and desire arise. *Designs by: Keith Miller, ASID.*

A number of single-level homes, townhomes, and condominiums are being built today with dual master suites. The arrangement of these houses, intended for two single roommates, works extremely well for aging-in-place individuals who wish to share a home with another for companionship or to reduce living costs. These houses also work well for smaller multigenerational families. With two large bedrooms, each with a better-than-average-sized bathroom and closet, members of a small family can spend time together or retreat to their own privacy when they wish.

A home planned with the future in mind will adapt successfully as your clients age and their needs continue to change. The private spaces should just as easily offer rest and rejuvenation for the client, a welcome place for family or friends arriving for an overnight stay, or a sense of home for older family members moving in

7.30 While the bedroom provides a sanctuary from daily life for all, it is even more important that the space be attractive and functional for those who may spend more time in the space than in the past, recovering from more challenging times the client or resident may have. *Design by: Judith Sisler Johnson.*

permanently. In "future planning" for a client's home, always keep in mind the stages and changes that may occur in their lives over the years. Creating a private refuge from the public areas of the home, with serene views, effective lighting, easily accessible storage and bathing, having a comfortable place to lay one's head, and a relaxing sitting area, provides a private sanctuary within the walls of that haven your client calls home.

References

1. National Institute on Aging and National Library of Medicine, NIHSeniorHealth.gov www.helpguide.org/life/sleep_tips.htm (last reviewed June 15, 2007).
2. MetLife Mature Market Institute in conjunction with LifePlans, Inc., *The MetLife Market Survey of Assisted Living Costs*, Metropolitan Life Insurance Company: New York, NY (October 2006).
3. Ulrich, Roger, "Effect of Interior Design on Wellness: Theory and Recent Scientific Research," *Journal of Healthcare Design*, The Center for Healthcare Design: Concord, CA, Vol. 3. pp. 97–109 (1991).
4. Ibid.
5. Lien, Cynthia A., M.D., Associate Professor of Anesthesiology, New York Presbyterian Hospital, Weill Cornell Medical College, "Thermoregulation in the Elderly," *American Society of Anesthesiologists, Syllabus on Geriatric Anesthesiology*, www.asahq.org/clinical/geriatrics/thermo.htm (updated September 16, 2007).
6. Ibid.
7. Skamulis, Leanna, reviewed by Charlotte Mathis, M.D., "Can a Mattress Improve Your Health?" WebMD, www.webmd.com/content/article/85/98467.htm (medically updated June 27, 2005).
8. Ibid.
9. Simmons, Tavia and O'Neill, Grace, *Households and Families 2000: Census 2000 Brief*, (issued September 2001).
10. "NAHB Study Profiles Home of the Future," *National Association of Home Builders News*, www.nahb.org/news_details.aspx?newsID=4052 (accessed February 8, 2007).
11. Baker, Kermit, Ph.D., Hon. AIA, Chief Economist, "As Housing Markets Correct, Owners Looking for Less Space but Greater Accessibility, More Flexibility in Home Designs," *AIArchitect*, Washington, DC, Vol. 14 (May 4, 2007).

CHAPTER 8

Designing the Kitchen

*Anyone that's ever had their kitchen done over knows that
it never gets done as soon as you wish it would.*

—Ronald Reagan, President of the United States

THE BIG PICTURE: SO WHAT'S COOKING?

The kitchen is no doubt an essential component within a home. Created in a myriad of shapes, sizes, and locations within residences, kitchens serve as the go-to places for food storage, meal preparation, and clean up, not to mention the gathering place in which—for many centuries—family members, young and old, have come together to relax and reconnect.

To some degree, the kitchen is also a barometer of life in the United States. It is, of course, where we obtain daily nourishment. But it is a place for so many other activities related to the human experience. With our busy schedules and heavy agendas, it is often the only place where quality social exchange is spent with the rest of the family. We gather together in the morning in the kitchen to check on the rest of the family. "How did you sleep? How was your day yesterday?" For some it is a place to check on world events on the TV or in the paper at the breakfast table or kitchen bar. The kitchen is often a place to plan the day before heading out of the house. It is also a place to reflect on yesterday's events over a cup of coffee, as we remember the things we didn't accomplish this week and recall how much easier everything seemed to be back "in the good ole days."

Those who remember kitchens before microwave ovens, frost-free refrigerators, and automatic dishwashers also remember long hours of drudgery in small, often galley-style "cabinet-and-counter" environments. As American architecture in the mid-twentieth century began to revolutionize the contemporary American home, the residential kitchen became more to many than a place of daily utility.

CASE IN POINT

I remember as a young child being in the kitchen in my family home. It was your basic painted wood kitchen in your basic brick house in Chicago during the 1960s. Mom traditionally cooked all dinners even though her paralysis made it difficult to stand a great deal, even with her walker as support. So when I planned my new kitchen, I tried to remember the things that Mom had challenges with so I could maybe avoid getting into the same type of issues.

Because she had to sit most of the time, the counters were too high to comfortably work. She solved that problem by sitting down in her chair on big, fat telephone books. It also helped her to see up inside the wall cabinets and reach the dishes there on the lower shelf. The bottom cabinets made it difficult to reach inside just to see what was at the back or retrieve a skillet so she just started leaving the most often used pots and pans stacked on the cook top and counter. In fact, most everything was pretty much scattered about and on top of the counters. A few years back, Dad surprised her with a new refrigerator, but because it had the freezer section way at top, Mom couldn't really get up inside it either. Mom just made do most of the time and never really complained too much. . .except about the new fridge. (She hated the avocado green.)

—From a client interview, 48 years young

Adjoining family rooms, encompassing great room spaces, sheltered garden rooms and patios, and larger breakfast rooms combine with kitchens featuring state-of-the-art appliances along with telephones and televisions, computers and the Internet, and music and entertainment to make it a hub of family activity.

In the past, the kitchen was designed as a fully enclosed environment, isolated from other parts of the house. But it has gradually been opened up to the rest of the house. Large window-style openings between kitchens and dining areas called "pass-throughs" became popular during the 1960s, allowing easier serving, not to mention direct communication between cooks and diners. Better ventilation and lighting, specialized food preparation machines, and furniture-quality cabinet storage make it an appealing place to "hang out."

And, in the last three decades or so, architects, kitchen designers, and contractors have peeled away what remains of the cooking box and—by removing walls and combining food preparation, dining, and entertainment in one large area—have created the ubiquitous "great room" in which kitchen islands and bar counters define cooking environments from the rest of the interior.

Today, as designers, builders, and architects designate more floor space than ever for kitchens—sometimes by sacrificing space in living room and sleeping room areas—they also are creating kitchens with fewer physical barriers that can accommodate people of all physical abilities. Tech-savvy baby boomers, as well as would-be gourmet chefs of any age, also have welcomed the integration of kitchens into larger single spaces.

Responses to a recent survey by the American Society of Interior Designers clearly indicate a desire for kitchens that feature a full array of restaurant-style appliances, including commercial-style refrigerators, multiple ovens, built-in coffee grinders and espresso machines, heavy duty mixers and bread-making machines, multiburner cooking surfaces, and high-capacity ventilation systems.[1] And the kitchen is poised to become even more multifunctional as the central communications core and administration center for the home: In today's high-end projects, kitchens include computer workstations with high-speed Internet access, business-quality voice mail phone systems, closed-circuit video security systems, and wireless controls for a fully integrated electronic household.

On the horizon, appliance choices will include a refrigerator with a television built into the door so the cook can check out the latest recipe on the cooking channel; a video/audio monitoring device connected to the phone line that notifies retailers when supplies of beverages or food items need to be replenished; Internet monitoring through digital audio and video that can remind a resident to take medication or perform limited medical procedures, such as taking a temperature or checking a heart

8.2 Innovative, creative spaces such as this kitchen appeal to the progressive baby boomers that appreciate good design, and open-planned spaces, while being able to adapt to their lifestyles as the years go by. *Design by: Adrienne Gamba. Photo by: Michael Giscombe.*

8.3 Kitchen spaces that open up to adjacent great rooms, solariums, and family entertainment spaces make the entire area look larger. Without full and half walls, doors and vestibules that create barriers for easy passage, it is easier to get into and out of the kitchen and enjoy group conversation or to watch over an ailing family member. *Design by: Pamela Goldstein Sanchez, Allied ASID, CKD, CBD. Photo by: Gerlick Photography.*

rate; and a sophisticated alert-and-alarm system, a kind of motion detector system that can "observe" the whereabouts within the house of an older individual and alert health personnel or family members if movement is not sensed within a space.

Open-plan kitchens and great rooms, now an accepted style in today's residential architecture, not only make entertaining more convenient for hosts or watching young children at play trouble free for parents who are preparing meals, but these rooms also make it easier to monitor or engage in conversation with an older parent or relative seated in an adjacent space.

And while a growing number of seniors are intent on preparing nutritious meals that will contribute to their longevity, and some are interested in entertaining and learning new cooking skills, larger kitchens can address other important issues that are vital to an older person's self-esteem. A kitchen designed for easy and efficient meal preparation and cleanup can allow a resident to feel in control and independent, just as the ability to choose what and when to eat also can contribute to an increased sense of well being important components to a successful aging-in-place design solution.

Homes in which three or more generations are together under a single roof increased by more than 38 percent between the years 1990 and 2000. The reasons for such growth are increases in the levels of immigration, higher costs of housing, and because certain cultures are accustomed to sharing quarters with extended family members.[2] With more multigenerational families living under one roof, the great room/kitchen concept will likely remain a popular design with home buyers, both young and old, for years to come.

ARCHITECTURAL HISTORY REPEATS ITSELF

Although it might seem that this open-plan and great-room style of kitchen design is a recent trend in American residential architecture, the one-room concept actually began two centuries ago in one form or another.[3] Designers who understand the evolution of the American kitchen have a perspective on the role of kitchens today beyond that of merely food preparation and cleanup.

From the mid-1700s through the nineteenth century, most American homes—the center of family life—were rural, functional one- or two-room structures built from whatever indigenous materials a region provided.[4] With the exception of the homes of the very wealthy, there was no separate kitchen or food preparation area in most early American homes. An open firebox or fireplace, which was usually positioned at one end of the main room and constructed with an extended brick or stone hearth to keep flying sparks from burning the adjacent wood floors, was the primary means for cooking and for heating the interior. A typical brick or stone fireplace was often painted or whitewashed and included iron hooks for hanging heavy pots and pans on a large mantle made from whatever wood or stone was available.

As each member of a family was expected to contribute to maintaining the household, if a family member was incapacitated due to an injury or was disabled with a chronic illness, that person became a burden on the rest. Consequently, aging in place could mean a life of segregation for the elderly or disabled in the early days of this country.

Because of the threat of fire, those early households that could afford to do so built their kitchens as separate structures apart and often "down wind" from the main residence. These buildings, which included cooking fireplaces, were exclusively for cooking; smoke curing meat, fish, and game; and for preserving and storing fruits and vegetables.

In the mid-1800s, while the heavy burden of American domestic life often fell to the women, the laborious tasks were eased with the invention of the cast-iron cooking stove, which burned coal or wood. As Ellen Plante suggests in her book *The American Kitchen, 1700 to the Present: From Hearth to Highrise*,[5] the cast-iron stove "altered American cookery methods and meal planning, while at the same time relieving the housewife or cook of multiple backbreaking chores, such as lifting and moving heavy iron cookware."

After the Civil War, in the absence of slave labor and as electricity and indoor plumbing became more prevalent in cities and towns, manufacturers of domestic products responded to an increased demand for appliances of all shapes, designs, and types that would make kitchen life easier.

Ultimately, it was women who began to think about how to design the ideal cooking environment. Among them, Catherine Beecher, along with her sister Harriet Beecher Stowe, developed concepts that encouraged the development of the kitchen as a model of efficiency. In their book, *The American Woman's Home*,[6] published in 1869, the Beecher sisters outlined a systematic kitchen plan based on ergonomics.

The Beechers' concepts included larger work spaces and wall-mounted shelves for storage as well as other types of dedicated storage areas. They also proposed that food preparation should be compartmentalized away from cooking by moving the cast-iron stove into its own individual space adjacent to the main kitchen.[7]

According to Plante, American kitchen design took new shape during the Victorian era. "It was a period of enormous change," she says in her book. "The Victorians loved anything innovative—they wanted the latest, the newest and the most modern. Anything that would improve the household, they would embrace." Eat-in kitchens and kitchens adjacent to informal dining rooms became popular

CASE IN POINT

I can remember that when I was first married to my wife, there would be these wonderful dinners on the table when I got home from work. Now these days, she has many other obligations than to take care of her husband in the manner he grew accustomed to. So I figure that I would buy her a whole new kitchen. Maybe with new cabinets, new appliances, counters, and all the latest gadgets, she would be home cooking me dinner. So we planned and shopped and compared prices and then lived through the disruption of remodeling the space. We hired this kitchen designer who told us about using space wisely in our otherwise very large kitchen.

We installed drawers and more drawers—drawers that are refrigerators and drawers that are dishwashers, and small drawers that pulled out from cabinets. The pantry has swing out racks; the lower cabinets have pullouts. We have two big drawers that are our recycling center. We put in countertops that were "green," but that wasn't because of the color and then something that is called a "pot filler."

And yet I am an old man that is still not being served a decent meal because now, the only thing she makes for me is "dinner reservations." If I had known that this would be the result of all this money spent, I could have been just as happy with a big old fireplace, a few logs on the fire, hot dogs on a stick and a six pack.

—From a client interview, 69 years young

at the onset of the twentieth century, providing spaces where family members could team up to prepare and serve meals for their families in more informal dining experiences.

From its humble beginnings as a fireplace at one end of a single-room colonial American structure to its status as the showpiece in today's large-scale residences, the kitchen has brought structure and routine to the American household.

BUILDING NEW SPATIAL RELATIONSHIPS AND OPENING BARRIERS

Throughout the evolution of American kitchen design, however, what have not changed are the conventional relationships, traditional arrangements, and standard dimensions and placement of kitchen components: cabinetry, plumbing, electrical, ventilation, and appliances. In most cases, these standardizations prohibit spaces from being fully accessible to those with physical disabilities.

Fresh, healthy food is vital to everyone, including seniors. For those with limitations to their range of motion, however, preparing a nutritious meal can be especially difficult when the kitchen's traditional structure limits how the space is used and who gets to use it. But for design to fully support the independence, health, and well being of older clients, changes, adaptations, and new ways to

8.4 Large drawers in base cabinets make for easy access to dinnerware, glasses, pots, and pans, rather than the traditional arrangement using a series of wall cabinets, which can be difficult to reach up and into.

8.5 Pantry storage systems, such as this one, not only organize the food but also pull out for selection, which makes it easy to look for something that might otherwise be tucked away in the back part of a dark cabinet.

coordinate kitchen components are needed to ensure that good, healthy nourishment is easy to prepare and consume; cleanup should also be less laborious.

Beyond basic kitchen design, there are a number of challenges to good nutrition and health maintenance that design professionals should be aware of. Reactions to specific medical treatments, such as chemotherapy, can sap strength and energy, discouraging an individual from preparing a meal, even if that meal consists of microwavable or prepackaged food. Some prescription medications for a variety of health-related issues also can reduce appetites. Some individuals with food allergies or family members who might have specific dietary requirements and food preferences may have special requirements for refrigeration of medicines and storage of specific food stuffs. Even the task of grocery shopping, not

8.6 Kitchens that are inviting, organized, and well illuminated would benefit anyone, and for elderly clients, they can encourage them to get into the kitchen, prepare and cook meals, and clean up if the design makes it easy to perform these tasks. *Design by: Ann Huff, ASID, CAPS. Photo by: Jim Robinette.*

to mention restocking kitchen cabinets, can be a significant undertaking for individuals unable to drive or for those with physical disabilities or loss of strength.

Diminishing eyesight that sometimes accompanies aging also can be a significant challenge with food preparation, which is even more difficult when the kitchen lighting is insufficient to read dietary information or cooking instructions on packaging. In some instances, poor lighting quality, which can include glare or hot spots from under-cabinet lighting, can actually make fresh food appear unappetizing. Inadequate lighting can also lead to poor sanitary conditions: Poorly cleaned countertops and sinks can promote food-borne disease.

When planning a new kitchen or renovating an existing one for older clients, designers should consider an individual's physical limitations, such as the inability to stand for long periods of time to unload groceries, prepare food, set the table, or wash dishes. Accessing heavy bowls and platters, portable appliances—such as mixers, waffle irons, or counter-top fry pans—or even large containers of food or condiments stored in cabinets can be especially difficult for people who have lost upper body strength or have limited range of motion because of arthritis or other joint conditions. And just as someone might select what to cook by how large the package is or where it is stored, that person may also make food choices based on his or her ability to grip and open a container.

8.7 When possible, plan for more drawers than door cabinetry so that the storage is placed at a height that is comfortable for anyone. Dividers and peg systems keep the contents of the drawers well-organized and accessible to retrieve. Lazy-Susan storage racks make the best use of corner cabinetry, especially when there is limited storage capacity. *Design by: Pamela Goldstein Sanchez, Allied ASID, CKD, CBD. Photos by: Gerlick Photography.*

> Good design is as much about listening as it is about creating. This is particularly true with aging clients, whose fears include dependence, loneliness, depletion of financial resources, and inevitable medical problems. As designers, we must move beyond the traditional emphasis of beauty and elegance to consider critical issues of mobility, security, and access. By doing so, we can make sure that beautiful choices go hand in hand with practical choices so that each transition in life is met with both acceptance and confidence.
>
> —ADRIENNE GAMBA-SCHNITTMAN, ALLIED ASID, INTERIOR DESIGNER

RECIPES FOR SUCCESSFUL KITCHEN DESIGN

Good planning is a basic key. As with any space, whether it's new construction, or small or large-scale remodeling, careful and thoughtful use of space provides a greater return on the client's—as well as the designer's—investment. It is especially critical to plan for and select cabinetry, counters, and appliances that

adapt to the abilities of all users of the kitchen. Small adjustments such as changing cabinet hardware, adding drawer-style rollouts to the base cabinetry, or improving lighting can reap benefits to everyone, especially when a client's budget or time frame is limited.

When planning a new space, start with a reasonable, not overly large kitchen footprint. Although large kitchens are visually appealing and are great places to entertain, a vast space can challenge someone with limited mobility. The extra square feet of space doesn't necessarily make it easier to navigate, even when a walker or wheelchair is needed.

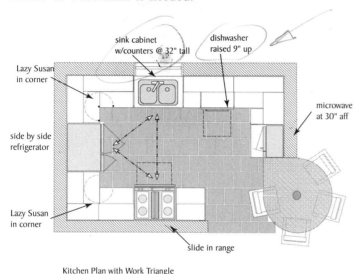

8.8 This plan view of a kitchen shows a basic but effective use of space. The work triangle is moved away from the kitchen entrance to avoid conflicts when others come into the space while a meal is being prepared.

Kitchen Plan with Work Triangle

Place the main appliances, the refrigerator and cook top, into a work triangle coordinating access to the plumbing for the sink. Plumbing is often one of the most expensive mechanical elements to change if it is not right. Cabinets and counters follow, making sure there are sufficiently sized landing pads around the three points of the triangle. Add electrical power to the kitchen system and light the space with ambient and task fixtures.

When remodeling a kitchen, look for ways to maintain an efficient work triangle and shift the mechanical systems only as needed, keeping in mind to balance those costs of electrical, plumbing, and ventilation with the overall client expenditures. Costs in these areas can quickly consume a client's budget, leaving fewer dollars for the cabinetry and counters.

Plan Both Cabinet Capacities and Efficiency of Use

The standard kitchen work triangle, developed by the University of Illinois' Building Research Council[8] in 1949, is made up of the three work centers: (1) a primary cleanup and food-prep sink, (2) a refrigerator, and (3) the stove or cooking surface. According to guidelines established by the National Kitchen and Bath Association (NKBA), the sum of the three sides of the triangle should be no more than 26 feet, with no less than 4 feet and no more than 9 feet in travel distance from one side to another. Traffic patterns into and out of the kitchen should not cross the work triangle. If there is only one sink in the kitchen, it should be located across from or between the refrigerator and cook top, rather than at the far end of one extended leg of the triangle.

For maximum accessibility, maintain a minimum distance of 42 to 48 inches between counters when planning aisles and travel areas between cabinets, and anticipate future needs by planning "comfort zones" (i.e., space needed for standing or walking with or without assistance) when determining cabinet and appliance locations.[9]

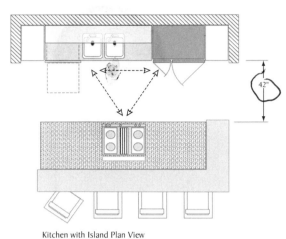

8.9 Kitchen islands are a great addition in a larger space as they can be used to open the cooking area to the rest of the house. Maintain a minimum of 42 inches between counters to give space to move about.

Kitchen with Island Plan View

Kitchen islands can provide additional counter space and cabinets, but if poorly located—for instance, in the middle of the work triangle—they can be significant obstacles to individuals with limited mobility. Specify the placement of a kitchen island either to one side or completely out of the primary work triangle.

Although attractive and convenient, open-plan kitchens sometimes have limited wall space for cabinetry, which can mean limited storage space as well. To compensate, plan for as much base cabinetry as possible and include drawer dividers, trays, and rollout drawers behind doors to organize essential, frequently used cooking implements and food items. Include rollouts and full-extension

8.10 When limited space requires the use of wall storage, consider the installation of the wall cabinets at 15 inches above the base cabinets and counter. Base cabinets may still be outfitted with plenty of rollout drawers to maximize efficiency and access for the most frequently used items.

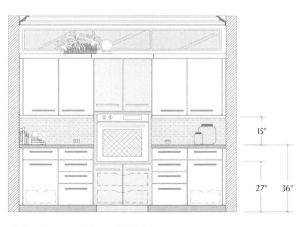

Kitchen Elevation with Lowered Wall Cabinets

C-1 This loft-style home for baby-boomer clients shows how design for aging in place can be functional, high style, and unique. Open spaces, common floor materials, and series of unencumbered windows help to create sight lines that make the space feel larger. *Design by: Patti Watson.*

C-2 Using classic lines of furnishings and fixtures in the design of this living and dining room, the designer took the timeless traditional design of the sofa, chairs, and tables and breathed new life into the pieces with bright fresh fabrics contrasted with dark finishes and a neutral flooring. *Design by: Susan Nilsson.*

C-3 The room is reminiscent of an era when parlor palms, woven rattan furnishings, and slow-turning ceiling fans filled verandas and parlors in homes large and small. This design is perfect for an aging client who recalls those times and the feeling of nature it can provide during any time of the year and no matter the season. *Design by: Lawrence-Mayer-Wilson Design Team. Photo by: Rosemary Carroll.*

C-4 Clean wide open spaces and classic contemporary furnishings define the basic elements of design for this great room for a baby-boomer client who realized the need to make housing plans for the future sooner rather than later and for a time when getting around the house may not be the easiest task accomplished every day. But level surface flooring will help to maneuver in and around the furnishings. *Design by: Susan Cozzi. Photo by: Michiko Kurisu.*

5 Though arms on chairs give
lid support for getting in and out
seats, these armless chairs posi-
oned in a tandem arrangement,
ithout tables at the sides, permit
n easy transfer from walker or
heelchair into one of two conver-
ational seating groups. A very flat
sal and a wool area rug help to
sually define the grouping in the
pen floor plan. *Design by:*
nn Huff, ASID, CAPS.

-6 A neutral textured floor of 18"
 18" Mexican shell stone runs
rom the entry and the living and
ining rooms into the kitchen and
reat room of this home that unites
ne spaces with a common neutral
ackground. Furnishings and rugs
n contrasting materials, finishes,
nd colors break up the spaces
nto more defined areas.

C-7 These contemporary chairs have arms that extend to the front edge of the seat and legs that allow feet to be pushed back under the seat aid in user to push up with their arms and stand up from the seat. The chairs are easy to move and can be brought closer into conversation with someone on the sectional. *Photo by: Jim Robinette.*

C-8 For this client, a small den and bathroom was remodeled to include a home theater system and cabinetry to showcase the client's expanding art glass collection. The audio system, cable box, and VCR and DVD players were positioned to the side and at a comfortable viewing height from the floor; the adjoining bath (not seen) was replaced with a walk-in wine cellar.

C-9 A swivel chair and ottoman on one side of the sectional and chaise-style seating on the other give this elder couple each their own preferred seat in the house, whether to gaze out of their condominium overlooking the boats in the bay or to sit for extended periods to watch their favorite basketball team play on a big screen flat panel TV. *Photo by: Michael D. Baker.*

C-10 The clients who commissioned this oceanfront guesthouse enjoyed the retreat that was created so much that it became more a retreat for the couple from their estate home elsewhere on the property. Ser-viceable and hardwearing fabrics slipcover over cushions, making them easy to remove and clean.

C-11 This living space is inviting and well balanced with good distribution of patterns, colors, and textures throughout the space, resulting in a more formal feel to the room. The timeless classic lines when coupled with uncomplicated design will keep this room from showing its age. *Design by: Lawrence-Mayer-Wilson Design Team. Photo by: Rosemary Carroll.*

C-12 The designer was thoughtful to include handrails in the hall but disguised them as a chair rail, a millwork element compatible with the overall theme of the interior. The arch top to the pocket door leading from the hall to the dining room echoes complimentary lines found in the breakfront. *Design by: Jo Rabaut.*

C-13 Bonus rooms are spaces built without a defined purpose planned, letting the owner and resident decide how the space will be used. Spaces such as these, therefore, can have many purposes and be easily converted to whatever need may arise, including a private space for live-in assistance. *Design by: Shannon Shillings. Photo by: Gerlick Photography.*

C-14 Strong organized geometric lines contrasted with abstract art combine in this residence of a baby boomer who decided to age in place in a home of his own choosing, achieving a clean contemporary design warmed by the textures of the concrete floor, woven fabrics on the seating, and creative lighting. *Photo by: Michiko Kurisu.*

C-15 The dramatic window treatment in this dining room frames the view through the glass to the landscaped yard and garden beyond. Lighting in good quantity and from a variety of light sources was necessary to illuminate the volume of space. Flat oriental carpets, such as this one under the dining table, can help to reduce the noise level often associated with tall ceilings. *Design by: Rita Goldstein. Photo by: Gerlick Photography.*

C-16 Kitchens should have strong visual appeal while still remaining fully functional for anyone to use, and this one does. Metal-framed doors with patterned glass inserts on sliding tracks serve as suspended, floating doors that visually conceal but not fully hide the dishes placed on wall-mounted shelving. This design makes it easy to locate, use, and replace what is stored on the shelves. *Design by: Adrienne Gamba, ASID, IIDA LEED AP. Photo by: Michael Giscombe.*

C-17 This guesthouse kitchen was designed for a client who planned to have an aging parent come live with them for as long as she needed or desired. The kitchen has various counters heights to accommodate anyone with or without disability, whether standing or taking a seat at the sink. The wall cabinets are placed slightly lower than conventional installations to make access into the lower sections a bit easier to get to. *Photo by: Jim Robinette.*

C-18 It is hard to tell, but the rear wall of this open kitchen houses a lot of appliances and becomes a center of activity during the couple's family dinners. Dual drawer-style refrigerators are installed under a single door refrigerator making cold storage easy no matter what goes inside. Dual freezer drawers are located adjacent disguised as drawers of their own. An oven stack on the right features side hinged doors that permit full access into the interior. *Photo by: Jim Robinette.*

C-19 Rollouts make the best use of base cabinet not only for increasing capacity but also for making it easier to reach for pots and pans that might otherwise be difficult to pull out to use. The top drawer is not a drawer but a full butcher block slab on a side-mounted full extension drawer that glides and gives additional food prep space and is at a lower counter height for someone who may need to sit to prepare a snack. *Design by: Ann Huff, ASID, CAPS. Photo by: Jim Robinette.*

C-20 Baby-boomer clients appreciate a touch of the exotic with a touch of tech. Special features in this master suite feature a flat panel TV located in the footboard of the bed that rises up and pivots around so that it can be seen from the seating area near the floor to ceiling window wall. Motorized window blinds controlled by wireless controls system operate behind the stationary draperies to block out much of the light for someone who is taking a nap in the daytime. *Photo by: Randy Smith.*

C-21 This bedroom suite has its own kitchenette and bath spaces, features that anyone would want or need for an extended stay whether as a visitor or a caregiver for an elder client or family member. *Design by: Judith Sisler Johnston.*

C-22 A strong accessible design is seen in the clean open spaces of this bedroom suite designed for a baby boomer that chose to age in place but without the usual clutter. Dividing walls are arranged to create large walk-in closets without doors and open-style bathrooms adjacent to the sleeping space. *Design by: Susan Cozzi. Photo by: Michiko Kurisu.*

C-23 This bathroom showcases the use of a number of assistive devices, including a high-styled grab bar and vertically mounted mini-grab pull in the fully accessible shower. *Design by: Great Grabz. Photo by: Brynn Brujin.*

C-24, C-25 The original plan of this bathroom had walls that cut up the space into smaller less desirable segments. After the remodel of the space, the bathroom now is a singular open interior space. With a level entry into the circular design of the shower and a vanity with rolling cabinetry, the new plan makes better use of the space while keeping it functional for the designer's elder client. *Designs by: Robert Wright.*

C-26 Baby boomers have expressed a desire for spa like bathrooms that can include plumbing accessories like multiple body sprays that can be as invigorating as a massage. Textured stone materials on the shower plan were chosen to give the client slip-resistant flooring that is complimentary to the main bathroom stone materials. *Design by: Ann Huff, ASID, CAPS. Photo by: Jim Robinette.*

C-27 With the continuity of a single floor material like concrete, the bathroom appears larger but is much more accessible for any client of any age and ability. The sliding door panel at the shower is from a decorative translucent material framed in metal hung from a ceiling mounted sliding track system. *Design by: Adrienne Gamba, ASID, IIDA LEED AP. Photo by: Michael Giscombe.*

C-28 This dual sink vanity can be adapted to fit the needs of someone who might need to brush their teeth or wash their face from a seated position. The recessed toe kicks are actually fully removable panels and doors are hinged to open up and pocket back in to the sides of the cabinetry. *Photo by: Jim Robinette.*

C-29 This clever cabana bath design was created by first removing the conventional shower curb, then extending the window down to the shower pan and installing semi-textured oval river rocks on the shower floor. Additional river rocks continue the visual experience and appear as ground fill in the landscape beyond making a direction connection between inside and out. *Design by: Ann Huff, ASID, CAPS. Photo by: Jim Robinette.*

C-30 This client anticipated his need for an accessible bath when his doctor advised that replacement knee and hip surgery would be required. To make his home user-friendly, the design called for a fully accessible shower with the standard fare of plumbing accessories, a bench, and a heated floor. *Photo by: Jim Robinette.*

CASE IN POINT

I'm barely 4 foot 10 inches and my husband is 6 foot. When we renovated our kitchen a few years ago, we had the contractor hang the cabinets at 15 inches and fill in the space at the top with deep crown molding. It made a world of difference in what I could reach, and [it] didn't bother my husband a bit!

—Julie Warren, writer, editor

drawer glides on all drawers to make the drawer boxes completely accessible and to maximize storage capacity. Soft-close devices help manage the noise made when wood doors and drawers meet wood cabinet and cases.

To make wall cabinets more accessible for seated users or for those with limited upper body range of motion, set the bottom of the cabinet box at 15 inches above the counter, rather than the conventional 18 inches. This height provides enough space between the countertop and cabinets for canisters and small appliances, like coffee makers and toasters, and brings more storage space within easy reach of those with limitations.[10]

Install easy-to-grasp hardware, rather than knobs, on cabinet doors and drawers. In cases where the client has extreme difficulty grasping, as with some arthritis patients, drape or hang small towels or straps around the hardware to help facilitate opening drawers and doors. To make it easier for those with poor eyesight to see drawer and door handles, specify contrasting finishes on hardware and cabinetry.

Cabinets built with conventional dimensions can suffer damage from walkers and wheelchairs. The standard American kitchen cabinet is customarily built with a three- to four-inch toe kick that is set back about three inches from the face edge of the case. The footrests of wheelchairs can not only bang into cabinets but also can prevent a seated individual from opening base cabinet drawers and doors without having to move to one side.[11] To allow adequate space for footrests under a cabinet box, specify cabinets on toe kicks that are from 9 to 10 inches high and set back 6 inches or more from the face front. Also include at least one knee space under a counter surface for people who must sit while performing kitchen tasks. Another knee space might be also required at the kitchen sink.[12]

Even if your clients don't have any significant physical limitations at this time, specify sink and cook top cabinetry now that can be removed in the future as a single unit without disturbing the cabinets on either side. Knee spaces should be a minimum of 27 inches high, 19 inches deep, and 30 inches wide—although a more generous 36 inch width offers additional maneuvering space, which can be especially important in smaller kitchens.[13] Specify that the floor covering be installed under cabinets for possible future exposure or other rearrangement.

A number of other unique devices can make kitchens more accessible for people with various abilities, such as

8.11 Pull-out stools that tuck back into a knee hole allow an individual who may not be able to stand for extended periods of time to sit and prepare a meal or talk on the phone.

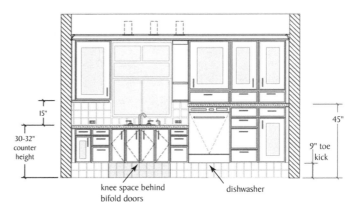

8.12 Building taller toe kicks permits the foot rests of a wheelchair to fit up to the cabinetry without damaging it, but in this elevation, it shows the dishwasher raised up from the floor, reducing strain to the client's back when he or she is loading the dishes.

Kitchen Elevation with Raised Dishwasher

wall cabinets mounted on adjustable cleats that can be vertically raised or lowered when necessary; pull-down shelving racks that pull out and down make getting into wall cabinets easy by lowering their contents to near counter height; and base cabinets or counters that can be raised or lowered mechanically or manually to accommodate a seated user.

Consider including a rollout or pullout counter, a cabinet with a folding drop leaf, or a cart on wheels to provide additional counter space for seated users. Because kitchens should accommodate standing users as well as those who are seated, don't recommend installing an entire kitchen at a lower-than-uniform height.

8.13 This kitchen showcases an effective design that is not only good looking but also has counters installed at various heights, so any member of the family can use the space in ways that suit his or her preferences. *Design by: Pamela Goldstein Sanchez. Photo by: Gerlick Photography.*

Counters

While the standard 36-inch counter height above the finished floor—and for which most standard major appliances are designed—is fine in most applications, we recommend including more than one counter height in kitchens to accommodate both seated and standing users.[14] Thirty- to 34-inch-high counters are more comfortable for those who are preparing meals while standing or seated, while 27-inch-high counters are more comfortable for someone to be seated in order to actively prep food by mixing, whipping, and kneading.

HOW GREEN IS YOUR KITCHEN?

It would be remiss during the process of selecting kitchen cabinetry if "green" or sustainable design were only considered for both the cabinets, but not also throughout the kitchen and the rest of the home environment. While aging in place addresses many safety, mobility, and barrier-free issues, creating effective aging design should also include healthy, sustainable design philosophies and practice. Green cabinets made from wood harvested from managed forests, medium-density fiberboard (MDF) free of all formaldehyde, and wood products fabricated from recycled materials or renewable resources are responsible selections. It is also a comfort to know more about the manufacturer of the cabinets. Ask a few questions: How green are their manufacturing processes? How is the waste disposed of? Will the finishes be free of volatile organic compounds (VOCs)? But choosing all the other kitchen design components with the same criteria is as important.

Green countertops can be fabricated from compressed paper and recycled glass, reclaimed woods, natural stone, slate, and concrete. Responsible flooring materials include cork, tile, wood, and stone as long as the green value of the material is not offset by the energy spent to ship and deliver the goods to the job site. Design for non-slip matt or textured ceramic tile, but specify those with a minimum of 50 percent recycled content. Other green considerations: energy-efficient HVAC systems, ventilation with filters that trap, wall and cabinet paints and finishes with low or no VOCs, ENERGY STAR–rated appliances, efficient lighting (including LEDs and fluorescent lamping), and special recycle centers that encourage their use.

At this point, with the evolution and acceptance of sustainable design in this country and around the world, it is important to take a larger, perhaps more philosophical view. It is relatively easy to think about the parts and pieces that can be green, or make a goal to use recycled materials when practical. But take a holistic approach to aging in place. Integrate sustainability in the design criteria. As Bernadette Upton, ASID, LEED, an interior designer who passionately advocates for environmentally friendly design states, "Green design is not a color. And it is not an option." It is this type of stewardship that will enhance the well being of the end user and others.

There are many countertop materials available, including metal, natural stone, natural and manmade tile, and manmade composite products. To ensure the best countertop for a specific application and budget, put ease of cleaning and regular maintenance at the top of your list of criteria.

Few other materials have as much visual impact as natural stone, marble, and granite, which are preferred materials for kitchen counters by many consumers. Granite is especially durable and does not conduct heat or cold. If these surfaces are not carefully treated with food-safe topical sealants and regularly maintained, however, minute food particles and liquids that collect in natural veins and fissures can promote the growth of bacteria. And individuals with diminished eyesight often have difficulty thoroughly cleaning these visually textured surfaces.

Natural and manmade tile, such as glass, ceramic, and porcelain, offer designers opportunities to create pattern and texture in a kitchen. Grout lines should

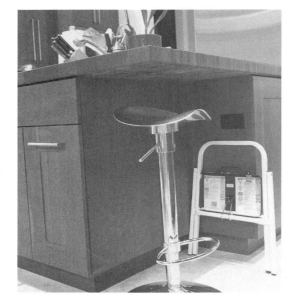

8.14 This island counter is made from mesquite, a sustainable wood species that will stand up to hard use. The counter then cantilevers over an open corner of the island that was removed from the cabinet lineup, providing a new niche, a place to sit down on a stool, and a place to tuck a small step ladder. *Photo by: Michael D. Baker.*

be routinely treated with a food-safe sealer to prevent stains and retard bacteria growth.

Solid-surface, manmade materials—fabricated from resin, acrylic, and polyester compounds—are exceptionally resistant to impact, stains, and bacteria and offer distinct advantages from other substances: Sections can be bonded without visible lines at the seams for longer runs of counters; burns and deep scratches can be easily repaired; and contrasting colors can be laminated together to create unique visual effects or edge details to give users a visual cue where counters begin and end. Since colors and patterns are solid throughout the material, solid-surfaces can be worked like wood, molded into unusual shapes and patterns, or installed in unique places.

Laminate surfaces are user-friendly and economical choices for countertops, particularly when combined with a backsplash of natural or manmade accent tile materials. By way of digital technology and high-quality printing, these counter surfaces are available in

8.15 Natural stone materials like Jerusalem stone, a type of limestone, have a natural matte finish that will eliminate glare from bright under-cabinet lighting. Materials such as these require some routine maintenance, such as using penetrating sealers to keep it looking fresh and new and resisting stains and build up of bacteria. *Design by: Ann Huff, ASID, CAPS.*

realistic visual representations of marble, granite, tumbled stone, and other textures. Colors and textures are only on the surface of these materials, however, so they are highly susceptible to scratches and burns that are not easily repaired.

Agglomerate marble as a countertop material is exceptionally hard, has minimal absorption, and is easy to clean and maintain. Fabricated from a mixture of 90 to 95 percent marble and 5 to 10 percent polyester resin, agglomerate marble is a good choice for countertops that will be subjected to heavy use.

Stainless steel, in either 14- or 16-gauge, makes an excellent choice for kitchen countertops because it is exceptionally easy to clean and sanitary. Metal counters, however, are susceptible to scratches or scuffing from heavy or careless use, and they do require routine maintenance to prevent stains and corrosion from etching the finish. Cost and availability of quality metal fabrication may be factors in choosing stainless steel or other metal materials.

Other possible countertop materials include concrete and wood. Although concrete countertops require routine maintenance using food-safe sealers, concrete is a good sustainable alternative over nonrenewable natural materials such as quarried stone and petroleum-based synthetic solid-surface products. Countertops made from maple or mesquite woods—which require regular application of food-safe mineral oil to preserve the appearance and prevent stains from water, oil, and acid—are an attractive option for achieving a "butcher block" look.

8.16 Concrete counters have found popularity with the design community as a "green" product, but as with natural stone materials, sealers will need to be used. The contrast created between this counter and the floor helps define where the counter ends, giving a great visual clue for those with sight impairments.

Sinks, Faucets, and Plumbing Choices

There are many options and combinations for sinks and faucets.

Sinks come in a variety of sizes and materials: large and small, round or square, single bowl or double, metal or porcelain, composite or plastic. There are also many different shapes and installation types. Faucets as well come in a large menu of choices: wide and small spread, deck or wall mounted, tall and short, and single or dual handled. They have a broad range of finish options to mix or match with the sink choice.

Before making the choice of what sink and faucet, first consider the range and ability of the most frequent user.[15] Then choose based on their physical ability to reach out, across the counter, over the sink, and down into the bowl. Large sinks may be perfect for a family with lots of dishes, but it may make it difficult for an elder to stretch out an arm, open a hand, and reach to the other side to turn the faucet on and off.

Very deep sinks present their own problems. They may be a great place to stack a lot of dishes and keep them out of sight prior to hand washing or going into the dishwasher. But this may present problems for someone who is in a seated position and can't easily see down into the sink pan to set dishes and glasses securely onto the bottom. For individuals who have lost upper body strength, it may seem nearly impossible to lift a large vessel out from the deep bottom well, especially when it is filled with water. Place such decisions at the top of the list before moving forward in choosing sink style, form, or color to achieve better access for everyone.

For better access from a seated position, install a kitchen sink in a cabinet that will have a finished counter height at 27 to 34 inches above the floor.[16] This

8.17 Even with a lowered counter height, access is not always that easy. In this example, a knee hole under the sink allows someone in a seated position or wheelchair to get in and under the counter. Careful planning will also help keep the plumbing lines and drain hidden from contact. This cabinet has a wood panel that does the trick. *Design by: Pamela Goldstein Sanchez, Allied ASID, CKD, CBD. Photo by: Gerlick Photography.*

8.18 Sinks such as this stainless version are available at many different prices, but the better ones will have insulation applied on the bottom outside surface to minimize the noise when washing dishes or scrubbing pans.

dimension accommodates minimum knee space for a wheelchair-seated user under a shallow-basin sink. Cleanup around under-mount sinks is much easier than drop-in sinks because there is no rim to catch food or liquids. Space and budget permitting, add an additional single-bowl sink in an island cabinet or in another area to provide food prep space away from cleanup tasks. A small square, round, or trough-shaped sink installed in a somewhat out-of-the-way location can create a functional work space to sit down while peeling vegetables.

Design professionals have a number of material options when choosing the perfect sink, but the best kinds of sinks are those that will last years without losing their luster or quality. The thickness, or "gauge," of the metal is an important factor in choosing a metal sink. The lower the gauge number, the thicker the metal. Those with a thicker gauge will also be less prone to dings from a pan that gets dropped from an arthritic hand by accident. Metal sinks with a lower gauge rating will also transmit less noise when the metal surface meets the metal of the pots and pans. It is a generally accepted guideline that a sink made from 18 gauge material is an acceptable basic choice. However, 15 or 16 gauge metals may make a sink cost more initially but will return better aesthetics and function over the years.

Metals such as copper and stainless steel are accepted materials by designers and consumers in higher-end projects. While copper is beautiful to the eye and touch, maintenance can be a chore for sinks that get a lot of use. Stainless-steel sinks, as with counters, require little maintenance but can easily show and retain even moderate scratches, marring the aesthetics. Many vendors offer metal sinks with insulation that will deaden the sound of water pouring from the tap or dishes and flatware moving about. Avoid highly polished finishes because with use and time, the finish may develop a spotty, foggy appearance as the years go by.

Other commonly available sink materials include porcelain over cast iron, manmade acrylics and resins, and bowls that are formed into sinks using composites, such as the solid surface materials often seen in countertops. All of these provide the consumer and the designer with more color choices than the "coldness" of metals.

Porcelain sinks are the standard of choice for many homeowners given that there is little maintenance other than washing and wiping them down to prevent water stains. However, their finish can be etched by foods with a high acid content, so regular and careful attention is required by the end user to make sure the finish does not dull as a result of contact with fruits and juices.

Acrylics offer less expensive, economical options and can provide years of service when limited care is taken. Generally sturdy and able to resist abuse, their colors can oxidize over a period of years, which is especially noticeable in very light colors. An acrylic surface can be burned when it comes in contact with a hot pan or skillet directly from the cook top. Care is required when using shiny or glossy finished acrylics as they will show wear. Using metal racks that rest on the floor pan of the sink will keep the bottom finish "showroom new" and also allow for better drainage.

Solid surface materials are another good choice because they will accept daily use and occasional abuse. They can be installed with a seamless under-counter method that makes cleanup easy. They can be repaired if scratched or burned, but quality labor and materials means higher costs to the client.

In the selection of sinks, also make note of the location of the drain.[17] Many sinks have the drains in the middle of its bottom. This can create drainage problems if dirty dishes and pots are placed over the drain hole. Some manufacturers have designed sinks with the drains to one side or in the corner, making it easier to set a casserole dish down into the bowl for cleaning without covering up the drain.

Single- and double-handle faucets are easier for everyone to use than faucets with knob controls. Faucets also may have options for individual hand-held sprays, making it easier to wash out the sink and clean up the dishes because the end of the faucet is in close proximity to the front of the counter. Choose one that has a head that can be easily gripped and the spray operated without a lot of pressure from the hand or fingers. To make reaching the faucet controls easier for a seated user, have the faucet and controls installed to one side of the sink basin, rather than at the back.

Faucet options might include a full range of finishes, spread sizes, special filtration, integral pullout sprays, and self-cleaning aerators that will fight off salt or mineral deposits in water. For certain special needs, faucets can be controlled using foot pedals installed at the front of the cabinets to make operation simple. Temperature settings on these control systems should include standard preset temperatures to avoid scalding from an accident with hot water.

8.19 Faucets come in all shapes and finishes, but select those that have handles rather than knobs because operation will be much easier for someone with wet hands. This version also features a pull-out spray and is in closer access to the front of the sink rather than a separate spray often installed along the back of the sink. *Design by: Pamela Goldstein Sanchez, Allied ASID, CKD, CBD. Photo by: Gerlick Photography.*

Appliances

Because appliances account for a substantial portion of any kitchen budget, it is essential to consider all criteria when specifying the refrigerator, dishwasher, range, oven, and microwave to achieve the best results for your client. Base selection of kitchen appliances on manufacturers' reliability, energy consumption of individual units, location of electrical and plumbing sources in the room, and how and what kind of cooking will be done, as well as on the client's style preferences. When considering installment locations, remember to anticipate that appliances may need to be accessed by a seated user.

Refrigeration

The choices and options of refrigeration are vast. Certain models, however, are easier to access than others for people with disabilities. Double-door or side-by-side refrigerator/freezers, units with shallow interiors, large-capacity refrigerators, and some newer French-door models—which have equal-sized doors on an upper refrigerator over a drawer-type pull-out freezer—provide good interior access whether the user is standing or seated in a wheelchair.[18]

In most cases, however, an individual who is seated in a wheelchair has limited access to over-and-under style units, such as those with the freezer in a bottom pull-out drawer, because the user must move out and away from the appliance without running into another obstacle behind or to the side so the refrigerator door or drawer can be fully opened. Similarly, it is difficult for a seated individual to reach an upper freezer or refrigerator section.

Under-counter refrigeration units, including icemakers, wine storage centers, and drawer-style refrigerators can be placed anywhere—and at any height—within kitchen cabinetry. Drawer-style units put frequently used food and beverage items within easy reach of everyone. As with other standard refrigeration, these units can be installed with decorative panel faces to blend with other cabinetry. Remember, however, to install or specify contrasting handles or pulls that clearly indicate where the appliance opens.

8.20 Double-door refrigerators like this one permit nearly a complete view of what is inside, whether from a standing or a seated position. The freezer on the bottom may be challenging for some to lift heavy frozen foods up and out of, but this is still better than a freezer located on the top. *Photo by: Michael D. Baker.*

8.21 This kitchen wall features a series of under-counter refrigeration and freezing drawer-style units, blended into the cabinet with optional wood appliance panels, and all is within easy access to the microwave and oven. *Photo by: Jim Robinette.*

Since opening refrigerator doors to retrieve items can be particularly challenging for those with loss of strength, the inability to grip, or limited use of both hands, the location of the refrigerator is as critical as the type or model. Be sure to place the unit away from corners, walls, or cabinet doors that prevent the refrigerator doors from opening a full 90 degrees. If the only place available is in a corner or next to a right-angled wall, separate the refrigerator from the wall with a small cabinet end panel or a filler to ensure the widest door opening possible.

Sometimes refrigerator doors can be especially difficult to open when cold air seals them or food items in door shelves add extra weight. To compensate for these and other situations when limited physical strength is an issue, specify oversized door handles or outfit existing doors with loop-style hardware. And consider other unique features in refrigerators, such as in-the-door ice and water dispensers with built-in water filtration, audible "door-open" alarms, and filter and defrost indicator lights.

Cooking and Ventilation

Select a range and cook top based on the source of power that is available— either gas or electric—as well as the unit's particular features, and review safety features with the client before writing the final specifications. While many people prefer gas for cooking because it is easier to control, cooks food more quickly than electric heat, and offers the ability for users to prepare meals during power outages, the open flames produced by gas stoves present a number of hazards. Gas stoves are particularly dangerous for elderly clients who rely on portable oxygen supplies when moving about their homes, and individuals with impaired senses of smell are unable to detect gas leaks. If a client insists on a gas cook top, investigate units that feature sealed burners that are recessed below the surface of the range to protect the user from an open flame.

Electric ranges and cook tops are available with two types of surfaces: coil-style radiant elements that plug into the range top and smooth or radiant surface models that provide a more even heat distribution and are easy to clean. In either case, choose a range or cook top with a warning light or another visual cue that indicates when a burner or surface area is too hot to touch. Since electric power has no visible flame to warn a user to turn off the heat, there is a higher risk of leaving a burner on once cooking is completed and containers are moved away.

For an additional measure of safety, select range and cook top models with controls along the front and/or at the side to avoid burns or spills caused by reaching across or over burners or hot pans to adjust burner controls at the back of the stove.[19] Always plan for a fire extinguisher to be placed within easy reach of the cooktop and oven, especially for those with impaired mobility and dexterity.

8.22 Gourmet style cooktops appeal to the elder population and their newfound love of cooking. In the selection of appliances, ensure that the ventilation system is correctly matched to the higher output and intensities of heat and vapors that these types of cooktops give out. *Photo by: Jim Robinette.*

8.23 For many cooks, gas appliances give more control of the cooking to the chef because they heat up faster and cool down quicker. But side or front controls are critical for safety because reaching over a burning flame to turn off the unit can result in a severe burn very easily.

Select control knobs and buttons that favor the level of ability of the most frequent user. Lever- or blade-style knobs, which do not require grasping to turn on and off, usually have a tapered shape that offers a visual clue by pointing the control's position. Touch controls require little force to operate and don't require gripping or twisting. Touch controls, however, are not a good choice for those with visual impairments and, as with all electrical devices, will not work in a power outage. Consider specifying a stove or cook top that offers controls or panels with large displays in contrasting lettering or raised markers.

Specify adequate ventilation directly above the cook top that is ducted to the exterior to efficiently remove cooking odors, vapors, and smoke. The recommended minimum vent size removes 100 cubic feet per minute (CFM).[20] Higher capacities are recommended beginning with a minimum of 150 CFMs. In certain cases, a larger ventilation motor can be installed in a remote location and ducted to the range hood when noise reduction is critical for a hearing impaired resident. Include a minimum clearance of 24 inches between the range hood and the cooking surface, and extend the hood beyond the width of the cook top a minimum of 3 inches on either side. Install control switches for fans and any auxiliary lighting within easy reach, such as on a side wall or at the front edge of a nearby base cabinet on either side of the cook top or range.

As with all appliances, operable parts, switches, and handles should be operable with a single hand. Select control and pull hardware that does not require pinching, grasping, or turning of the wrist in order to operate. The force to activate controls should be a maximum of five pounds.[21]

Ovens

As with ranges and cook tops, select the type and number of ovens based on the available power source. Oven features, such as self-cleaning capacity, interior lights, adjustable rack systems, rotisseries, and digital controls and displays are especially convenient accessories for aging-in-place environments. Wall-installed ovens, rather than those found in freestanding or drop-in ranges, are more accommodating for those with disabilities because heights above the floor provide easier access.

Although the standard wall-oven installation height is 30 to 40 inches above the finished floor to the bottom of the unit, it is important to install the appliance at a height that accommodates the individual user's preference, puts the controls within easy reach, and provides for knee space if the user is seated in a wheelchair.[22] Consult with your client to

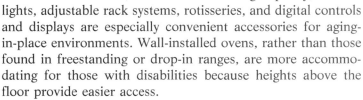

8.24 This oven has a door that folds down but is designed to support the weight of the pan or broiler filled with several pounds of turkey and dressing or lasagna. The wire shelves are perfectly aligned to meet the wire grid mounted to the door, allowing the food to be slid onto the door, rather than the user having to pick up a pan directly from the oven racks. *Design by: Keith Miller.*

determine the appropriate above-the-floor height for his or her oven's placement, and allow sufficient room around the oven for the most frequent user to either move to the side or back away to open the oven door. A good guideline to follow to provide easy transfer of hot food from the oven to the countertop is to position the wall oven so that the most-used oven rack is at the same height as the countertop. Be sure to install a heat-proof surface or add a pull-out shelf adjacent to the oven where hot baking dishes can be placed quickly.

When specifying conventional drop-front door ovens, plan for and specify adequate open floor space on either side and in front of the open oven door. For a side-hinged or swing door, include open floor space below the oven door and on the side of the oven closest to the oven door handle. The minimum requirements for unobstructed open space around an oven door are:[23]

- 27 inches (29 inches for wheelchair armrests) in height
- 19 inches of depth
- 30 to 36 inches in width

And as with the selection of the range and cook top, select controls, knobs, and buttons based on the level of ability of the most frequent user.

Microwave Ovens

With a microwave oven, a user can quickly and easily cook or warm food, especially in small quantities, a particular advantage for households with one or two residents. While the customary location for the microware is above the cooktop, a better location for accessibility is either on the counter or in the cabinetry below the counter. The primary requirement for any microwave's location should be the range of reach of the most frequent user. Remember that the location above the cook top requires a user who is able to stand.

For a user seated in a wheelchair, a counter location is suitable as long as the appliance is not placed too far back and there is knee space directly under the microwave or to one side for easier access. Install a cabinet-mounted microwave at a minimum of 15 inches to a maximum of 54 inches above the finished floor based on the range of reach of the most frequent user. Keep in mind that the height of the control panel should not exceed 48 inches above the finished floor (AFF).[24]

Although microwave controls are available as either dials or electronic touch panels, the former can be a chal-

8.25 Microwave ovens make it simple for someone to prepare or warm a meal, which is especially important for someone who doesn't have the ability to stand for a long time. Knee-holes under the oven provide easy access in and out of the appliance and onto the counter.

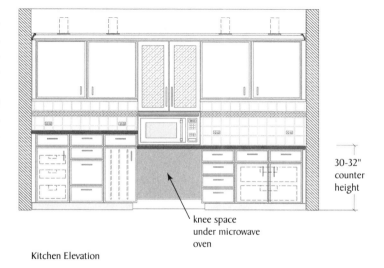

30-32" counter height

knee space under microwave oven

Kitchen Elevation

8.26 While this microwave appears to be built-into the cabinetry, it actually is sitting on a shelf. This flexible design permits the appliance to be moved down to the counter when access is needed from a seated position.

8.27 Dishwashers that are installed off the floor from 9 feet to as many as 18 feet will make loading and unloading much less of a chore, and with cabinetry close by, a breeze to move clean dishes into their spaces. *Design by: Pamela Goldstein Sanchez, Allied ASID, CKD, CBD. Photo by: Gerlick Photography.*

lenge for users with limited small motor skills because of the grasping and twisting motion required. Dials with raised markers, however, work well for those who are visually impaired. Touch-panel controls that feature single-touch operation require little effort for most users. In any specified model, however, the controls should have some method of providing feedback to ensure its intended and proper use such as a clicking sound when the dials are moved and/or a visual display to confirm operation.

Dishwashers

Like other appliances, dishwashers have become kitchen necessities and are especially helpful for those with minimal upper body strength, as well as for those who cannot stand for extended periods. A unit that is installed from 6 inches to as many as 18 inches off the finished floor requires less bending and thus, less stress on a user's lower back and legs to load and unload. When selecting controls, follow the same guidelines as those for the range, oven, and microwave, and look for models with grip handles on the inside as well as the outside of the door to make frequent opening and closing less of a chore.

Drawer-style dishwashers that are installed in base cabinets are not only easy to access but energy efficient as well. These small-load models save on water consumption, are particularly well-suited to households with only one or two occupants, and are very functional when installed in cabinets anywhere within 36 inches from the cleanup sink. The demand by consumers for these appliances continues to grow as prices drop due to more competition from worldwide manufacturers that offer even more model options and features such as timers, remote controls, and soft-touch button operation.

Lighting Can Be Very Illuminating for Elder Clients

Diminished eyesight is the most common physiological change as we grow older.[25] Studies document and affirm how dramatically eyesight can diminish with age so there is a lot to consider when selecting the right combination of light fixtures and lamps for an aging-in-place kitchen. A person age 50 or over with diminished eyesight or eye disease requires more light to perform the same tasks as younger individuals. The type and arrangement of lamping, beam spread, wattage, and fixtures are essential to the proper selection of lighting.

Kitchen lighting should be nonglare and in sufficient locations throughout the room to provide a maximum of task and ambient illumination. According to guidelines put forth by the Illuminating Engineering Society of North America (IESNA), to adequately illuminate for basic meal preparation, dishwashing, and general cleanup there should be at least 30 foot-candles of light in the kitchen.[26]

When deciding between incandescent or fluorescent lighting for designated kitchen work areas, keep in mind that both types of bulbs are available in a wide range of colors and color temperatures and should be selected appropriately for specific tasks. The soft light of a standard "cool-white" fluorescent light, when used as under-cabinet lighting, can make raw red meat appear brown and unappealing. Another lighting choice can produce a more appetizing visual result.

Local and state building codes that regulate energy compliance may limit the choices and quantity of lighting fixtures and lamping, but with the right type of fixtures, equipped with an appropriate lamp, the area can be illuminated properly for nearly all kitchen tasks.

Specify overhead, surface-mounted, or recessed fixtures over and around the main workspaces—the sink and cleanup areas—as well as around the major appliances.[27] Breakfast bars and dining spaces should have separate light sources from the kitchen space and might need to include task lighting in which to read the morning newspaper. Standard-sized and miniature track-lighting fixtures make good task accent lighting but should not be used as the only source of illumination.

Include individual switches to control the various fixtures placed throughout the kitchen to enable users to select which fixtures to turn on for specific activities. Dimmers and rheostats not only extend the life of bulbs but also save energy costs. Long-life bulbs are an especially wise investment for elderly residents who can't reach ceilings or other out-of-the-way fixture locations to change bulbs.

Halogen lamps, such as those found in low-voltage, under-cabinet fixtures, are acceptable solutions when used in certain ways. They have very bright, white color and sharply define objects within their range. These lights, however, can create intense hot spots when used over mirror-like counter surfaces, such as polished granite or marble, so their use might be limited to areas where reflections are minimal and glare reduced. Some fixtures that accept halogen lamps can be equipped with diffusers or lenses that are softer and impart less glare than when the lamps are left bare and exposed. Another note when considering halogens in an aging-in-place environment: People with limited ability to grip and twist small objects may find it difficult to change small halogen bulbs.

Kitchens are as much about efficiency as they are about function. And because a kitchen can be one of the most costly residential investments, it is essential to carefully address each client's current needs while thoughtfully anticipating his or her potential future requirements. Discuss with your clients who in the household—whether themselves or a caregiver—will do the food shopping, prepare meals and clean up, and how food, cookware, dishes, and utensils will be stored. Also discuss your clients' physical abilities as well as their

8.28 Good lighting is key in all parts of the residence. But in the kitchen, it is even more important that creative applications of ambient and task light sources illuminate the work and food prep areas well, while accent lighting provides a strong visual appeal to the space, as in these illuminated wall cabinets. *Design by: Susan Cozzi. Photo by: Hal Finkelstein.*

prognoses and expectations. Information and insights gathered from these conversations will ensure that the space you design will be functional, accessible, and—as technology provides consumers with more options—adaptable now and far into the future.

References

1. American Society of Interior Designers, *Aging in Place: Aging and the Impact of Interior Design*, Washington, DC (2001).
2. Jayson, Sharon, "A Changing Family Picture," *USA Today*, McLean, VA (June 27, 2007).
3. Friedman, Arthur; Pile, John; Wilson, Forrest, *Interior Design: An Introduction to Architectural Interiors*, Elsevier: New York, NY (1982).
4. Fletcher, Banister, *A History of Architecture*, The Butterworth Group: London, (1987).
5. Plante, Ellen M. *The American Kitchen 1700 to the Present: From Hearth to Highrise*, Facts on File: New York, NY (1995).
6. Beecher, Catherine Esther and Stowe, Harriet Beecher, *The American Woman's Home*, Harriet Beecher Stowe Center: Hartford, CT (2002).
7. Ibid.
8. Building Research Council, *Kitchen Planning Principles*, University of Illinois at Urbana-Champaign, School of Architecture, Champaign, IL (1993).
9. National Kitchen and Bath Association, *Kitchen and Bathroom, Planning Guidelines with Access Standards*, Hackettstown, NJ (2007).
10. Mace, Ronald L., *The Accessible Housing Design File*, John Wiley & Sons: New York, NY (1991).
11. Ibid.
12. Ibid.
13. Remodelers Council, National Association of Home Builders, *Remodeling for Today & Tomorrow*, Washington, DC (2002).
14. Ibid.
15. Ibid.
16. National Kitchen and Bath Association, *Kitchen and Bathroom, Planning Guidelines with Access Standards*, Hackettstown, NJ (2007).
17. Wright State University, *The Accessible Kitchen*, www.cs.wright.edu/bie/rehabengr/kitchens/fintro.htm (accessed October 8, 2007).
18. Ibid.
19. Remodelers Council, National Association of Home Builders, *Remodeling for Today and Tomorrow*, Washington, DC (2002).
20. National Kitchen and Bath Association, *Kitchen and Bathroom, Planning Guidelines with Access Standards*, Hackettstown, NJ (2007).
21. Ibid.
22. Ibid.
23. Mace, Ronald L., *The Accessible Housing Design File*, John Wiley & Sons: New York, NY (1991).
24. National Kitchen and Bath Association. *Kitchen and Bathroom, Planning Guidelines with Access Standards*, Hackettstown, NJ (2007)
25. The Pepper Institute on Aging & Public Policy, *Facts on Aging: Aging & the Senses*, Florida State University, www.pepperinstitute.org/Facts/ (accessed October 8, 2007).
26. The Illuminating Engineering Society of North America, *Lighting Education Fundamentals*, New York, NY.
27. Ibid.

CHAPTER 9

Designing the Bathroom

*If I want to be alone, some place I can write, I can read, I can pray,
I can cry, I can do whatever I want—I go to the bathroom.*

—Alicia Keys, singer

Design by: Ann Huff, ASID, CAPS.

ONE HIGHLY IMPORTANT PLACE IN THE HOUSE

The bathroom, arguably the most important room in the home, is a unique personal space that provides privacy and intimacy that other interior spaces do not. A bathroom can be an oasis, a respite, a retreat, as well as a place to refresh and revitalize the body. But it also can be a treacherous space filled with obstacles and barriers that challenge one's independence. Combining the functional requirements of the space with safety and aesthetics will result in a successful solution to what is often one of the bigger challenges in designing a bathroom space.

As the legendary Chicago architect Louis Henri Sullivan said, "Form ever follows function."[1] But he also believed that form and function are not separate entities when he said, "Not so much the importance of function over form, but rather that the two are intricately intertwined and never inseparable."

As health diminishes as a result of the aging process, some senior adults often spend a good deal of time in doctors' exam rooms, hospitals, and clinics, and they know the harsh, sterile appearance those places often have. Most have had at least a minimal exposure to doctors' offices, hospitals, and physical therapy clinics. The last place that should remind anyone of such places is the bathroom in his or her private residence.

Elderly or disabled citizens can have meals delivered or hire others to prepare meals; they can hire others to clean their homes, do the laundry, and run errands. Caregivers, family members, and friends can provide emotional and social support when needed. Nothing, however, can replace the independence associated with what takes place in the bathroom—the last place in the home that anyone would want to relinquish the privacy that comes with remaining independent.

It does not matter how attractive a bathroom is if one is unable to get to and then through the door, or if it has barriers inside the space that make maneuvering difficult. Most individuals who cannot access the bathroom by themselves face not only the loss of independence and privacy but also ultimately, the loss of self-esteem as well.

9.2 Creating safety in a bathroom is critical to the health and well-being of the client. Installing assistive devices, including grab bars, provides a higher measure of safety in the event someone slips, stumbles, or falls in the space. *Design by: Great Grabz.*

BATHROOMS GROWING IN NUMBER AND SIZE

During the last century, advances have been made to residential bathroom design in the United States. In the first half of the twentieth century, it was uncommon to find more than one bathroom in a home. In the years that followed World War II, the number of homes being built with two, three, and as many as four bathrooms grew along with the amount of square feet of the homes.

During the late 1970s through the 1980s, new construction offered homebuyers of new houses a number of upgrades and options, and the size and number of bathrooms per residence increased dramatically. In some cases, the size of a bathroom could be greater than the size of the adjacent bedrooms.

Today, options for customizing bathrooms also have expanded dramatically and include multiple vanities; dual showers; separate spaces for toilets and bidets; exercise, massage, or meditation steam showers; showers with multiple water sources; saunas; flat-screen television sets; fireplaces; audio systems; and even chromatherapy equipment. Despite the evolution in bathroom design, however, very little consideration has been given to making these spaces safer, more secure, and free of barriers.

9.3 This is an example of a bathroom that is both attractive yet functional for anyone with or without a disability. Wider openings to the shower, level thresholds, benches, and textured floor materials are key basic design elements.

THE MOST DANGEROUS PLACE IN THE RESIDENCE

In addition to being the most private room in a residence, the bathroom also can be the most dangerous—especially for the elderly or those with disabilities. Slippery surfaces or inadequate lighting can contribute to or cause falls, and scalding water or steam can burn or blister residents of any age and ability. The bathroom can become even more of a danger to the elderly or disabled if it isn't designed to accommodate anticipated age-related physical challenges, such as diminishing eyesight, difficulties grasping, or issues of balance, to name a few.

According to a study by the U.S. Centers for Disease Control, more than 1.8 million people age 65 and older are treated in hospital emergency rooms annually for injuries related to falling. More than 420,000 of these injuries require some type of hospitalization.[2] Older adults are hospitalized five times more often for injuries related to falling than from other causes, according to an article in the *American Journal of Public Health*.[3] And 20 to 30 percent of those adults who do fall suffer moderate to severe injuries that reduce mobility and independence and increase the risk of premature death.

The most common nonfatal injuries and reasons for hospital admissions include broken arms, hip fractures, and concussions.[4] Where younger bodies are resilient enough to recover from such injuries, injured senior adults may be faced with extended periods of hospitalization or months of physical therapy—or both. And, tragically, falls are the leading cause of injury-related deaths among older adults.

CASE IN POINT

As a successful designer, I usually work 50 or 60 hours a week, which leaves little time in the schedule for a personal life. But events change your schedule, perspective, roles, and responsibilities when you least expect them to.

Like me, Mom was an independent soul throughout her life. And something like breast cancer wasn't going to stop this feisty lady from living her life the way she wanted to. But the cancer had traveled through her body and was in the bones, making them fragile. One day she fell in the bathroom in her home, breaking her neck as she stepped from the shower. While she amazingly survived the fall and the subsequent surgery, her head and neck were fitted with a metal halo, an instrument that locks the head and neck in a fixed position while the bones heal. She took it all in stride, however, despite the prognosis and the thought she would be in the hospital for six weeks.

As I anticipated my new job as her "caregiver," I began to design how to get her home in shape to allow for her to return one day. I told myself, "I'd certainly get rid of that curb in the shower that started all this in the first place. And maybe turn the main living and dining rooms into a single room for her hospital bed." She could have live-in help to fix her meals and take care of her.

But I never got that chance of a lifetime to design and remodel her home for my most important client, my mom. Neighborhood children playing with matches accidentally caught her place on fire, and she lost most of all she had assembled in 70 years of life, just three days after her surgery. But once again, my mom proved to be a strong soul throughout the ordeal. She told me that ". . . everything, every person, every event is a lesson."

Without a way to bring her into my small rental apartment, the only choice was to place her in a nursing home—a sad place that was to be her home of last resort for her remaining seven months. After my own lesson in being her caregiver, I am much more conscious of designing my current place and those of my clients with much more flexibility to accommodate the unexpected events that at one time or another happen to us all. I have learned my lesson, Mom. I won't forget.

—Interior designer, caregiver

Consequently, designers always should be thinking about safety, as well as aesthetics, when it comes to designing bathrooms. It is especially important for designers to approach bathroom design for aging clients differently. Placement of plumbing, plumbing fixtures, and cabinetry is certainly the first consideration, but it is also essential for designers to anticipate anything that might be placed within a bathroom that would present a potential hazard to an aging adult.

For instance, inadequate lighting, curbs at the shower, polished hard-surfaced flooring, and low-profile toilets are just a few of the typical obstacles that can contribute to accidents in bathrooms. Many solutions are simple: Brighter light-

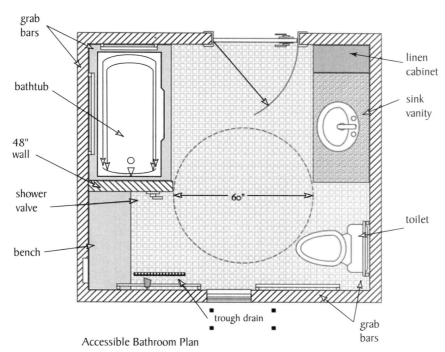

grab bars

bathtub

48" wall

shower valve

bench

linen cabinet

sink vanity

toilet

trough drain

grab bars

Accessible Bathroom Plan

9.4 When possible, plan the bathroom space to have a turning radius of five feet to allow for the potential use by an individual in a wheelchair. This plan shows a shower that is integrated into the bathroom without walls or shower doors.

ing; zero-entry showers with grab bars; hand-held showerheads; taller toilet seats; anti-scald shower controls; lever-style faucet handles at the vanity; textured or non-slip, hard-surface flooring; and bathroom telephones are some features that can contribute to safer bathroom environments and should be considered as standard accessories for any residential bathroom. Wise design professionals will point out to clients that such items can make bathrooms safer for everyone, not just those who are experiencing age-related physical challenges.

PUTTING THE BATHROOM PLAN TOGETHER

So where do we go from here? Clearly, in new construction it is possible to plan for a resident's current or anticipated needs. When it comes to remodeling bathrooms to accommodate occupants, however, changes can range from the very simple, such as resurfacing a highly polished floor to those that are more complex—and sometimes costly—adaptations, like making doorways and hallways wider, changing the direction of door swings, and swapping locations of toilets, sinks, bathtubs, and showers to provide better access.

9.5 By code, entrance doors to a shower are usually required to swing out from the shower and into the bathroom, rather than into the stall. In planning, allow plenty of room for the door to swing out fully 90 degrees or more for someone to exit easily from the shower. *Design by: Sharon L. Sherman. Photo by: Peter Rymwid.*

The size of an existing bathroom, as well as its configuration and relation-ship to adjacent spaces, can have a lot to do with the extent of its remodeling. And any owner of a multistory home without a bathroom on the main floor should consider adding such a room. An accessible bathroom on the main level of a residence is a definite convenience for any resident, not only those with age-related problems: Consider a new mother who has given birth by Caesarian and is limited to the number of times per day she can take the stairs; or a toddler who is learning to use the bathroom but who is too young to manage the stairs alone; or a younger family member who has sprained an ankle playing sports and must traverse the stairs with crutches; or a frequent disabled visitor, such as a grandparent, to the household. Elderly family members and other guests may not be able to visit because a bathroom is located down a narrow hall or up a flight of stairs.

Remedies to the lack of a main-floor bathroom include adding a bathroom within the existing footprint of the house on the main floor; building an addi-tion to the residence that includes a main-floor bathroom; installing a chair lift on an existing staircase or—space permitting—an elevator; or—most disruptive of all—moving to a new home that already has a main-floor bathroom.

CREATIVE DESIGN SOLUTIONS START WITH THE BASICS

Thoughtful, imaginative designers can produce visually appealing and safe designs for highly accessible bathrooms. While there is a growing number of universal-designed fixtures and equipment available, a designer's creative application of standard, off-the-shelf products can provide attractive, high-impact, functional bathroom designs that will stand the test of time.

9.6 and 9.7 Make entrances to the bathroom a minimum of 32" of clear unobstructed space between the doorjambs, but when space allows, make the doorways and openings as wide as possible, which will result in open clear space around the vanity. *(top) Design by: Lisa Brooks, Allied ASID. Photo by: Gerlick Photography. (right) Design by: Thyme & Place Design.*

Planning the Basic Footprint

The bathroom entrance can be one of the most significant obstacles in a home. More often than not, bathroom doors are too narrow for a wheelchair or a walker to pass through, and narrow hallways and those with sharp right-angle turns also make access difficult for individuals who use walkers, crutches, or wheelchairs.

Ideally, entrances to bathrooms should be a clear minimum of 32 inches wide, a measure that permits an individual in a wheelchair to pass through a door without banging his or her knuckles on either side. Doorways that are 34 to 36 inches wide permit even better access.

If there is sufficient room for the bathroom door to open without bumping into a cabinet, wall, or fixture, the simple installation of hinges that permit the door to swing clear of the jamb is all that's needed to make entering easier. Replace existing hinges with either an offset hinge or a clear-swing-style hinge to provide as much as one to two additional inches of clearance. Another way to make an existing door opening wider is to plane down the jamb to a half inch or replace it altogether with a stop that has a smaller profile. Pocket and barn-style doors are other effective solutions for expanding access to a small bathroom.

Experienced aging-in-place specialists strongly recommend that bathroom doors be hinged to open out toward the hall rather than into the bathroom.[5] Imagine someone stumbling on a wet bathroom floor and falling against the entry door. If the door swings into the bathroom, then anyone trying to help is prevented from entering the space. And pushing on the door from the outside to gain entrance could cause additional injury to the person inside, not to mention some stressful moments for everyone concerned. The problem is compounded if the individual inside the bathroom suffers from dementia. If the door swings out into the hallway, a caregiver can enter the bathroom without the difficulty of communicating to the person inside to move away from the door.

CASE IN POINT

Some things should be basic when you think about it—like having a bathroom you can get into. My 77-year-old Dad had a heart attack one day when going to the bathroom. He got up from the toilet, stumbled, fell against the sink cabinet and onto the floor. Crumpled up, he must have laid there for some time before I noticed he wasn't around the house.

When I finally went to check on him, he wasn't responding to my calls to him through the closed door. I tried opening the door, but his body was wedged between the cabinet and the door. Running around to the outside of the house, I peered through the small, frosted window and could see the outline of his body. Using a brick from the garden, I broke the glass and climbed through the window. Glass was everywhere. When I finally got to him, he was alive, but his limp body was pure dead weight. I struggled to move him so I could get the door open and call 911 for help.

Something as simple as the direction of the door swing was never on my mind when we remodeled that bathroom so Dad could come live with us and have a place of his own.

—From a client interview, 55 years young

9.8 The design of this open-planned bathroom showcases plenty of counter space, lots of clear floor area under the cabinetry for cleaning and ac-cessibility. The large sets of windows do a good job capturing the natural light. *Design by: Lena Brion, ASID/Brion Design Group.*

Bathroom door thresholds should not exceed one-quarter inch in height unless the threshold between the bathroom and the adjacent room is beveled to blend the varying heights. Thresholds should never exceed one-half inch in height even if the sides are beveled.[6]

It is critical to have at least a 5-foot turning radius for a wheelchair—should one ever be needed—to maneuver once inside the bathroom. There also should be room for someone who is seated to easily access the three main bathroom components: the vanity sink, the toilet, and the bathtub or shower.[7]

Designing the Cabinetry

Traditionally, bathroom vanity cabinets were built with a finished height of 30 inches above the finished floor (AFF). In recent years—perhaps taking into account that the average American is likely to be taller than in previous generations—the trend has been to install taller cabinetry so that counters are as

9.9 This bathroom vanity is installed with counters that are 30 inches above the fin-ished floor. It also has a knee-hole under the sink with a slanted back panel to safely hide the hot and cold water lines and the drain, making it easy to access. *Design by: Lisa Brooks, Allied ASID. Photo by: Gerlick Photography.*

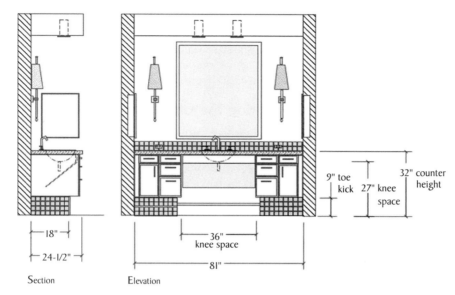

18"

24-1/2"

Section

36"
knee space

81"

Elevation

9" toe
kick   27" knee
space

32" counter
height

9.10 While 30 inches of knee-hole space under a sink and counter is acceptable, the plan for this vanity includes a space that is 36 inches in width, an opening that is much more functional to use. The slant back panel and taller toe kicks work well for someone to sit down at the sink and get ready for their day.

high as 36 inches AFF. Taller vanity heights allow users to get closer to the sink opening without having to bend over, a position that puts stress on the lower back and legs. Since there is no standard recommendation for vanity cabinet height in residential applications, the height should be based on the size and height of the most frequent user.

With aging in place in mind, however, design professionals should anticipate the use of the vanity and sink from a seated position. Even if the most frequent user is not confined to a wheelchair or is able to use the sink while either standing or seated, it might be prudent to include two levels of cabinets and counters.

Another option for the configuration of the base vanity cabinets is to include taller toe kicks—as much as 9 inches with a 6-inch setback from the face edge of the cabinet—to keep the footrest of a wheelchair from damaging the vanity. Removable doors or doors that pocket back into the vanity cabinet also give a good measure of flexibility when combined with detachable toe kicks, making it possible to open up the base of the cabinet to provide access for a seated individual who needs to get close to the sink. Remember to include insulation or pipe protection panels to prevent users of such cabinet configurations from coming into contact with any sharp or hot surfaces.

While traditionally located in hallways adjacent to bathrooms, linen storage is best when located within the bathroom, space permitting. Plan for as much storage space as possible for towel and linen storage—a convenience for users of any age or ability, as well as caregivers.

Sliding or pullout shelves, rollout drawer systems, laundry hampers, and portable or mobile storage pedestals contribute to a well-organized bathroom, amplifying its use and comfort. By including multiple medicine cabinets and/or

9.11 It seems that storage always comes at a premium, but in this project, a 9 inches wide and 80 inches tall cabinet directly next to the tub gives additional space for towels and easy access when there are no doors to swing open. *Design by: Ann Huff, ASID, CAPS. Photo by: Michael D. Baker.*

tall, shallow storage units installed between stud walls—rather than the single traditional medicine cabinet—designers can provide more than adequate storage space for medications, toiletries, and other bathroom necessities for all users.

Encountering the Countertops

Base the selection of countertop materials on ease of maintenance, as well as aesthetic appearance and the client's budget. Marble, onyx, and granite cost more than other manmade materials, such as laminates, composites, and cultured marble but are as easy to maintain.

Solid-surface materials, such as Dupont Corian® and Silestone®, which are made from quartz mixed with polyesters, are nearly maintenance free and can be easily repaired if scratched, stained, or marred. These surfaces are also more resistant to bacterial growth than other products.

Wood makes a serviceable counter when sealed with a water-resistant finish such as a urethane or a type of marine varnish commonly used on boats. Porous natural materials, such as slate, limestone, and crosscut travertine, should be treated at the time of installation with a penetrating sealer to help keep the surface stain- and bacteria-resistant. Routine follow-up applications of the sealer are also highly recommended. Ceramic and porcelain tile are also ideal materials, but grout lines should be sealed to prevent stains.

9.12 Long runs of counters can be broken into shorter segments with sit down vanities between runs of cabinetry as seen in this plan. The sinks are positioned in counters at 32 inches tall and off centered to make them easier to reach from the lowered vanity kneehole. Counters at the kneehole are 28 inches above the finished floor. *Photo by: Michael D. Baker.*

9.13 This bathroom vanity is smart looking and yet affords a measure of accessibility. The wood top is a departure from the conventional materials and contrasts well with the elongated sink basin. *Design by: Susan Cozzi. Photo by: Hal Finckelstein.*

Specifying the Sinks and Faucets

When selecting a sink from the wide variety of styles available, much depends on the client's personal preference. Whatever style is selected, however, the sink is best installed toward the front of the cabinet, rather than in the middle of the countertop. Sinks mounted from under the counter are much easier to clean than drop-in or vessel models. A cantilevered sink that sits over the front edge of a cabinet and countertop is another imaginative option. Although they lack storage space underneath, a pedestal sink with a slim base that can be installed close to the wall, or a wall-hung sink, which can be installed at a low height to provide accessibility, are other viable alternatives.

9.14 and 9.15 Sinks come in all sizes and shapes from vessel style bowls to cantilever designs, but they should be installed at a height that will be easy for any individual to use while standing or sitting. *(right) Photo by: Michael D. Baker*

Of the wide selection of faucets in the plumbing marketplace, the wisest choices are those with lever or paddle handle controls. Knobs, discs, and ball-style faucet handles are difficult for anyone with wet or soapy hands to operate and are especially difficult to maneuver for those individuals with limited use of their hands because of arthritis, stroke, or other ailments.[8]

Whether a client or designer chooses single- or dual-control handles for the faucets, the location of the valves can increase usability. Installing the faucet handles closer to the front of the cabinet—which can be accomplished by following the curved line of the sink—or bathtub makes them easier to use.

A Place to Sit—Toilets

Although it goes without saying that toilets and bidets generally are selected to coordinate with other adjacent plumbing fixtures and finishes, the seat heights of these fixtures is a critical consideration. Low-rise, one-piece toilets may be attractive, but their typical seat heights of 14 to 15 inches make getting on and off the seat stressful on users' knees and back. Such low seat heights also can make transferring from a wheelchair to the toilet—and back again—problematic.[9]

9.16 Toilets that have taller seat heights than the norm mean less strain on the back, legs, and knees of users when standing up off toilet seats. Leaving a clear space next to the toilet makes the use of the toilet much easier when someone needs to move from a walker or transfer from a wheelchair to the seat. *Design by: Kristi Choate. Photo by: Gerlick Photography.*

Toilets with seat heights of 16 to 19 inches—what some plumbing manufacturers refer to as "comfort height"—are usually found in two-piece sets. Designers should keep in mind, however, that while taller toilet seats are an advantage for some users, higher seats might pose problems for young children or adults who are short in stature.

9.17 Manufacturers of toilets may call them by various names such as "comfort height" or "accessible seat," but verify that the seats are between 17 inches and 19 inches to the seat above the floor line. Grab bars can be placed on the front and back as shown, but actual placement should be decided with the client for the best locations.

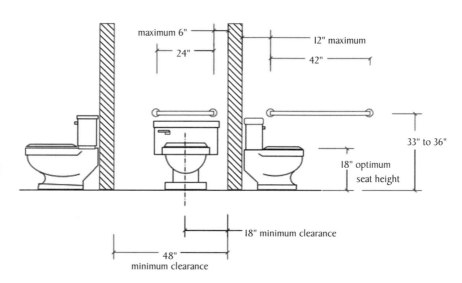

One of the biggest challenges in bathroom design is locating the toilet so there is sufficient space to transfer from a wheelchair to the toilet and back. Use the following American National Standards Institute (ANSI) and Uniform Federal Accessibility Standards (UFAS) guidelines to achieve the best use of available floor space:

> 4 feet × 4 feet, 8 inches for a side approach when the sink is adjacent to the toilet
>
> 5 feet × 4 feet, 8 inches for a front or side approach with no sink next to the toilet
>
> 4 feet × 5 feet, 6 inches for side or front approach with sink adjacent to the toilet

Toilets should be at a minimum of 18 inches from vanity cabinets, bathtubs, or sidewalls,[10] which is a more generous allowance than the standard recommended dimension of 16 inches.

While toilet paper holders customarily are built into walls either to the side or behind the toilet, freestanding toilet paper holders provide more flexibility and convenience.

Tubs and Whirlpools

As with other fixtures, there are numerous styles, shapes, and colors of bathtubs, but take special care when selecting those for elderly or disabled clients. Choose a bathtub that can be built into a deck or some type of normal chair-height surround that provides a place to sit while safely rotating first the legs, then the body, into the bathtub interior. When designing the bathtub area, design professionals should also think about easy access to faucet handles once the user is seated in the bathtub.

When designing the platform around the bathtub, include 10 to 12 inches of seating space. Choose bathtubs that can be mounted from under the bathtub deck and, to avoid a raised rim that can be an additional barrier, don't select drop-in style bathtubs.

Freestanding bathtubs, such as those with classic oval shapes or traditional ball-and-claw feet, may be attractive, but stepping over their tall sides to get in and out can be tricky at best, not to mention dangerous for those who are mobility impaired. Adding grab bars on the wall can greatly help to provide support.

9.18 For a measure of safety, there should be a place to sit down along the edge of the tub in order for a client to swing his or her feet into the tub and slide down into the water. This is a very important detail when the tubs are recessed into a platform or are extra deep. Stepping directly over the edge of a tub is a dangerous, slippery operation at best and an accident waiting to occur when getting out of the tub.

9.19 Footed tubs, such as this, are great to look at but not always easy for someone with a disability to get into or out of. Grab or assist bars securely mounted to the wall around the tub will help to make the transfer safer. *Design by: Jo Rabaut, ASID.*

Although whirlpool bathtubs with pulsating water jets can be physically beneficial and comforting for users with aching joints and muscles, design professionals should make certain that getting into and out of the bathtub is easy for users. Specify versions that include the on-and-off controls within an arm's reach, once a user is in the tub. Since rapidly moving water loses heat more quickly than standing water, consider adding an inexpensive in-line heating unit to keep the water temperature at a consistent level. Design professionals should also take into account the force of the water jets, which, if too powerful, can alter what is meant to be a relaxing, soothing experience into an uncomfortable battle.

One recent innovation is a bathtub with a watertight side door that makes getting into and out of the bathtub relatively easy. This is an option that can replace a standard or whirlpool bathtub. When specifying this product, however, make certain that the bathroom space is able to be sufficiently warm so the user won't get chilled during the several minutes it takes to fill and empty the water from the bathtub.

9.20 Innovative designs in grab bars not only make a safer bathroom experience but also help to avoid any reference to an institutional appearance when shapes and finishes are complemented with faucets and spouts. *Design by: Great Grabz.*

A number of bathtub styles include built-in seats at the sides, which elevate the user off the bottom of the bathtub to a more comfortable seated position. Bathtub seats not only make getting into and out of the tub easier for the user, but they also make it easier for caregivers to assist the user. Other mechanisms that fit down into the bottom of tubs can lower and elevate the individual into the water.

Designing an Accessible Shower

Older American bathrooms include bathtub/shower combinations, which provide in one fixture the options of either sitting down in the bathtub or standing to shower. Climbing in and out of bathtubs can be cumbersome for anyone, particularly people with disabilities or medical conditions that involve limitations to mobility.

Many homes built in the last few decades, however, include separate showers either as a complement to a bathtub in the same room, such as those found in master bathrooms, or as the only bathing option in a smaller secondary bathroom where space is limited, giving residents a variety of bathing options based on their personal preferences and levels of independence.

The variety of today's shower equipment and fixture options can make bathing a pleasant daily event: Showerheads can be fixed, adjustable, installed from the ceiling, or mounted on an adjustable rod; shower valves can be set for predetermined water temperature and pressure; and, with sufficient available water pressure to drive them, water jets can invigorate and massage tired muscles and sore joints.

Shower spaces can be enclosed with something as simple as a vinyl shower curtain mounted on a rod or partially enclosed with by-pass or tempered glass doors that not only retain water but also hold in warmth during showering. Designers should take note, however: Curtain rods must always be permanently and securely mounted to the walls adjacent to the shower or to the shower jamb, and shower doors should always be installed so that they swing out into the bathroom.

9.21 Many options are on the market for shower fixtures, including multiple sprays, handheld adjustable shower heads, and hot and cold water valves that allow for the pre-adjustment of the water temperature. *Photo by: Gerlick Photography.*

9.22 If shower curtains are to be a part of the design, use the type that can be securely installed directly into the wall and not the spring-loaded, tension types. With larger expanses of shower as in this design, individual curtains are easier to push back and forth. The textured slate floor pitches toward the drain, making it possible to avoid all curbs or barriers into the space. *Design by: Keith Miller, ASID.*

9.23 While shower doors contain the overspray of water, with proper placement, doors can be eliminated so that doorways remain unencumbered, free, and open for use.

Steam showers, which can be therapeutic, call for floor-to-ceiling shower doors and wall panels that completely enclose shower stalls to contain the steam. Exhaust or ventilation systems always should be installed with steam showers to remove the excess moisture that otherwise would escape into the bathroom and contribute to making floors slick and surfaces susceptible to mold.

Showers also can be designed without any enclosures at all as long as provisions are made for adequate waterproofing and drainage. Keep in mind, however, that in the absence of any enclosure or shower curtain, as the air in the shower is heated by the shower water, it rises and is replaced by the cooler air from the bathroom, creating a potential chilling effect for the user.

A bench within a shower is a definite benefit—a safe place for someone to sit or prop up a leg or foot while showering. In most cases, shower benches should conform to the typical seat height and depth of a chair, although personal preference and the available physical space will dictate the actual dimensions.[11] In the absence of sufficient space for a built-in bench in the shower, designers should consider creating a portable seat or bench fabricated from teak or another attractive, water-resistant material to avoid having to rely on other more institutional-looking options.

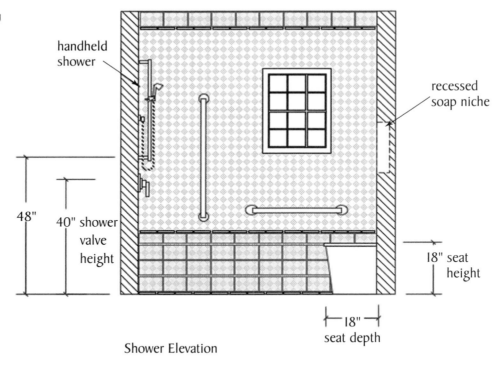

9.24 Whether existing or new construction, including a bench in the shower area is a great feature for all households and showers. Benches should be approximately 18 inches tall and 18 inches deep, and the vertical elevation slanted slightly back to allow for the feet to be positioned slightly behind and under the user.

handheld shower

recessed soap niche

48"

40" shower valve height

18" seat height

18" seat depth

Shower Elevation

The placement of plumbing fixtures also can contribute to a more pleasant showering experience. Most shower valves are located directly under the showerhead, a placement that requires the user to get into the shower before turning on the water—and probably experience an initial shot of cold water. Locating the shower controls just inside the shower enclosure where a user can reach them to adjust the water temperature before stepping under the water makes more sense.

While many newer homes have recycling or closed-circuit hot water systems that bring and return water to the hot water tank to help with energy and water consumption and provide quicker filling times, an inexpensive heater option is important to use when water is already in the tub. Using line voltage, a heater can be connected to the pump and can maintain the temperature of the water because the whirlpool action can quickly reduce temperatures.

A hand-held showerhead on a flexible hose mounted on a removable bracket or a wall-mounted slide bar permits the user to choose a shower height of his or her preference.[12] Hand-held showerheads also can better control overspray and allow the user to adjust the water pressure or to turn off the water temporarily when needed. Adjustable units also make for easier showering from a seated position, as well as for easier cleanup.

A diverter control valve should be installed when a hand-held showerhead is used in combination with a fixed showerhead. Installing a separate control valve for each showerhead may be more cost effective and easier to plumb, however.

To avoid bumping into the shower valve and accidentally turning up the hot water or causing a sudden shift in the water temperature when a toilet is flushed elsewhere in the house—either of which can potentially scald someone using the shower—it is essential to include in each set of plumbing specifications fixtures and valve selections that restrict high water temperatures and/or provide a balanced flow of water at a fairly consistent temperature level.[13]

Customarily, architects, builders, and contractors have designed, specified, and built curbs at shower entrances that require users to pick up their feet and step over and into the shower pan. In some cases, the floor of the shower pan is lower than the floor of the bathroom. Stumbling over curb heights of four or more inches to get in or out of the shower is a likely occurrence for individuals of any age who suffer from a loss of mobility, balance, agility, or strength. Perhaps this traditional but potentially unsafe construction practice is based on the misconception that if water should ever back up in a shower pan because of poor or inadequate drainage, the curb would prevent the water from running out onto the bathroom floor.

With well-executed framing and appropriate plumbing and drainage installation, however, it is possible to build showers without curbs and thresholds that not only do not leak but also meet building codes.[14] A curb-less, zero-entry or "freedom" shower entry eliminates one of the major barriers—and most dangerous obstacles—in a bathroom, while successfully preventing stray water from permeating the area surrounding the shower.

Costs for building a curb-less shower usually do not exceed costs for a shower with a traditional curb. The successful construction and plumbing of a curb-less shower, however, does require careful attention to installation details and adequate supervision of the various contractors involved, especially when subcontractors may have little or no experience with this type of construction or may be resistant to change.

9.25 With a level threshold at the shower entry, changes in texture and patterns in the flooring material—both in and around the space—will provide a visual clue where the shower pan begins and the main floor ends.

CASE IN POINT

A few years ago, I had a new contractor (with his plumber) actually tell me that getting rid of curbs at the shower is against building codes and that is why he went ahead and put one in place anyway. Now as a design professional, it takes a lot to pull the towel over my face when it comes to designing a safe bathroom for my clients. I figure that it was just something that they didn't know how to do and decided that he could use building codes as an excuse. Creating a flush, flat entry where clients can move out of a wet, slick shower pan without stepping over something is just basic on my design agenda and is not an option.

—Anonymous designer, 45 years young

The most important consideration in designing a curb-less shower is to determine the appropriate size[15]: The overall length and depth is critical. In general, the smaller the footprint of the shower, the more difficult it is to contain water that might spill out beyond the shower curtain or shower enclosure. More important, the deeper the dimension from the entrance to the back wall of the shower, combined with the location of the showerhead, the easier it is to prevent water from damaging adjacent walls and floors.

While most accessibility standards define the minimum depth of a curb-less shower to be 30 inches, a more generous minimum depth of 36 inches is recommended.[16] An even larger depth of 42 to 48 inches not only permits easier drainage, but also allows someone in a wheelchair to enter the shower and retain complete range of motion for bathing and accessing the water controls.

Although it is suggested that shower spaces be 66 to 72 inches of length for a roll-in shower, the standard minimum length is at least 60 inches in all directions, providing adequate space for a caregiver to assist someone in a wheelchair.[17]

9.26 To ensure proper drainage of the water in a curbless shower, the shower floor should have a slope toward the drain 1/4 inch to 3/8 inch for every foot of floor. Ideally, position and locate the drain at the point farthest from the entry area, even if it is located near an interior corner of the floor.

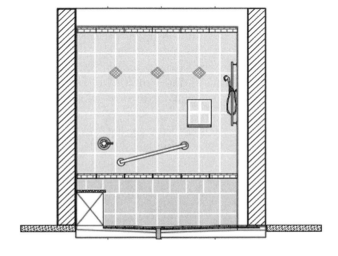

Curbless Shower Elevation with Floor Drain

The position of the shower drain is another vital component in bathroom design, and the larger the shower, the easier it is to gradually slope the shower floor to the drain.[18] Location options that can reassure any skeptical designer, contractor, or client include installing the drain in a corner of the shower opposite its entrance, along the back wall of the shower, or as a trough-style drain around the perimeter of the shower enclosure.

The minimum slope of the shower pan from the entrance to the drain should be one-quarter to three-eighths inch for every foot in length, and the transition between the bathroom floor and the shower floor should be flush. If the shower is especially narrow or small, or if there are concerns about overspray or drainage, an acceptable compromise is to create a small bevel (1 to 2) in the shower floor just inside the entrance that permits a wheelchair to roll over the bevel.[19]

The Grab Bar: You Have to Have One

One icon, good or bad, that represents the needs of those with physical limitations or disabilities is the grab bar. Ever present in ADA-compliant public bathrooms in offices, restaurants, and other public venues, grab bars also are reminiscent of medical institutions and extended-care facilities.

Grab bars are critical elements to mobility: They can aid in the safe transfer of someone on and off the toilet; they provide a secure grip for someone getting in and out of a bathtub or shower; and they provide balance for someone who is bending over to towel off or dress. Because, more often than not, grab bars are installed in a residence only when the need arises, such as during the recovery period after surgery or a stroke, little thought is given to their appearance. The style or type of grab bar, however, can do a lot to diminish its institutional look.

9.27 and 9.28 Figuring out the framing location where the grab bars should be placed should be the preference and desire of the client so plan ahead and know where to place plywood or wood blocking during the framing stages of the project. A better solution and one that gives more flexibility is to frame the entire walls of the shower. With plywood covering the entire walls behind the tile or stone face, placement can be made anywhere and at any time.

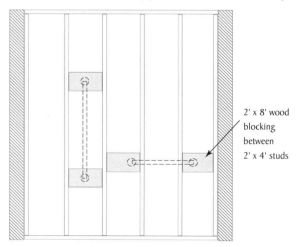

2' x 8' wood blocking between 2' x 4' studs

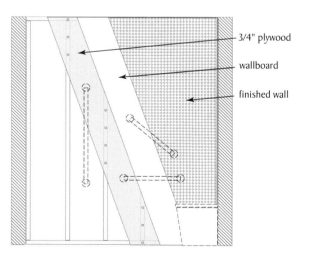

3/4" plywood

wallboard

finished wall

Shower Walls with Blocking for Grab Bars   Shower Wall with Plywood Backing on All Walls

No matter what styles are selected, however, it is essential that grab bars be firmly and securely installed directly into wall studs, into walls that have been reinforced with wood framing, or into walls faced with a minimum of one-half to three-quarter-inch plywood. The latter is preferred as support material as it allows more flexibility in the placement of grab bars along a wider expanse of wall. Grab bars should never be installed with wing nuts or molly bolts alone.

While no laws exist that regulate the placement and location of grab bars in private residences, designers and contractors should consider the following guidelines before specification:[20]

- Specify no more than one-and-a-half inches of space between the wall and a grab bar. A user's arm could slip between larger spaces between the bar and the wall, possibly causing injury.

- Select bars that are of one-piece construction or those that do not move or rotate during use. Select bars with a textured grip as an added safety measure.

- Specify installation of grab bars on the walls at the front and/or at the rear of the bathtub at 33 to 36 inches AFF.

- Specify installation of grab bars around toilets to be 33 to 36 inches AFF and a minimum of 12 inches away from the rear wall.

- Specify grab bars that, once installed, can support a weight of up to 250 pounds.

Consider the individual client's physical needs when determining where and how to place grab bars. ADA guidelines may not suggest the best placement for a particular individual.

ILLUMINATING THE BATHROOM

Designing bathroom lighting for users of all ages is routine for most designers, but a few important age-related considerations could increase usability of such spaces for older adults.

A number of age-related conditions can impact eyesight. Older adults often lose the ability to process light through the retina, a condition frequently complicated by presbyopia, or the inability to focus. Other vision complications include age-related macular degeneration (AMD), a disease that impacts the macula, the part of the eye that allows close-up and detailed sight, and cataracts, the clouding of the cornea or lens of the eye. AMD, which often begins with blurring of the sharp, central vision, creating a fuzzy image in the direct sightline that is sometimes referred to as the "dead-ahead view," advances slowly and usually requires a physician's examination to identify.

With cataracts, the cornea becomes thicker, preventing light rays from passing through. The word "cataract" literally means "waterfall," and those who are so afflicted describe seeing as trying to look through a sheet of running water. Other age-related vision problems can include poor vision in dim or darkened interiors, faded or bland colors, nearsightedness, and sometimes, periods of multiple vision.

To create a safe bathroom interior for clients challenged by any of these vision conditions, designers should specify materials with well-defined, con-

9.29 With aging eyesight, a common ailment, good lighting is important above and around the sink and makeup mirrors. Sconce lighting is a good way to avoid shadows around the bottom of the face that overhead lighting alone will not give.

trasting colors to increase the distinction between counter edges, corners of cabinetry, steps, or changes in floor levels. For example, a soft, neutral-colored limestone tile specified for a bathroom floor to blend with the limestone used on a countertop can make it difficult for someone with even moderately blurred vision to determine exactly where the counter begins and ends. By using contrasting materials, the designer makes the lines of demarcation more apparent.

Design professionals should keep all such age-related conditions in mind and choose appropriate light fixtures and lamping for bathrooms to accommodate elderly clients who may not yet realize they are experiencing vision loss. General room lighting, as well as task-specific lighting around the sink and make-up areas, should be as bright, clear, and glare-free as possible.

Consider adding natural light via skylights, especially in interior bathrooms without windows. Depending on their location, skylights also can help capture solar heat during cooler weather. Washing entire walls with light provides drama but gives the space more ambient lighting as well.

To illuminate pathways to and from bathrooms, use dimmers, rheostats, or motion-sensitive switches on light controls with soft impact accent lights. Also consider installing small, recessed wall fixtures or "theater aisle" fixtures just above the floor line or adding lighting at the toe kick of a cabinet.

Although combination lighting/ventilation fixtures are available, when a large amount of steam and humidity needs to be removed from the bathroom—as with large bathrooms or sauna and steam rooms—specify a single, large vent with multiple vent openings located in an attic or crawl space. Other options for ventilating bathrooms include vent fans with motion- or humidity-sensitive controls and fans with quiet operation.

Other electrical components—once regarded as luxuries but now considered standard items—that can enhance a bathroom and help keep its interior evenly warm include heated towel bars; radiant heating throughout the bathroom floor, shower pan, and shower bench; and toe kick heaters under the cabinetry. When the distance is great from the bathroom to the hot water tank, supplementary electric-powered water tanks, small enough to tuck into a bathroom cabinet or an adjacent closet, can supply hot water immediately.

In addition to traditional wall-mounted sheet mirrors located behind vanity sinks and faucets, magnifying mirrors with or without built-in lighting are another nice bathroom accessory for those with diminishing eyesight. These mirrors, either wall-mounted or freestanding, can help a user see details without having to lean over the sink to get close to the mirror and can make looking in a mirror easier when seated at a vanity.

CHOOSING THE RIGHT FLOORING MATERIALS

Selecting flooring material for any space is important, but it is a critical decision for bathrooms. When wet or moist, highly polished marble, ceramic, or porcelain tiles can be very slick, contributing to falls. A wide variety of materials are available that have matte, honed, or moderately textured finishes that can increase or contribute to better traction.

To make an existing glossy floor safer or, if the client insists on installing a highly polished or shiny floor, apply a treatment such as those manufactured by Slip Tech that will increase the slip coefficient when the floor is damp or wet. Often used on large commercial installations of marble, granite, and tile, this finish is applied easily and, with routine applications, will offer a more secure footing without affecting the appearance of the floor.

The dimension of floor material and how it is installed over the subflooring are also important considerations. Grout lines not only contribute to a decorative pattern on the floor, but they also provide additional traction—and thus,

9.30 This design features a textured, patterned wall that is effectively lit from above with wall washer-type light sources, adding both accent and ambient light to the bathroom's interior. *Design by: Susan Cozzi. Photo by: Michiko Kurisu.*

stability—to bare feet when the floor gets wet. Generally, the smaller the floor tile or stone material, the more grout lines there will be; and the more grout lines, the more texture—thus traction—the floor has.

Designers should also pay special attention to flooring materials within shower enclosures. Since they tend to move accumulated water toward the floor drain more efficiently than larger tiles, specify smaller-sized tiles, especially those from 1 to 6 inches, such as those found in mosaics and textured natural materials, as standard for residential showers.

Undoubtedly, water will get on the floor of any bathroom, so floor base molding materials around the perimeter of the space should give protection to the lower portion of the walls. The taller the base materials, the more protection there is for walls and wall coverings from moisture, as well as from bumps by walkers and wheelchair foot rests.

Older physiques tend to be more sensitive to cooler surfaces, so designers should investigate and consider the variety of radiant floor heating available. While some systems are installed easily and can warm an entire bathroom environment, some can be easily placed in the shower pan and under the seat of a shower bench.

Floor drains, which provide another measure of bathroom safety, are especially effective when used in open bathtub/shower areas or curb-less showers.

No matter the size or shape; the cabinetry, sinks, or toilet chosen; or the layout of the shower or tub, the safety of the bathroom is always the highest priority. It is more than just the addition of grab bars. When properly outfitted, the bathroom can give the client the assurance that this space will continue to support his or her independence, while reducing the potential for injury or death. With form and function combined together during the design process, the bathroom can be a place that is attractive yet functional and secure.

9.31 Shower pan flooring should be of a type that is slip resistant in texture and style. Smaller tiles mean more grout lines, and they not only increase the measure of safety but also allow for a better angle and slope to the drain that larger tiles will not do effectively. *Photo by: Jim Robinette.*

References

1. Twombly, Robert and Menocal, Narcisco, *Louis Sullivan: The Poetry of Architecture*, W.W. Norton & Company: New York, NY (2002).
2. U.S. Center for Disease Control, *Fatalities and Injuries from Falls Among Older Adults—United States, 1993–2003 and 2001–2005*, www.cdc.gov/mmwr/preview/ mmwrhtml/mm5545a1.htm (accessed October 8, 2007).
3. "Preventing Disability and Falls in Older Adults," *American Journal of Public Health*, (November 1994).
4. U.S. Center for Disease Control, *Fatalities and Injuries from Falls Among Older Adults—United States, 1993–2003 and 2001–2005*, www.cdc.gov/mmwr/preview/ mmwrhtml/mm5545a1.htm (accessed October 8, 2007).
5. National Kitchen and Bath Association, *Kitchen and Bathroom, Planning Guidelines with Access Standards*, Hackettstown, NJ (2007).
6. Remodelers Council, National Association of Home Builders, *Remodeling for Today & Tomorrow*, Washington, DC (2002).
7. Ibid.
8. Mace, Ronald L, *The Accessible Housing Design File*, John Wiley & Sons: New York, NY (1991).

9. Ibid.

10. Ibid.

11. Remodelers Council, National Association of Home Builders, *Remodeling for Today & Tomorrow*, Washington, DC (2002).

12. National Kitchen and Bath Association, *Kitchen and Bathroom, Planning Guidelines with Access Standards*, Hackettstown, NJ (2007).

13. Ibid.

14. Remodelers Council, National Association of Home Builders, *Remodeling for Today & Tomorrow*, Washington, DC (2002).

15. Ibid.

16. National Kitchen and Bath Association, *Kitchen and Bathroom, Planning Guidelines with Access Standards*, Hackettstown, NJ (2007).

17. Mace, Ronald L., *The Accessible Housing Design File*, John Wiley & Sons: New York, NY (1991).

18. Ibid.

19. Ibid.

20. Ibid.

CHAPTER 10

The Rest of the House

A man builds a fine house; and now he has a master, and a task for life: he is to furnish, watch, show it, and keep it in repair the rest of his days.

—Ralph Waldo Emerson

AGING ALL THROUGH THE RESIDENCE

So often aging-in-place issues focus on the primary living areas in homes—kitchens, bathrooms, bedrooms—yet there are many specialty areas that also need to be adapted for aging in place. The term "aging in place" sounds sedentary, but for those who plan to do so, aging in place is anything but. Today's seniors are active, involved, and not likely to be sitting on the sidelines, and this is especially true of the baby boomers. Many in the ubiquitous "boomer" group—and some who are slightly older—have already officially retired from their first careers only to have taken on second careers or avocations, started businesses, or gone back to school for advanced degrees. Therefore, their homes need to be designed to accommodate the variety of interests and activities they presently embrace—and will continue to do so in their later years. Spaces can include game rooms, exercise areas, home theaters, and summer kitchens—all of which can be great looking and accommodate the needs of a variety of users.

AARP research indicates that these days American seniors—those who are age 50 and older—will not be sitting idly on their front porches in their retirement years.[1] Rather, in terms of home features, seniors are designing and selecting their homes to "remain active, engaged, and in touch."[2] The impact that boomers have had on American society has been observed, documented, and discussed frequently over the past 50 years, so what this population segment will do, buy, and influence when they reach their retirement years has been the topic of much speculation. Well, that time has come.

The first boomers reached their sixtieth birthdays in 2006 and, as they proceed toward the traditional retirement age of 65, there has been very little else

10.2 Aging in place doesn't stop at the bathroom or kitchen. It can and should extend to all rooms as in game, music, and entertainment salons. Flat flooring materials, lots of open spaces to move about, and great natural and artificial lighting is important to the success of all interiors. *Design by: Janis Sundquist. Photo by: Gerlick Photography.*

about them that is traditional. Offering them a rocking chair on the front porch will not satisfy their vision of the rest of their lives.

Rather, older Americans—like everyone else—want space in their homes for exercise or yoga, an inviting place to do laundry or crafts, an efficient and well-wired home office, as well as areas for outdoor activities and even home theaters in which to age in place. There's no doubt about it, seniors are remaining active and engaged—major considerations for designers who are planning aging-in-place homes.

The typical American household washes 400 loads of laundry per year, or an average of just over seven loads of laundry per week, according to the Consumer Energy Center,[3] and even though the amount of laundry should decrease as the number of people in the family decreases, there always will be laundry to wash, dry, fold, and/or iron. With the variety of fabrics on the market, there is often a need to pay close attention to the specific needs of each of these fabrics when laundered, thereby increasing the time spent performing this task.

10.3 Laundry spaces often do double duty as sewing, hobby, and craft spaces, so plan to include counters for laundry sorting and folding, as well as separate places to lay out art materials without using the same counters. *Design by: Candace McNair. Photo by: Gerlick Photography.*

The location of laundry rooms in the basements of homes can also mean a number of trips up and down the stairs. Even those laundry rooms that are on the same level but at the furthest end of the house from the bedrooms, where most of the laundry is gathered, can require many wasted steps back and forth. One such location is often in, or adjacent to, the kitchen. The value of this location is often "sold" with the idea that the cook could then multitask and be able to do the laundry while working in the kitchen. In reality it meant that the washer and dryer were actually farther from where most of the laundry is gathered—in the bedroom areas. Having the laundry so close to the kitchen also meant that when working in the kitchen, any conversation was in competition with the background noise from the washer and dryer.

Frustration with washers that do not seem to remove all the soap residue in the final rinse cycle and clothes that appear dingy after being washed often lead clients to put their clothes through two wash and/or rinse cycles. The extra laundering adds up in higher overall costs—more dollars are spent on energy for the additional cycles, more soap may be used, and there is the increase in water usage. Added to these energy costs is the increase in physical energy used by the client or his or her housekeeper when spending even more time on the laundry.

For a job that can usually involve a good deal of time, little time may have been spent on the design of the surroundings. Lack of storage and counter space for sorting and folding clothing are challenges posed by many laundry area locations and designs. With a possibility of dreary utilitarian surroundings, and the probability of no window for natural light and view, it is easy to see why doing the laundry is not high on the enthusiasm list of many clients.

Exercising at home is taxing when your client must rearrange a room every time they want to work out. When there is no specific area designated permanently for fitness, it just adds to the reasons why exercise can be ignored.

Multi-purpose rooms can be an efficient use of space in a home without having to add on to the house, and often the home office is installed in other areas of the house to do double-duty. The problem with this arrangement is that if it conflicts with the other use of the space, say in a guest room where the client cannot use the office when entertaining overnight guests, then it is not an efficient use of space. The same holds true when a home office outgrows its original electrical or wiring capabilities.

In addition, outdoor living spaces do not lose their appeal just because a client is temporarily on crutches, has arthritis, or may end up needing to use a wheelchair. People who loved to garden when they were younger will not necessarily lose that enjoyment just because their physical abilities may be lessened. Clients should also be able to include all of their friends and family in outdoor entertaining. What a shame when some members can never be a part of those enjoyable outdoor activities because the areas are not accessible for everyone.

WASH AND WHERE?

Although the prospect of doing laundry does not necessarily bring joy to everyone's mind, when the area in the home designated for the task is well designed, the drudgery of the chore can certainly be reduced. In the past 15 years, the number of American homes with a separate laundry room has increased from only 17 percent to well more than half (56.7 percent). The average space devoted to laundry areas is 47 square feet, and the more affluent the household, the larger the size of the room.[4]

In a survey conducted by the National Association of Home Builders (NAHB), 95 percent of respondents indicated they desired separate laundry rooms in new homes and wanted such spaces to be multi-functional and to be adjacent to areas where laundry accumulates, such as kitchens, bedrooms, or bathrooms.[5] With the laundry room moving out of the basement, it can be in more direct view of visitors, and so simple practicality is not enough for clients. Additionally, those spending any time in the laundry room are looking for more pleasant surroundings.

A well-organized and inviting laundry room should include a number of important components in addition to the standard washing machine and dryer, although with the many improvements in appliances on the market, "standard" no longer needs to be used to describe even these two staples. A number of the developments in laundry appliances today can improve on the efficiency of the process as detailed in the following pages.

Certainly the larger-capacity washers and dryers that are available can equate to fewer loads of laundry per week, and high-performing products, such as more efficient dryers that offer several alternative drying methods, appliances that target stain removal or those that can handle a variety of fabrics and materials, help to avoid repeated cleaning and keep clothes from wearing out as quickly. Many appliances now are less stressful to operate, with front-loading washers and dryers mounted on pedestals and designed with the controls at the front of the units, making it possible for anyone, particularly in multi-generational homes, to do the laundry.

Since consumers want these products to withstand the demands of repeated use over a long time, they expect reliability and durability in laundry equipment, and that is what many of the manufacturers are now advertising. Additionally, the improved appearance of laundry equipment, with a variety of colors available and some units that can be installed so that they are hidden behind cabinet doors, are significant improvements toward designing rooms that are pleasant places to perform laundry tasks.

Most appliances are now easier to operate and have improved features, such as program and temperature selection and identifying how much detergent to use. Some machines on the market today can discern not only the type of fabric in the load and the care needed but also the weight of the load and how dirty it is. These machines can then automatically select the appropriate water level, wash action, wash cycle time, and spin and rinse cycles. Such machines, by so efficiently using energy and water, are also environmentally friendly.

10.4 Small laundry spaces can still be designed for effective use. Stack washers and dryers. Many models are available that will handle full size loads, and they will free up some space that can be used for other tasks.

10.5a Front-loading washers and dryers can be installed in an under counter installation, freeing up more counter space for other tasks; however, the resulting height of the counters can be as many as 42 inches above the finished floor.

10.5b Recent updates in appliances include matching bases that will raise the washer and dryer up off the floor, making it easier to get heavy loads transferred between front-load-style appliances. Front-loading washing machines are generally more energy efficient, using less water and detergents. *Design by: Candace McNair. Photo by: Gerlick Photography.*

a

b

To address consumers' demand for better performance and convenience in laundry appliances, some models of washing machines and dryers today are designed with the technology to "communicate" with each other, as well as with the user. The washer communicates electronically with the dryer, presetting dry cycles for improved clothing care as well as increased time savings. Once the user selects the wash options, there is no need to program the dryer because the load information is delivered automatically to the dryer, which then automatically determines which settings will deliver the most effective results. Not only do clothes last longer when washed in machines that thoroughly rinse items and leave little or no residue, but also fewer rinse cycles mean less energy is used. Programmable dryers that effectively dry clothes and notify the user when the clothes are ready to be removed without wrinkles also save energy, as do wrinkle-free clothes that require little or no ironing. Some units can also be set up on time delay, allowing the client or housekeeper to set the laundry to start the following morning even before the household is awake.

Planning the Laundry

Proximity and Location

There are many advantages to one-level living, including eliminating the decision of what level will house the laundry room. When planning to adapt a multi-storied home for aging in place, however, it is critical to carefully evaluate where the laundry room should be. What may have been a suitable location when the home was first built—in many cases, the basement—may not seem as ideal as residents make repeated trips up and down stairs carrying loaded laundry baskets. A laundry chute can aid in getting dirty laundry from upper to lower levels, but it does not solve the problem of the upward climb with clean items! There is a renewed interest in dumb waiters as a means of ferrying a variety of common items from one level of a home to another, such as groceries, firewood, and even mail—not to mention laundry—which people frequently carry up and down stairs.

Moving the laundry area out of the kitchen, another "historic" location, can also be beneficial. Not only is the background noise removed, but also the kitchen location is often a small space behind closet doors with little to no counter or easily accessible storage. Moving the laundry area out of the kitchen also frees up more space that can be used for kitchen storage or work area, as well as possibly allowing for a more efficient layout of the kitchen itself.

In homes with a master suite on the opposite side of the home from the rest of the bedrooms, thought might be given to locating the main laundry area with the majority of bedrooms, but adding a smaller laundry center near the master suite. With this arrangement, as clients age, they have easier access to the laundry near their bedrooms, yet there is an additional laundry area if the home is shared by multi-generations or if they should ever have a live-in caregiver. The same benefits hold true for adding another laundry center near the main-floor master suite if the main laundry area is on the upper floor near the other bedrooms.

Storage Issues

To help reduce packaging waste, consumers are being advised to buy the largest available size of laundry supplies. Studies also show that as homeowners look for convenience they often purchase larger sizes of laundry supplies, such as detergent and other cleaning products, to avoid repeated trips to the market to replenish these items.[6] Such buying habits then create a need for sufficient, easy-to-access storage for the larger containers and quantities, as well as smaller storage near the point of use.

Many homeowners may also use the laundry room for other activities. Clients may incorporate a family studio for craft projects, a garden center, or even a place where the family pets reside when the homeowners are out of the house. In that case, further consideration needs to be given to storage needs as well as the possibility of adding cabinetry to hide the appliances when not in use. Clients may also want an outdoor view to bring in natural daylight.

Drying Challenges

To prevent damage from over-drying, shrinking, and pilling, several dryers on the market use sensors to determine automatically when clothes are dry. An alarm is sounded to notify the user that the job has been completed. Some of the latest additions to the dryer market include steam dryers, using a combination of mist and heat. Clothes can go from the washer to the dryer as in the past, or when clothes just need a quick freshening, the unit can be used to eliminate wrinkles and remove odors from clothes within minutes.

Reacting to the fact that there are some clothes that cannot be put in a dryer, manufacturers developed "air drying cabinets" that circulate air within the cabinet to reduce drying time. They did not stay on the market, but we will probably see improved versions in the near future as people are becoming more "green." Even though some people are reverting back to line drying to save energy, there are challenges with that also. During times of the year when homeowners could not hang clothes outdoors, they used to be able to use the basement laundry area. Now, however, with moving the laundry area out of the basement, we need to consider some sort of line drying area as well as a flat drying area in designing clients' laundry rooms. It still might be within a "drying cabinet," but the cabinet will need to be custom designed. When the door is closed, it can then blend in with the remainder of the laundry room cabinetry. The ideas used by the appliance manufacturers in creating a hanging space above with slide-out flat drying surfaces below were good ones and might be useful to imitate.

Counters and Surfaces

A common complaint associated with small laundry rooms is a lack of clear surface area for folding and organizing laundry. Offering surfaces for sorting and folding clothes can be very much appreciated by the client when designing a laundry area. Though having sufficient counter space would be a first choice, some of the newer, stackable washing machine/dryer units—which can also be installed as a convenient second set for multiple-level homes—include a pull-out shelf for this purpose, a bonus feature for tight spaces.

Ironing and Steaming

Even in this era of easy-care fabrics, there are still times when we need to do some ironing, another chore that justifies a pleasant environment. Where to plan space for ironing depends on the user's needs, of course, but it's a good idea to plan for at least two places: A primary ironing area—with the available option

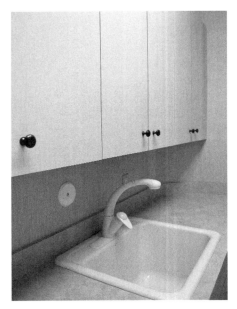

10.6 Laundry sinks are a great addition to the laundry area and give the client the ability to rinse very small loads of clothes, wash the dog, or water plants without going to the kitchen sink.

of sitting or standing—is within the laundry room itself that includes a television or a view through a window and a pull-out or pull-down ironing board in the master bedroom dressing area for quick touch-ups before dressing or packing a suitcase. The ease of fold-down ironing boards has expanded to include built-in ironing cabinets complete with task lighting, electrical outlets, adjustable-height ironing boards that swivel 360 degrees, storage for hot irons and hanging areas for freshly ironed items—and doors that conceal all of this efficiency when not in use. It's all about choices and convenience, something everyone—not just seniors—are looking for.

A rotary iron, with its wide, heated rollers, is another great way to press tablecloths, napkins, bed linens, and some clothing. A seated user operates the appliance with a foot pedal, and the speed can be adjusted to the type of laundry being pressed as well as the individual user's pace. When not in use, the portable unit can be folded and rolled into a storage cabinet.

Laundry Sinks

In addition to the traditional laundry sink, which is important for a variety of tasks such as hand washing delicate items, there are several alternative appliances that can deal with washing items that require extra care. A sink installed next to the washing machine, particularly when paired with a hands-free faucet, is helpful for spotting clothing before washing. Jetted sinks, which hold up to nine gallons of water, have a gentle, adjustable agitation and can wash anything from one fine, hand-washable item to a small load of laundry—an additional convenience in the laundry room. Again, to save steps, consider including a jetted sink in the master bedroom suite for washing delicate items or small loads without traveling the distance to the laundry room. It is often a long walk in houses where the laundry is on a different level or at the opposite side of a large home.

Other Uses—Crafts and Hobbies

When space elsewhere is not at a premium, extra counter space for folding laundry can serve a variety of other uses, like wrapping gifts, sewing, potting plants, or doing other crafts. Craft areas can be effectively combined with laundry room space and, with ample storage, a utility sink, and plenty of work surfaces, clients' fluctuating interests can be easily accommodated. As in other work areas, designers should provide counter surfaces in varied heights—as well as legroom for a seated user—so residents can choose to stand or sit while working. A mobile table is always a versatile item to include, particularly if its height is adjustable, making it especially flexible.

A last thing to consider in multi-functional laundry rooms: a pet spa. Tubs, complete with jets to soothe their aging muscles, are designed specifically for bathing pampered pooches that might be aging in place right along with their owners. For large dogs, consider adding a curb-less, walk-in shower with a hand-held showerhead. Moreover, if the laundry room will be used to house pets when clients are out, consider a window with a sill low enough for them to see outside. They will enjoy a view just as much as the homeowners!

10.7 With fitness and exercise being a popular activity, home gyms and fitness rooms make it very easy for elderly clients to work out without having to drive to their gym or club. By making it easy to use, it encourages them to maintain their muscle tone.

WORKING OUT AND STAYING FIT

We hear a great deal about baby boomers' extended life expectancy and their active lifestyles, and—as the group moves toward retirement—researchers are keeping a close watch on members of this population segment and how their health compares with their parents' at the same stage. One such survey, Growing Older in America: The Health & Retirement Study (HRS),[7] follows more than 20,000 men and women over the age of 50. This leading resource for data on the health and economic circumstances of older Americans, which is sponsored by the National Institute on Aging under a cooperative agreement with the University of Michigan, reports that boomers may be the first group to enter their golden years in poorer physical shape than their parents were at similar ages.

HRS also states that boomers are more likely to report being challenged by routine activities, such as walking a few blocks or climbing stairs, in addition to having continual health problems, such as high blood pressure, cholesterol, and diabetes. The report also indicates that though boomers plan to be very active in their senior years, members of this age group need to improve or maintain their physical health and stamina to match their abilities with their expectations. As the health of the pre-baby boomer elderly Americans continues to improve, there are some who feel that younger generations have been ignored and fear we may face more challenges with healthcare in the future.[8] If the boomers decide to make some changes toward improving their physical health with the addition of an exercise routine, then it stands to reason that their desire for, and use of, home fitness areas will also increase.

Members of the baby boomer segment are more focused on healthy eating and weight loss than those born after 1964, according to HRS, yet overall, they struggle with weight gain,

10.8 Weight and cardio training machines are now made in a scale that can fit in most any place. An extra bedroom or lower-level space can be an instant gym in no time. *Design by: Keith Miller.*

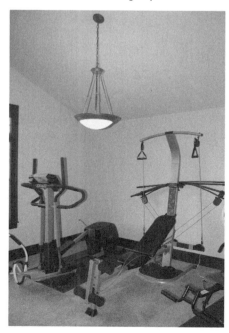

issues of poor health, and have somewhat of a love/hate relationship with exercise, leaning toward "hate."[9] According to the International Health, Racquet and Sportsclub Association (IHRSA), in 2006 those 55 and older purchased 20 percent of all gym memberships, with the majority of those having never been in a gym before. Moreover, baby boomers exercise fewer hours overall than those in younger age groups and are more sedentary—attributable to long hours at desk jobs and long commutes to and from work—than prior generations.

Baby boomers' interest in joining gyms may not necessarily be because they want to reverse the negative effects of aging, but rather to improve their physical ability to help ensure they will be able to age at home and not depend on care by others. Many of them have seen their elderly relatives lose their independence and do not want to repeat that scenario themselves. Many of those in the first wave of boomers have grandchildren and also seem to want to be able to keep up with them and continue to enjoy favorite activities. A number of health clubs, aware of boomers' unique approach to exercise, are reevaluating and renovating facilities to include more spacious rooms, improved lighting, softer music, and equipment suitable for body strengthening.

Reports of two recent studies emphasize the benefits of exercise for seniors and demonstrate that it is never too late to attain those benefits. In a study by the Buck Institute for Age Research at the McMaster University Medical Center in Hamilton, Ontario, a group of healthy seniors undertook a regimen of resistance training and improved their strength by nearly 50 percent. At the beginning of the study, the seniors (from the ages of 65 to 84) were 59 percent weaker than younger adults in the study (from the ages of 18 to 28); after training for six months, the seniors were only 38 percent behind younger subjects in the study. Once the study was completed, most seniors in the group, through continued training at home, maintained their improved strength and retained muscle mass.[10]

The second study dealt with the relationship between the loss of insulin in older adults and the loss of muscle mass, which can lead to frailty. Conducted by researchers at the University of Texas Medical Branch at Galveston (UTMB) and the University of Southern California, Los Angeles, the study discovered that with moderate aerobic exercise, such as "45 minutes of fast walking 20 hours before exposure to insulin restored the muscle-growth-stimulating effects of the hormone to levels comparable to those seen in normal young adults."[11]

Staying Active in Creative Spaces

The findings above, as well as results from related studies,[12] such as those conducted by Yankelovich, Inc., a leading consumer research company, indicate that baby boomers, as they seek the ability and means to be in control of their health through many forms of keeping fit—including working out at home, fitness club memberships, and regular participation in outdoor activities—prefer convenience, choice, variety, ease of maintenance, and "bells and whistles."[13] These reports suggest, then, that in-home fitness rooms should be an essential component in an overall aging-in-place design.

The National Institute on Aging (NIA) reports that when older people become less active during the winter months they could be losing stamina, strength, and flexibility.[14] Such seasonal inactivity also applies to those who reduce their activity during the hot summer months as well. To assist these people—who should move their physical activities indoors, but may not have a plan for how to do so—the NIA has produced an exercise video that targets endurance, strength, flexibility, and balance. When designers provide designated areas and incorporate audio and video equipment—such as VCRs and DVD players—for exercise, they help motivate their clients to take advantage of such opportunities and to keep fit all year long.

Designers should also plan in-home exercise areas to include ample natural daylight and a pleasant view, and provide variety and choice of audio and video equipment, such as voice-activated software so clients can "surf" the Internet while exercising or access a virtual personal trainer. Don't forget to provide lighting in this area with levels that can increase as the client ages and their eyes require higher levels of light. As in other areas, it is important that glare-free light be provided so that they will be able to see clearly enough to avoid accidents while exercising.

Karl Knopf, Ed.D., professor of Adaptive/Older Adult Fitness at Foothill College in Los Altos, California, and an expert in older adult fitness, suggests that those with limited—as well as full—mobility should take advantage of water exercise.[15] In addition to water aerobics classes at numerous public indoor pools, seniors—and their designers—should consider the various therapeutic pools designed for private residences. These pools, which include "counter-current" or "resistance" features, do not require a lot of space and can be installed outside or indoors for year-round use.

10.9 Patios with pools and spas are luxury items that require weekly maintenance, but the benefits for the homeowner and client justify the cost when it is easy to end the day with a few laps in the pool or sit in the spa. *Design by: Susan Cozzi. Photo by: Michiko Kurisu.*

Not all houses are large enough for a specific room to be designated as the fitness area, so designers can include in any suitable room exercise equipment that can be folded up and put away or—depending on the geographical location of the home—create an outdoor fitness area. For clients who prefer outdoor activities such as tennis, cycling, hiking, walking, or jogging, designers should provide adequate, well-organized storage for equipment near the most often-used exterior door. Be sure that when designing a multifunctional space that will include fitness equipment, that will be folded up when not in use, it can be accessed and put away with little effort. If great energy is needed just to get to the equipment, then the use of it for the actual exercise will probably wane. In addition, the fact must be considered that as the client ages, their strength will probably decrease. For storage provided for outdoor activities, the same thought should be taken to make access easy.

WORK FROM HOME—IT'S NOT ALL BUSINESS

For the more than 20 million people who work at home at least once a week,[16] research suggests a growing need for designated spaces within homes for offices. Reports published by the American Association of Retired Persons (AARP),[17] the American Society of Interior Designers (ASID),[18] and other organizations suggest that aging in place may not include retirement as usual. Many older Americans are requiring some type of residential work area. Validation for this need also comes from a study conducted by the Internet Home Alliance Research Council, a network of leading consumer product and service companies serving the home technology market.[19] Among other factors, "the study found, for example, that more than half (63 percent) of seniors have home offices in their new homes. Seventy percent have broadband Internet access at home and 45 percent have WiFi access. In two-thirds of the homes, builders have installed wiring for computer networking. Fewer than 10 percent of the surveyed homeowners have no Internet access."[20]

A zest for additional challenges, as well as economic motivations, may lead many future retirees to leave one job only to go on to another in a very different field, and these new ventures may create a need for a home office. Even many who do retire completely need space, adequate light, and equipment for managing household and personal accounts and working on correspondence.

10.10 Dedicated home offices are a common component to many residences these days. Many can be outfitted for multiple purposes, including running a small business or as a get away from the rest of the house.

You must be able to communicate with your client and understand all the limitations involved in the aging process. We professionals know how many products are available in the market and how they can be incorporated into our design to enhance our clients' lives. It is up to us to listen to our clients and create an environment that will enhance their lives as they age and start to lose some of their abilities.

When a client faces the fear of getting old and not being able to do things without help, I tell him/her that getting old is not a crime, but a privilege. Not everyone has been given the privilege of living for so many years and with all the new products and technology available in the market, his/her freedom can be emphasized.

—Andrea Vollf, Allied ASID, Interior Designer

A home office typically needs—at a minimum—space for a phone and a computer, a clear flat area for writing, and plenty of good ambient and task lighting. Even as laptop computers have become more popular, a computer usually includes a monitor, a processor or CPU, a modem for Internet access, a keyboard, a mouse, a printer, various cables, and possibly a scanner. Additional office equipment may also include a fax machine and, of course, adequate storage for documents. And when a home office is truly intended for business conducted from home, there will be additional needs specific to the type of business. Storage areas that are hidden behind doors or in drawers can help the appearance of business disappear when work is completed.

10.11 Small walls in a bedroom or den can become a place to pay the bills, catch up with news and shows on the TV, and display many framed pictures of the family.

As we have come to rely on the Internet for both business and personal correspondence, so have we created the need for wireless equipment—modems and routers—as well as spaces to house them. When using a laptop, most people do not move from room to room with their computers but rather tend to use them in specific areas, though those areas may differ with each household, and within each household, with each user. Daily use of a laptop may necessitate adding either a wireless keyboard or additional monitor to relieve stress to the body. According to the *Ergonomic Guidelines for Arranging a Computer Workstation*, published by the Minnesota State University Moorhead,[21] when the laptop screen is at a comfortable height and distance for the user, the keyboard is not and vice versa.

With CAT5—as well as structured—cabling included in most new homes, and with wireless products that make it possible to retrofit older homes, home offices can now provide faster Internet access as well as a better work space layout. And as computer technology is constantly and rapidly changing, it is imperative for homes to have cabling that can adapt to the future demands of developing technology. When clients upgrade their computers, they expect their homes to accommodate those improvements. Well-wired homes, such as those with home networking packages that frequently incorporate home entertainment features, offer users the ability to work anywhere in their residence, including outdoor living spaces. And of course, it is much less disruptive to install wiring and wireless systems before clients move into the home, even if they intend to add additional equipment in the future.

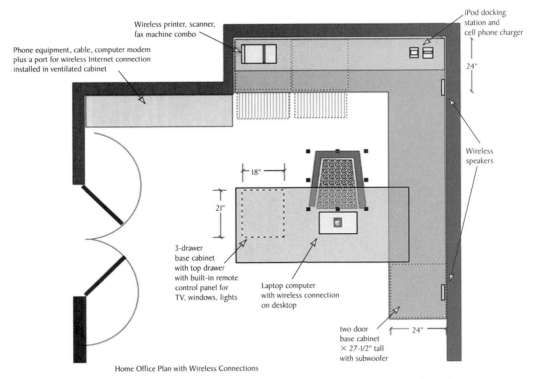

Home Office Plan with Wireless Connections

10.12 Using wireless connections to network the computer, printer, and modem, the desk area remains uncluttered except for what the client brings to the table. It is important to know the types and quantities of equipment at the beginning of the design process, as appropriate places need to be planned well in advance of the electrical, phone, and cable wiring. Because wire is so inexpensive, consider adding a second run of phone and cable wiring at the same time to create redundant systems that also might allow for expansion.

CASE IN POINT

My wife and I moved to Florida when I retired from my surgical practice. Due to my failing eyesight because of macular degeneration, I was no longer capable of performing surgery as I had done for the last 30-some years. My long-term prognosis is not good, but I am not ready to turn over and play dead yet. And other than my sight, my mind is active and I swim at the club a few times a week.

In order to read, I had to make an investment in equipment. So now I spend a lot of time in my desk chair, with my Apple Computer and this rather huge video reader that sits next to the keyboard that allows me to see printed images at 50x magnification or larger. Since I do love to read the daily paper, check my stocks, email the grandkids, I can go into my new little office and with all the equipment for me to see, do the things I have always enjoyed. I can even read the print on my medicine bottles and that is so great.

I had to make some accommodations with the cabinetry for the big reader to sit next to the computer and printer, but it all turned out really well. I needed a lot more counter space and a much larger kneehole so that I could move back and forth from the reader to the computer. I wanted the electrical plugs and telephone connections to be also right on the countertop so I can easily use them. And while I can no longer sit in a chair and read any of my books without the use of the reader, I still enjoy knowing that they fill the bookshelves around me. My books are a part of who I am, just like in the old house.

—From a client interview

With boomers often retiring and then starting up other jobs, a well-wired home would allow them to telecommute from their back patio as easily as driving to an office. Furthermore, the computer offers the opportunity to communicate with family and friends across the globe, and so your client will appreciate being able to access the Internet from a variety of areas in the home, including out by the pool or anywhere in the garden. If they have mobility challenges, having the ability to connect whenever and wherever they want provides additional independence. They are not "tied" to one area of the home while working or catching up with emails. Remember that access to the Internet includes connection to medical professionals, educational opportunities, and entertainment.

In a study conducted in Finland, subjects between the ages of 70 and 80 years were asked to evaluate the height and comfort of selected work- or task-related furniture and fixtures. The respondents indicated that adjustable furniture and fixtures allowed them to choose heights and positions suitable for their own personal needs. The study also revealed that as people age their range of motion, range of reach, joint flexibility, balance, and coordination often decline.[22] In spite of these advancing limitations, older workers tend to ignore any discomfort and continue to use chair and table positions they are accustomed to, even though those positions are less comfortable.[23] Since baby boomers have a reputation for not readily putting up with the status quo, this kind of habitual acceptance may change in years to come. Furniture and fixtures that are flexible and adaptable are more practical for aging-in-place clients as their abilities change, and designers should consider specifying flexible seating, adjustable-height work surfaces, and adjustable keyboard trays and monitor arms to add to the efficiency of the home work area.

Aches and pains in backs and shoulders increase proportionately with the length of time a person sits at the computer, and with so much time spent at computers both for work and entertainment, a comfortable, well-designed, adjustable chair is an essential item to specify for a home office. The Occupational Safety & Health Administration (OSHA) describes a good chair as one that will provide needed support to the back, legs, buttocks, and arms, while reducing stress.[24] Be sure the chair seat height allows the user to keep both feet flat on the floor while seated and that armrests are adjustable up or down to allow the user's shoulders to remain relaxed.

Ergonomics, the science of creating a safe and comfortable workspace that fits the body, can be applied to home office design in a variety of ways.

- Keep frequently used items within easy reach to eliminate the need for the user to stretch beyond his or her natural range of motion, which can cause shoulder strain.

- When using a separate monitor, set it at an appropriate height for the user to avoid neck strain by having to look up or down to see the screen.

- A phone headset is not just a convenience; it is also an excellent way to avoid neck strain that is often suffered by those who hold the phone between the ear and shoulder. A hands-free headset not only supplies the user with the ability to multi-task, but it is an excellent convenience for anyone of the 46 million Americans with arthritis and other rheumatic conditions.

Designers also should always incorporate individual client preferences and work styles as they develop aging-in-place solutions to home offices. Where one client must spread out his or her work, another must be able to move easily between the computer and a writing surface, access files, and check reference books while seated at the work area.

Next to thoughtful, adequate furniture and equipment, ample accessible electrical outlets should be at the top of the list for designing in-home offices. As clients' physical abilities and mobility change, they will be less likely to crawl under a desk to access the electrical outlet or climb on a ladder to adjust or change a fixture. Designers should help clients plan for future needs in home offices by locating sufficient outlets and switches within easy reach of a seated user and eliminating as many visible cords and wires as possible. As mentioned in Chapter 6, there are products designed to cover the many cords and wires throughout our homes and offices that still provide easy access to them, yet look like a beautifully paneled wall.

Lighting is once again an important element in designing for aging in place, as the need for sufficient natural and artificial light is critical in a home office. Particularly when clients work at home, there should be plenty of windows to supply natural light, as well as a pleasant view. By the same token, glare is a common result of providing large areas of natural light. With the use of filter-

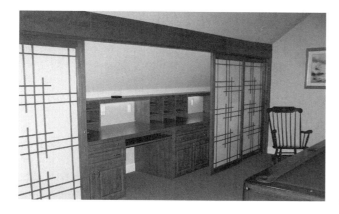

10.13 Large shoji-style sliding doors hide this home workspace that was created from attic space. The client can close up the paper mess of this workspace without having to let papers, files, and books remain out in the open for others to see. While wood-paneled doors are functional in these applications, they might have been heavy to operate for such wide widths; the translucent nature of the screens give a light and airy feeling to the desk space and are easy to pull across the desk. *Design by: Janet Kay. Photo by: RT Photography.*

ing window treatments, the glare can be eliminated without losing the value of the natural light. Specifying remote controlled window treatments allows everyone to more easily adjust the filtering effects as needed without having to move to the windows and sliders to open and close them.

Some window treatments can also be set to automatically adjust according to the time of day and/or direction of the sun. Either of these possibilities creates independence for those who previously had to rely on someone else every time they needed the window treatments adjusted. By being able to adjust for the glare at certain times of the day, without blocking the view and light, it is possible to position a desk facing a window without the challenges previously caused by glare. It still can be beneficial, though, to position the desk at right angles to the window in order to have the natural light come from the side, rather than directly facing into it. With this arrangement, one is still able to enjoy the view.

Position the computer monitor to avoid direct daylight hitting the screen. It is advisable to select task light that is adjustable, allowing light to be directed on the desk surface without hitting the screen. Designers should also specify non-glare surfaces, looking for those with a matte finish and avoiding surfaces that are bright white in color. Of course, people do not just work at a desk or computer during daylight hours, and as their eyes age and require even more light, it is important to plan for appropriate task and ambient light in this space. When specifying ambient light, be sure that the fixtures will conceal the bulb or tube from view or use a diffuser to help eliminate the glare. Select task lighting, whether table or floor lamps, with adjustable levels of lighting to provide higher levels when needed. For all lighting choices, consider how easy it would be for someone with limited mobility and/or limited reach or strength to operate the controls without needing help from others.

Acoustics can also have a huge impact on home office design, as effective sound absorption can improve concentration and eliminate distractions. For those with hearing loss, good acoustics are even more valuable to block out background noises. Particularly in an office area, there are often a number of hard surfaces that reflect rather than absorb sound. Because of this problem, consider the specifications of products to counterbalance it. Adding low-pile carpet or cork flooring, fabric wall hangings, soft treatments on the windows, or upholstered furniture are some of the choices that will help to provide additional acoustics to this area.

OUTDOOR LIVING—HEALTHY ALTERNATIVES

The health advantages of exposure to sunlight have generated a variety of research studies focusing on the relationship between sunlight and various illnesses. The positive influence of nature on humans is nothing new. In ancient Egypt, gardens were created to restore the spirit. And what of the writings of Emerson, Thoreau, and Whitman that expound on the serenity achieved from being exposed to nature? In the nineteenth century, Dr. Benjamin Rush, the "father of American psychiatry"[25] and a signer of the Declaration of Independence, reported that garden settings showed positive effects for people with mental illness.

And if views of nature through a window can provide health benefits, then moving outdoors to experience nature first hand should be exponentially more beneficial. Scientists at the University of Illinois reported that "park-like surroundings increase neighborhood safety." Exposure to parks and open space has also been proven to relieve mental fatigue, as well as feelings of violence and aggression that fatigue can trigger. The three classic symptoms of mental fatigue—inattentiveness, irritability, and poor impulse control—have all been previously linked to aggression. Spending time outside in a natural setting can restore concentration and focus, just as rest refreshes physical fatigue.

In a study published in the *Journal of Environmental Psychology*, researchers compared the reactions of two groups, one of which was allowed to view nature from interior spaces and participate in nature walks. Subjects in this group, when compared to those in the second group, which either remained in a windowless room or walked in an urban setting, reported fewer feelings of anger and more positive attitudes.[26] Similar research results have helped influence funding for parks in many inner-city neighborhoods.

But what of the many homes constructed in neighborhoods beyond downtown areas that lack substantial views or access to natural areas—and often have

10.14 Garden, patio, and solarium spaces extend the living spaces of the interior into outdoor living rooms where clients can enjoy the breeze and sunshine.

10.15 Planned communities with meandering walks, landscaped paths, gazebos, and parks encourage exercise and conversation with family, friends, and neighbors.

few or no trees, greenbelts, or views other than into other structures? Most of these homes are not in impoverished neighborhoods, yet they are surrounded by mostly structures and paved areas. Many of these areas lack parks nearby or other green spaces. Those who wish to age in place in these neighborhoods will have little to entice them out of their homes, either into their tiny outdoor settings or into the neighborhood in general. There is a lack of gathering space, for families or for neighbors. Studies show that people are looking more for "livable communities" in which to live and age in place. They are searching for homes or condominiums within walking distance of local shops, businesses, restaurants, and other gathering places. And we are told that the number one thing that influences people's decision in choosing retirement communities is the campus grounds—that search for green spaces again.

Today we are seeing horticultural therapy used and recognized as a practical treatment with many positive benefits for people who are both mentally and physically challenged. Some of these benefits that might relate particularly to the aging client include improving memory and concentration, easing emotional pain from bereavement or abuse, cultivating nurturing feelings, encouraging social interaction, and reducing stress and anger.[27] These benefits were in evidence in the rehabilitation of war veterans hospitalized in the 1940s and 1950s.[28]

According to William Haskell, professor of medicine at Stanford Prevention Research Center in Palo Alto, California, "gardening burns about three times more energy than being sedentary." Haskell also says that "gardening activity can help in preventing heart attacks and strokes, colon cancer and Type 2 diabetes."[29]

Recommendations to counteract obesity published by the National Institutes of Health (NIH), include gardening for 30 to 45 minutes or raking leaves for 30 minutes a day as physical activities.[30] A *Journal of the American Medical Association* study corroborates these recommendations, suggesting that 30 minutes of "lifestyle exercise," such as gardening, will offer notable improvements to

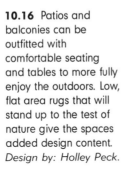

10.16 Patios and balconies can be outfitted with comfortable seating and tables to more fully enjoy the outdoors. Low, flat area rugs that will stand up to the test of nature give the spaces added design content. *Design by: Holley Peck.*

blood pressure and cholesterol ratios and can lower stress levels, decrease the risk of diabetes, and help to control weight. Depending on the type and extent of gardening, this activity can also build strength and improve endurance as well as increase the cardiovascular capacity.[31] Time spent in the garden digging, weeding, trimming shrubs, and mowing the lawn (no cheating here with a riding lawn mower!) can require the same energy as other physical exercise activities, such as walking, cycling, swimming, and other aerobic activities.

Researchers at the University of Illinois also discovered that residents who live near areas of outdoor greenery socialize with close neighbors more often and have a stronger overall sense of community. The number of shade trees in surrounding green spaces appeared to be essential to this improved sense of community: The more trees, the more the area was used by people of all ages. Studies also show that people who are considering aging in place are thinking not only of their personal residence, but also of the contiguous area—what AARP describes as "livable community."[32]

With all the evidence supporting the importance of creating outdoor living environments, designers should also remember that in designing outdoor aging-in-place spaces—just as in other areas of the home—accessibility for all ages and abilities is a critical component. For outdoor environments that truly welcome and assure enjoyment and provide access to

10.17 Garden spaces developed into well-landscaped oases give more reasons for elder clients to linger out of doors, making the connection to nature. Gardening can be a good physical and aerobic activity as well as social and mental therapy. *Design by: Susan Cozzi. Photo by: Michiko Kurisu.*

all visitors, no matter what their health or abilities might be, designers should work with a landscape architect to include a number of thoughtful elements that will involve all the senses. These might include incorporating a variety of textures, plants that draw birds or butterflies, plants or other materials that offer pleasing scents, an interesting array of colors, and water elements for their soothing acoustical quality. All are positive additions to any client's outdoor living space, but for those clients who, as they age, may have limited use of one or more of their senses, including these elements will help continue to enjoy their garden area. For example, texture, scent, and sound can help lead a sight-impaired client through the spaces, and color, texture, and scent can still be enjoyed by the hearing impaired, even if they lose the ability to enjoy the sounds of the garden. And then, of course, a well-planned garden can be enjoyed from the interior of the home as well.

Through the Doors—Gardening and Landscaping

Just as people with physical limitations and health issues are those who can benefit most from gardening, any number of health conditions, such as arthritis, back injuries, and a myriad of disabilities, can make gardening difficult—if not impossible—without special accommodations. To create well-designed, accessible gardens that have no physical barriers, designers should work closely with landscape architects or designers to extend aging-in-place principles to outdoor living areas. And although ADA guidelines are meant for the construction of public buildings, they are also a valuable reference for residential design.

Designers who are planning outdoor living spaces for aging-in-place clients should apply the same principles they use for interiors. Barrier-free exits to outdoor areas should be a priority consideration. Even a small, raised threshold can be anything from a tripping hazard for someone who uses a cane to a challenging barrier for someone who is seated in a wheelchair; all exterior doors of the home should be flush or nearly so.

Beveled edges with a slope no greater than 1:2 are indicated for thresholds higher than recommended allowances, as well as for changes of floor levels in common areas. Another approach, particularly in new construction, to creating barrier-free access and egress is to recess sliding door tracks. Use lever hardware on both sides of exterior doors, and consider the weight of doors themselves and how difficult it is for clients to open and close them. In some instances, automatic door openers can be used.

Once through the door, everyone should be able to enjoy the same view; interior designers should partner in outdoor projects with landscape designers or architects to guarantee the landscaping is accessible for all and to

10.18 Exits from the residence onto the patio, pool, and garden can be made level by decking up to meet the level of the interior floor, making egress easy.

10.19 Smaller accent gardens can be easy for one individual to take care of as a continuing project with the rest of the landscaping done by others. For the elder gardener, having a place to focus their talent and attention is less overwhelming than to scatter their work over a complete yard. *Design by: Susan Cozzi. Photo by: Michiko Kurisu.*

ensure maximum sensory enjoyment. Often gardens and outdoor spaces can be adapted to aging-in-place standards with only a few simple adjustments in grade, equipment, and landscaping.

The American Horticultural Therapy Association offers the following suggestions for designers who are planning gardens to accommodate people with a wide range of abilities:

- Construct wide, gently graded wheelchair-accessible entrances and paths.
- Use containers and raised beds.
- Adapt tools and containers that can turn a disability into ability. Some examples might be flowerpots on wheels, raised gardens, garden tools with padded guards to support weak wrists and arms, gloves designed to minimize pain for people with repetitive motion problems, adjustable cushioned handles, telescoping garden tools, and sturdy lightweight tools.
- Create sensory-stimulation environments by selecting and installing plants for their fragrance, texture, and color.
- Use accessible greenhouses that bring the garden indoors for year-round enjoyment.

Gardening satisfies a certain human instinct to nurture, and gardeners are certainly well rewarded for their efforts when they enjoy the fruits of their labor—either beautiful flowers or a bountiful harvest of homegrown fruits and vegetables. For those who want an active role in the garden in spite of their limitations and disabilities, raised beds and containers not only are more accessible for the seated gardener, but they add visual interest as well. Garden beds set 2 feet high and constructed with edges wide enough to sit on can bring touchable plants within reach and fragrances closer. And many tools that are especially designed to make gardening easier for disabled users would probably be the tools of choice for all users. Non-slip, wheelchair-accessible paths between beds make moving through the garden safer for all avid gardeners, no matter what level of mobility.

The sensory stimulation of a garden not only expands enjoyment of the outdoor space beyond the visual but can also help cue those who are sight or hearing impaired to interact with their surroundings.

Creating different areas, or "rooms," in the garden can increase clients' visual and sensory enjoyment of their outdoor living areas. A variety of scents in a garden can subtly alter a person's mood. For instance, the delicate fragrance of lilacs, roses, or lily-of-the-valley can be especially relaxing, while some heavy scents, like honeysuckle, jasmine, and wisteria, can cause sleepiness, and herbal aromas, such as lavender, rosemary, and lemon verbena, can energize and invigorate. And a stroll past culinary herbs, like oregano, sage, and thyme, will often improve the appetite.[33]

An assortment of different textures, including plants, stone, fabric, wood, water, and other organic materials, also can make exploring the garden extraordinary. Thoughtful use of texture can also supplement wayfinding for those who are sight impaired.

Garden sounds, another factor to enjoy in outdoor spaces, can influence moods and provide excellent audio signals to help orient sight-impaired visitors to the garden. The whisper of breezes through the limbs of weeping trees, such as willow and birch, can have a calming influence; the rustling of ornamental grasses and bamboo can convey a sense of excitement and stimulation. Waterfalls, fountains, wind chimes, and bird feeders are other possible acoustical garden accessories. And, as they have for generations in Japan, rain chains—some of which have been designed by musicians—are functional, yet beautiful alternatives to traditional gutter downspouts. The sound of moving water is an excellent stress reducer that not only can block out street noises and other noise pollution but can also create the impression of a larger space. And a small reflecting pool can mirror light and plant color throughout an outdoor living area.

Although the sounds of the garden may be lost on the hearing impaired, the colors will not be. Even for those with limited sight, in a well-planned garden, year-round color variations can help distinguish specific areas—again, a good wayfinding technique.

When evaluating outdoor spaces, paths and paved areas should be smooth, level, and firm, and should always have good traction. Wood, for example, can become very slippery when wet. The following list includes advantages and disadvantages to specific paving materials:

- Asphalt—Absorbs and radiates heat. Gets hot in summer, but snow melts off sooner.
- Wood decking—Slippery when wet.
- Brick—Expensive and must be installed properly.
- Decomposed granite—Readily available; suitable for people in wheelchairs but not for those on crutches.
- Concrete—Expensive; glare can be a problem for older people and those with visual impairments.
- Woodchips and turf—Use only for persons who do not require ambulatory equipment.
- Rubber—As long as it is not too soft, it can prevent tree roots from uprooting pathways and is a softer surface if someone should fall.

Also, for easy detection by those who are vision impaired, path edges should have distinct textural differences, such as concrete to

10.20 Decking and surface materials can be stone and tile, natural wood, and man-made composite materials, but the finishes need to be matte and with a texture that will be skid-proof outdoors.

grass or bricks to a mulched bed. A textured strip across a path can indicate a patio entrance, the location of seating, or a place to pause to enjoy a fragrant plant or interesting texture. Such wayfinding signals should be from 12 to 18 inches wide and contrast noticeably—such as a brick strip across a crushed stone path—from other paving materials. Avoid raised edging, which can create a tripping hazard.

Lighting a Fire—BBQ, Summer Kitchens, Fireplaces

With the popularity of outdoor living, the kitchen has expanded outdoors as well, as have dining and living areas and—in some instances—sleeping and bathing areas. Complete outdoor kitchens that rival those indoors are replacing barbecue grills and outdoor sinks. Through realistic project evaluation, designers can ensure that the spaces they create will be just as useful and attractive in the future: Is the outdoor living area close to the house? Is there enough well-sealed storage to eliminate or minimize trips in and out of the house? Are there sufficient electrical outlets for a variety of small appliances and ample outdoor lighting so the cook can see to prepare a meal after dark? Is there plenty of flexible, adjustable overhead covering, such as awnings or umbrellas, to protect the cook and guests from the elements, day and night? And finally, are the specified products and materials durable and of low maintenance?

10.21 The popularity of grilling has turned into an elaborate part of many upscale homes for the aging population. Summer kitchens, bars and bar appliances, and outdoor cabinetry have redefined the outdoor experience, and it needs to be accessible. In this case, keeping the knee space open under the grill makes it user-friendly for everyone.

10.22 In this colonial-style house, the brick sidewalk gently ramps up from the gardens to meet the front porch, welcoming friends and family, and then continuing on with full accessibility directly into the home.

When creating outdoor kitchens, designers should also apply many of the same considerations as those used to design indoor aging-in-place kitchens: working surfaces of various heights; work areas that can be used by someone who is seated; easy-to-access outlets, switches, and appliance controls; good task lighting; and outdoor fans and heating elements—there are a number of outdoor heating products—to regulate temperatures.

Fireplaces, considered by some as the center of the home, are also moving outdoors. From *chimeneas*, the somewhat portable clay fire pots that gained popularity a few years ago, to expansive fireplaces that are now gaining even more popularity, many of which include remote-controlled flames, these are not the outdoor fireplaces of the past.

With aging baby boomers hoping to remain independent and age in place with well-equipped laundry rooms, fitness areas, home offices, and outdoor living spaces, you have the opportunity to help them reach these goals by "future proofing" their homes.

Residential design for aging in place does not begin with grab bars in the bathroom and end with taller toe kicks in the kitchen. It is all through the residence, in every room and corner and space. It is inside and outside. It is up and down. Understanding the challenges and specific needs of the client as they maneuver all about the home is key to creating effective designs that make the most of the spaces for their intended use, no matter the client's ability or desire.

References

1. AARP, *Beyond 50.05. A Report to the Nation on Livable Communities: Creating Environments for Successful Aging*, Washington, DC (2005).
2. "Seniors' Design Choices Seen Reflecting Optimism," *CABA Researchers Report, K&B Design News,* (July, 2007).
3. Consumer Energy Center, www.consumerenergycenter.org/home/appliances/washers.html (accessed July 12, 2007).
4. GE Consumer and Industrial Press Room, Washers and Dryers; *Laundry List of Laundry Facts*, www.geconsumerproducts.com/pressroom/press_releases/appliances/washers_and_dryers/laundry_facts_07.htm (accessed July 12, 2007).
5. RIS Media, *Laundry Rooms Gain Respect in New Homes*, www.rismedia.com/wp/2004-05-28/laundry-rooms-gain-respect-in-new-homes/ (accessed July 8, 2007).
6. Kleber, Steven L., *How to Sell and Market to the Right Generations*, www.bathenclosures.org/press/How%20to%20Sell%20and%20Market%20to%20the%20Right%20Generations.pdf (accessed May 25, 2007). And Biesen, Erin. "An Expanding Laundry List," *Appliance Magazine,* (September, 2005), www.appliancemagazine.com/editorial.php?article=1091&zone=1&first=1 (accessed May 25, 2007).
7. Karp, Freddi (ed.) The Health and Retirement Study, *Growing Older in America*, National Institute on Aging: Washington, DC (March 2007).
8. Stein, Rob, "Baby Boomers Appear to Be Less Healthy Than Parents," *The Washington Post*, www.washingtonpost.com/wp-dyn/content/article/2007/04/19/AR2007041902458.html (accessed July 10, 2007).
9. *Healthy Living Among Boomers*, Harris Interactive Webinar, May 31, 2007, www.harrisinteractive.com/services/pubs/HI_CPG_Webinar_Healthy_Living_Among_Boomers.pdf (accessed June 21, 2007).
10. Melov, Simon; Tarnopolsky, Mark A.; Beckman, Kenneth; Felkey, Krysta; Hubbard Alan, *Resistance Exercise Reverses Aging in Human Skeletal Muscle*, www.plosone.org/article/fetchArticle.action?articleURI=info:doi/10.1371/journal.pone.0000465 (accessed June 21, 2007).

11. University of Texas Medical Branch at Galveston, "Aerobic Exercise Helps Maintain Muscle in Elderly, Study Suggests," *Science Digest*, (May 30), 2007, www.science daily.com/releases/2007/05/070530113120.htm (accessed July 10, 2007).

12. "Aging Baby Boomers: Will the 'Youth Generation' Redefine Old Age?" *CQ Researcher*, Vol. 17, Number 37, pp. 865–888, (Oct. 19, 2007), http://agingandwork.bc.edu/documents/Boomers.pdf (accessed Oct. 25, 2007).

13. Krotz, Joanna L., *What Do Boomers Want in 2006?*, http://www.microsoft.com/small business/resources/marketing/market_research/what_do_boomers_want_in_2006.mspx (accessed August 3, 2007).

14. National Institute on Aging, *Heat Up Your Indoor Fitness Program During Cold Winter Months with NIA's Over-50 Fit Kit*, http://www.nia.nih.gov/NewsAndEvents/PressReleases/PR20010101Heat.htm (accessed August 18, 2005).

15. "Aerobic Exercise for People with Limited Mobility—How to Get Aerobic Benefits When You Can't Move So Well," *Bottom Line's Daily Health News*, (August 7, 2007).

16. U.S. Department of Labor (May 2001); Sweet, Kimberly, "Home Technology and the Home Office," *Professional Remodeler*, (January 1, 2005).

17. AARP, *Beyond 50.05*, Washington, DC (2005).

18. ASID, *Aging in Place; Aging and the Impact of Interior Design*, Washington, DC (2001).

19. "Internet Home Alliance Releases Senior Housing Study Results," Business Wire, http://findarticles.com/p/articles/mi_m0EIN/is_2007_May_29/ai_n19172521 (accessed May 29, 2007).

20. Ibid.

21. The Minnesota State University Moorhead, *Ergonomic Guidelines for Arranging a Computer Workstation*, http://www.mnstate.edu/ehs/Ergonomics.htm#MINNESOTA_STATE_UNIVERSITY_MOORHEAD_ERGONOMIC_GUIDELINES_FOR_ARRANGING_A_COMPUTER_WORKSTATION (accessed August 12, 2007).

22. Kirvesoja, Heli; Vayrynen, Seppo; Haikio, Ari. "Three Evaluations of Task-Surface Heights in Elderly People's Homes," *Informe Design 2000*, http://www.informedesign.umn.edu/Rs_detail.aspx?rsId=1302 (accessed January 10, 2007).

23. Ibid.

24. U.S. Department of Labor Occupational Safety & Health Administration, OSHA Chair Ergonomics, *Work Stations*, http://www.osha.gov/SLTC/etools/computerworkstations/components_chair.html (accessed January 10, 2007).

25. *The History and Practice of Horticultural Therapy*, http://www.ahta.org/information/ (accessed April 2, 2005).

26. Ulrich, Roger, "Effect of Interior Design on Wellness: Theory and Recent Scientific Research," *Journal of Health Care Interior Design*, Vol. 3. pp. 97–109 (1984).

27. Worden, Eva C.; Frohne, Theodora M.; Sullivan, Jessica, *Horticultural Therapy*, University of Florida, Institute of Food and Agricultural Sciences, http://edis.ifas.ufl.edu/EP145 (accessed March 30, 2007).

28. *The History and Practice of Horticultural Therapy*, http://www.ahta.org/information/ (accessed April 2, 2005).

29. Fosdick, Dean, "Gardening Can Be an Avenue to Weight Loss, Better Health: Turn Cultivating, Weeding into Daily Exercise Routine That Includes Warm-ups," *Associated Press*, (January 23, 2005), http://www.dispatch.com/dispatch/contentbe/EPIC_shim.php?story=dispatch/2005/01/23/20050123-I13-00.html (accessed March 30, 2005).

31. National Institutes of Health, "HHS Tackles Obesity—Health and Human Services," *FDA Consumer*, May-June, 2004 http://findarticles.com/p/articles/mi_m1370/is_3_38/ai_116734853 (accessed March 30, 2005).

32. Krautkramer, Christian J., *The Physician's Role in Preventing Obesity*, American Medical Association, http://www.ama-assn.org/ama/pub/category/print/12631.html (accessed March 30, 2007); AARP, *Beyond 50.05—Livable Communities: Creating Environments for Successful Aging*, Washington, DC (2005).

33. Caplan, Larry, *Gardening for the Senses: The Sensual Garden*, Purdue Extension Service, http://www.ces.purdue.edu/vanderburgh/horticulture/4senses.htm (accessed April 2, 2005).

CHAPTER 11

Design Beyond Age

In most people's vocabularies, design means veneer. It's interior decorating. It's the fabric of the curtains or the sofa. But to me, nothing could be further from the meaning of design. Design is the fundamental soul of a human-made creation that ends up expressing itself in successive outer layers of the product or service.

—Steve Jobs, co-founder and CEO of Apple

DESIGNING A BLUEPRINT FOR AGING IN PLACE

Like any well-designed house, aging in place is built from many parts and pieces whose sum is altogether bigger than the parts. At its broadest foundation, aging in place is a design process with two parts. The first determines issues related to clients' quality of life when coping with the prospect of aging. The second specifies effective solutions that promote independence over a lifespan.

Building up from there, universal design principles define the structure, both inside and out, with walls designed to facilitate accessibility and adaptability. The "aging process" itself influences the design of this well-designed haven. Age is the part that most everyone tries to avoid discussing in depth, except perhaps in conversational jest with friends and family, because acceptance of one's own aging means acceptance of life with a beginning and an ending.

The aging structure takes form when it builds a heightened awareness for design professionals as to just what's at stake—of just how important it is to provide clients a choice and the type of living environment that echoes clients' preferences of where and how to live. When fully embraced, residential design for aging in place becomes standard practice, rather than the exception, giving future generations homes that last a lifetime.

Aging in place is not a trend but rather a growing and unique opportunity for the design and construction community to build a new way to practice design. By its growing demand, this design-adaptive practice will have a revolutionary impact on houses, homes, and havens much akin to the evolution of sustainable or "green" design. Each of these evolutions will make its own impact on how Americans live and enjoy life as they grow older. When combined with each other, these two design cultures will create a new blueprint for residential design.

BUILDING AN AGING ADVANTAGE

Imagine the opportunities for a 60-year-old couple to live anywhere they choose in America and select from a wide number of accessible and adaptable homes—as numerous as convenience stores on local street corners—ones that can accommodate their long-term living requirements. Universal design features would be standard. This couple wouldn't consider houses that lack thoughtful, inclusive design with features that are transparent: curb-less entries to showers, wider hallways and doorways, lever-style handles on doors, taller toilet seats, bathrooms and showers with turning radii for wheelchairs, faucet handles to the side of sinks and bathtubs, and light switches and electric outlets within everyone's reach.

This new standard "style" of residence would also include increased lighting levels and a full accessible bath and sleeping space on the first floor of every home. The couple could choose homes that include flex-space options, adaptable

11.2 Designing spaces that remain flexible should a change to a client's personal lifestyle require altering the function of a particular room means creating a well-planned design plan that can adapt with the user's needs.

11.3 With advances in building systems and new technologies, these homes can be wired together as a network using fiber optics to deliver phone, cable, and the Web, delivering age-related content at high speeds to a target market that has grown up in the time of electronic toys and needs to have time in later years.

guest suites, and detached guesthouses to provide space for live-in family members or essential caregivers, should either become necessary.

State-of-the-art technology would connect every village resident to the Internet, which could also provide a myriad of educational and entertainment opportunities. Unlimited topics would be available via virtual classrooms, and global positioning systems (GPS) would continually monitor the locations of individuals with unique cognitive needs.

Expanding the vision, such homes would be one choice among a variety of residences, including single-family houses, condos, duplexes, and townhouses that are featured in a village of shared resources. Central to such a village is the community center, a gathering place for socialization and recreation of all kinds. Near the center—and within walking distance or a short bike ride of all the homes—would be requisite shops: a farmers' market and local grocery store; a pharmacy; a bank; a post office; a dry goods store; hardware and bookstores; professional, social, and health services; and religious and spiritual facilities. Such a village would be artfully planned so that all amenities could also be accessed via convenient, safe public transportation that operated on clean fuel.

Inclusive communities in the years to come will base their own "new urbanism" formulas on successful places like Kentlands in Gaithersburg, Maryland, and Seaside and Disney's town of Celebration, both in Florida. These new hybrid places would not be a rehash of old concepts and plans of how towns and cities are currently designed but reflect a way of thinking first how residents live, work, build a family, and grow old together.[1]

11.4 In Abacoa, a city within a city in Jupiter, Florida, downtown living options combine with retail, office, restaurants, ballparks, and golf courses into a new urban community surrounding a college campus. A social focus of the development has been to bring together many generations together into a single setting.

One development has considered inclusive age-related design in its initial master planning for those exclusively over 55. The Villages, located in central Florida, is a 20-square-mile senior living community with 67,000 residents that has everything found in a similar sized town, from Starbucks to Wal-Mart, dozens of eateries, golf courses, entertainment, and a lifelong learning center that offers college-style courses on a wide range of topics.[2] As the largest single-site development in the country, the population is expected to grow to more than 100,000 by 2012.

Many multi-use housing developments have been built in the United States during the past two decades that feature village-style qualities. However, some lack an essential consideration: the inclusion of age-related design components within the houses themselves.

How is it possible to ensure that as people grow older they can continue to have freedom of choice in their housing? Acceptance, anticipation, analysis, and attitude might well be the paths that will foster change.

Acceptance Is the First Step

Only recently has consideration been given to the design of residential environments that will accommodate generations of families and adapt to special needs when required. There is much more that needs to be accomplished. The acceptance of the aging process should be a component of any design criteria, much in the same manner as code compliance—it is not an option and must become standard. Aging-in-place building criteria should be part of local building codes in much the same way that a certain percentage of low-income housing is required in newly developed communities. Visitability is one example of successful regulation.

11.5 This side entrance ramp added to this home takes over some of the driveway, but it provides great access to the front porch and entry door through its slow and steady rise.

According to the U.S. Census Bureau's 2005 American Housing Survey,[3] approximately one-third of the 124 million residences in the United States, many of them homes to baby boomers when they were still babies, were constructed before 1960. Between 1960 and 1980, another 36 million homes were added to the housing inventory. Yet, despite the number of existing homes, according to research by groups like the American Society of Interior Designers (ASID), the

National Association of Home Builders (NAHB), and the American Association of Retired People (AARP), not only is there currently a shortage of elder-friendly accessible housing, but also there is a critical need to adapt existing homes, as well as to build new residences to accommodate the huge baby boomer population.

Anticipation Is the Next Step

When a design professional anticipates a client's need for a safe, secure residence that will span a lifetime, the design program will obviously include elements of universal design, barrier-free accessibility, and other adaptable practices. By taking into account the molecular degeneration of human physiology that weakens body, mind, and spirit, combined with the way our American culture views age, the challenges are enormous. Concerns about an individual's potential loss of independence and control, coupled with the diminishing physical abilities, should be the primary motivation for both clients and designers.

An important case study reveals such concerns and reinforces these concepts. President Franklin D. Roosevelt, in anticipation of his own need to have a home where he could age in place, became a forerunner in designing and building accessible housing—perhaps the first accessible home in the United States and designed by one of only two presidents who had a hand in architecture. (Thomas Jefferson was the other.) In 1921, at the relatively young age of 39, Roosevelt was stricken with what was at the time believed to be polio, though it may have actually been Guillaume Barre Syndrome. His condition quickly deteriorated in the weeks that followed, and ultimately, he suffered permanent paralysis from the waist down.[4]

Roosevelt refused to accept his fate and fought hard to regain the use of his legs through a number of therapies. Outfitted with heavy braces on his legs and hips, eventually he was able to walk short distances with a crutch or cane. He was concerned with public perception of him as a disabled public servant and politician, so he was most careful never to be seen in public using his braces or crutches or to be photographed sitting in a wheelchair. As a result, few people ever knew the extent of his disability. While governor of New York, then later as a presidential candidate, and ultimately as president, Roosevelt would make public appearances standing upright with physical support and assistance from family members or aides.[5]

As he anticipated his retirement from public office during his second term as President, Roosevelt made plans to build a private residence on his family's expansive estate in Hyde Park, New York, where he could retreat from all but his closest friends and family to write his memoirs. "I began talking about building a small place to escape

11.6 President Roosevelt in one of the very few photographs of him in a wheelchair, taken on the rear porch of Top Cottage, Hyde Park, New York, about 1941. *Photo courtesy: FDRoosevelt Library.*

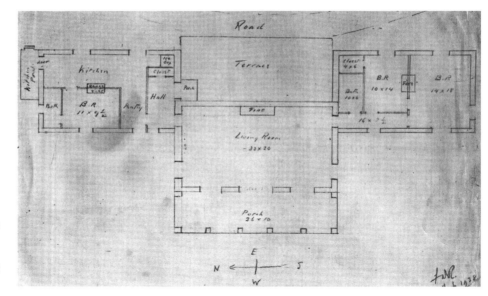

11.7 FDR's hand drawn sketch in 1938 for Top Cottage became the master plan for what some call the first universal design residence. *Photo courtesy: FDRoosevelt Library.*

the mob," he wrote.[6] Acting as his own architect, Roosevelt designed the house, which he named Top Cottage, to include the accessibility features he needed. Sited on a secluded hilltop overlooking the Hudson Valley, Top Cottage was one of the country's first barrier-free buildings.

Roosevelt partnered with Henry Toombs, a young architect, to formulate his ideas and complete the working drawings for Top Cottage. He then contracted with the building firm of Adams-Farber, whose principals fully understood Roosevelt's accessible criteria. Plans for the house, completed in 1939, included windows low enough to the ground so that Roosevelt could be seated in his wheelchair and still gaze out over the Hudson River and the mountains beyond.[7] Large wood-framed glass pocket doors that opened onto the rear deck were designed with door tracks that were fully recessed into the thresholds to make traversing by wheelchair barrier-free. Landscaping at Top Cottage included an earthen berm that changed the elevation from the rear deck of the house to the grounds so that Roosevelt could move out onto the lawn without having to be carried.

Although Roosevelt did not retire there as planned, he was especially proud of Top Cottage. The home provided solemn comfort when he was able to escape the

11.8 Top Cottage featured Dutch Colonial architecture, very much like what FDR had seen along the Hudson River where he grew up. With the building structurally restored, a visit to Top Cottage provides a quiet look back to a place and time when one man designed a specially adaptive retreat that would give him a place where he could escape and remain fully free and independent of others to get around. *Photo courtesy: FDRoosevelt Library.*

pressures of his third and fourth terms as President, and he privately hosted a number of international dignitaries there, including Winston Churchill, Madame Chiang Kai-shek, and King George VI and Queen Elizabeth.[8] It was a particular point of pride for Roosevelt, however, that he was able to welcome close friends and family to Top Cottage and entertain them with little assistance. As an example, he had an electrical outlet installed next to the living room fireplace at card-table height so that he could plug in a toaster and offer toasted bread and butter to guests at teatime.[9]

Top Cottage was structurally restored by historic preservation architects John C. Waite Associates during the 1990s and is now managed by the National Park Service.[10] This unpretentious house, which is reflective of the Hudson Valley area's Dutch Colonial architecture, exemplifies the independence that Roosevelt had aspired to in its design.

CAREFUL ANALYSIS TELLS THE CLIENT STORY

Results of surveys and data assembled by various organizations, including ASID, clearly indicate that most people want to remain in their current residence indefinitely.[11] That prospect may not be possible for everyone who needs more advanced care. However, much can be learned by analyzing the "aging" experiences of others. In each of the following studies, a number of complex, difficult issues must be addressed. In each situation, designers and their team of experts bring together all the facts, issues, and elements and explore the options with the clients to develop comprehensive plans.

11.9 Effective aging-in-place environments combine the aesthetic nature that appeals to the elder population with built-in, transparent, functional quality that will age with style and are safe and secure in the foundation. *Design by: Judith Sisler Johnson.*

CASE IN POINT: INTRODUCING EVELYN AND DAVID

Take for example Evelyn and David, a married couple living in a two-story home in the suburb of a large mid-western city. The once well-kept neighborhood and surrounding areas have fallen into disrepair with the economic decline of local industries. Evelyn and David, who are both in their mid-70s and in generally good health except for some minor mobility issues due to the first signs of arthritis, are active individuals. They have lots of friends whom they enjoy entertaining in large groups in their home. Evelyn and David's children have long since moved away and, of late, a number of their oldest friends have passed away, leaving the couple without many of the personal connections they once enjoyed.

Many decisions are at hand. Should they stay in place or go elsewhere? Although their house is paid for, it needs a fairly significant remodel to add a new master bedroom and full bathroom to the first floor. The couple may not be physically up for the remodeling effort if it means having to live in a construction site for a number of months. Remodeling or adding an addition to an existing residence in their neighborhood may also not make economic sense if the value of the real estate in the area is headed downward.

CASE IN POINT: MEET BARBARA

Barbara, nearly 75, recently experienced the death of both her husband of more than 50 years and her only child in an accident. Struggling with despair and depression, Barbara is unable to make decisions about either her current or her future living situations. Family members have offered her a place to live so that they can give her emotional support, but she " ... does not want to be a burden on anyone." Since her health is stable and good, she expects to remain independent for a long while and even talks fleetingly of traveling at a moment's notice to faraway places to find her new self.

Barbara is considering several options: Should she sell the house she and her husband had custom built just four years earlier and buy a condominium, which would give her less maintenance to worry about? Or, should she investigate buying a unit in a retirement community in Florida or Arizona? Her indecision is obscured with the anxiety of pulling up well-established roots to move several thousand miles away to live in a place with other "old" people who she does not know.

IT IS TIME TO CHANGE THE ATTITUDE

Each of these individuals now faces some difficult decisions, ones that may take a while to fully investigate. But none of them are thinking about a time when living in an assisted living center is even on the table for discussion.

CASE IN POINT: PRESENTING RICHARD AND LAURA

Both of these active baby boomers each enjoy a professional career and are currently raising two teenagers, the oldest of whom will go to college next year. The family is living in a comfortable, though somewhat crowded, three-bedroom, two-bath, single-story home. Richard's father, Bill, who lives alone in his own home a few miles away, was diagnosed recently with stage one Familial Alzheimer's Disease (FAD). Consequently, Richard and Laura are faced with a difficult decision: Since there appears to be no reasonable or cost-effective way to remodel their current home so that Bill can live with them, should they move to a larger house that can include Bill as a member of the household, or welcome Bill into their house and make the best of their current home, or help Bill remain in his own residence for the time being?

Not only do Richard and Laura need to evaluate their financial resources, but they also need to be realistic about their ability and desire to become Bill's caregivers. Including Bill as a member of Richard and Laura's household now may mean a major change to the family's already busy day-to-day routine. More important, once Bill is a part of their immediate family, will both Richard and Laura be able to continue their demanding careers, manage college expenses for both children, and still provide Bill with the kind of care he needs? Or is it more reasonable and cost effective to make accommodations for Bill to age in place in his current residence? What provisions are required now and in the future for live-in help to assist Bill with his activities of daily living (ADLs)? Richard and Laura's own personal retirement plans may have to be postponed for now.

People are disabled by circumstances and situations, as well as by attitudes. So a shift in attitude toward older people may very well be the most important step to success in building a new prototype for designing homes. The idea of senior citizens as a socio-economic group without useful skills, physical abilities, or substantial financial resources fosters ongoing negative attitudes. Although there is a growing awareness of the economic potential of marketing to older demographic groups, industries that design and build houses for the masses have been slow to adopt most new design concepts.

Whether as a result of the natural aging process or because of a chronic disease or permanent disability, at some point, many people will accept the fact that living alone is no longer possible. Many older people fear the consequences of stumbling or falling and not being able to get up. Having to relinquish personal privacy or having to rely on a family member or hired caregiver compounds the issue.

A needs assessment can guide designers and their clients as they develop and implement effective plans for creating more livable spaces. Immediate needs, of course, can be met in short order by applying the standard menu of grab bars, door levers, increased lighting, and non-slip floors. Clients and designers can accomplish mid-sized projects, including bathroom and kitchen remodeling or converting a little-used space into an extra sleeping area, or larger projects, including building an addition to or completely remodeling a residence—only

"Futureproofing" is a term used to describe planning for long-term value, not just short-term gain. In the building and design industry, such planning relates to integrating features that will improve the client's present life as well as ensure that the value of his or her home is maintained and even improved to serve the client in the future. A home holds value for the client as a major investment if it can adapt to the lifestyle and changes in technology that will occur in the future. To assure that a home's design is future-proof, designers and builders should consider the following:

- Better energy efficiency
- Better space management
- Better sound control
- Better building health and safety improved quality control and lifecycle costs[12]

when they are aware of all available options and can make informed choices based on time frames and costs.

To find an effective design solution for an especially complex project, design professionals and clients should start by gathering a team of client-focused aging-in-place advocates, including the interior designer, an architect, the remodeler, and the various contractors. Other valuable team members also can include a real estate professional, who can determine the fair market value of the current residence; a banker or financial advisor, who can provide a strategic financing plan; and any medical or healthcare professionals who can counsel the team on the clients' current and potential health maintenance issues.

MAKING THE BEST DECISIONS AND IMPLEMENTING SOLUTIONS

Evelyn and David decided to put their house on the market—a tough decision—and move closer to their children. Because of declining property values in their suburb, it made little financial sense to invest in a major remodeling project and risk not getting the best return on their investment. Evelyn and David were then able to focus on their other options and to define a new life for themselves, while the designers offered affordable suggestions to improve the exterior and interior of the house—including fresh paint, updated kitchen appliances, and new floor coverings, which are generally easy, low-cost projects that can be accomplished quickly—to maximize its sale.

Evelyn's wish list of features in the couple's next residence included either a house or condo with a single-story configuration, lots of storage, and a great room/kitchen combination for easy entertaining. David's criteria included low-maintenance and a space for his personal "office." To Evelyn and David, "old" means "ready for a nursing home," and because they don't consider themselves to be at that stage yet, they have no interest in grab bars, taller toilet seats in the bathrooms, or any other aging-in-place components in the new residence they are seeking. "Those bars remind me of some hospital, and we're not ready for that," David says.

Clearly Evelyn and David are not anticipating or planning for potential deterioration in their mobility that might require changes to any new home.

Barbara's life choices as an adult—where to live, where to vacation, where to work, who to socialize with—were always made in concert with her husband. Since his recent death, and without his valued input, Barbara finds herself with many options but no clear direction. Although friends and family offer advice, she is confused about future living arrangements, both from a financial viewpoint as well as the physical layout of the home. Her biggest dilemma? Would she be able to stay in the house and continue to pay the real estate taxes and maintenance on a home that is probably too large now for a single woman?

For Barbara, a team of professional advisors, who are more informed about costs and available alternatives than well-meaning family and friends can more objectively define a course of action for Barbara that will help her progress toward a more optimistic future. Grief counseling even might help her put things into perspective as she contemplates the future.

Barbara's options might include moving to a planned "over 55" community that can provide social support from people her own age and with her same interests should she want to give up wandering around alone in a large residence. She could also move to a development that offers measured home and healthcare services. That way she could continue to live independently and access available domestic services when she eventually requires help to clean, do laundry, and prepare meals.

As a resident, she will be able to tap into a menu of continuing-care health and nursing services that include assistance with her ADLs, if and when she requires it. Should more intensive healthcare be needed, Barbara could move across campus to a skilled nursing "environment," rather than moving to still another new residence at a more physically stressful time in her life. There are many small-group living environments available with private sleeping rooms arranged around a central core of public areas. These facilities, which are not unlike a family home environment, rather than the traditional institutional nursing home, make communal living enjoyable.

In any of these options, as her health declines in the years to come, Barbara will be in a place of her own choosing that is furnished with items that she and her husband collected during their life together.

Now to Richard and Laura, who have a number of critical short- and long-term issues to face. With the demands of raising two children and full-time careers at a peak for both, Richard and Laura's time is already fully committed. Putting one of their careers "on hold" to manage Bill's care is not a plausible option at this time. If Richard and Laura decide to become Bill's caregivers, they will have to be masterful at scheduling, as well as balancing the cost of their children's education and the additional financial responsibility of Bill's healthcare costs. They also know that Bill's Social Security and retirement funds will help to pay for some of the costs.

An assessment of Bill's needs might indicate that the best short-term solution is for him to remain in his current residence. During stage one of FAD, individuals suffer some memory loss and mood swings and tend to have less energy and slower reflexes. Since Bill is at this early stage, it is possible he can stay in his own home under the care of a visiting assistive care professional, who will monitor him daily to ensure he bathes, dresses, eats properly, and takes prescribed medications on time and in the correct dosage. Richard and Laura, along with their teenagers, can take turns spending evenings with Bill. As Bill's disease progresses, the family can hire nurses or other healthcare professionals to stay in the house with Bill at night to better ensure his safety.

In stage two of FAD, patients become easily confused and tend to wander. When Bill reaches this stage, he can wear a wireless monitoring device on a lanyard around his neck or on his wrist to alert his family and caregivers as to his activities and location. Exit door alarms on Bill's home would also give Richard and Laura some peace of mind.

Depending on how quickly Bill's condition deteriorates, Richard and Laura's long-term planning can include bringing him into their home at some point in the future. With the kids in college for another year or two, there would be some space available to have Bill stay with them, but the kids would have to double up in the remaining bedroom when they did come home.

Because they can't build out onto their property due to setback lines, another option might be to design and build guest quarters farther back on the property so that Bill can continue to enjoy independence while still under the concerned and watchful eyes of family members. Richard and Laura might also investigate facilities that specialize in caring for FAD patients in preparation for the eventuality of selling Bill's home and using the proceeds for his long-term care. As Richard and Laura have realized through their planning, without the help of full-time caregivers and a plan for long-term, facility-based care for their loved one, even the most devoted families find it difficult to meet the needs of an Alzheimer's patient.

As people grow older, it becomes more difficult for them to accept change. And next to fear of loss of independence, fear of change can make personal decisions, like those that Evelyn and David, Barbara, and Richard and Laura face in these case studies, so difficult and stressful. Evelyn and David ultimately decided to purchase an existing first-floor condominium in a seniors-only community in Arizona within an hour's drive of their family, a decision that will allow them to cultivate deeper relationships with their children and grandchildren. They are working with a design professional to make alterations to the property that will ensure accessibility for many years to come.

No doubt, packing a lifetime's worth of belongings and moving to a new city will mean a lot of effort for Evelyn and David. Their first step in accomplishing the move, as suggested by their designer, was to discard or give away unwanted and worn-out furnishings and household items and keep only a few sentimental, personal belongings accumulated during their more than 50 years of marriage to take with them to their new home.

Barbara chose to move to a gated community in Florida where she found support, companionship, and networking opportunities with like-minded adults, as well as a sense of safety. Not only was the condominium a wise investment, but it was a convenience as well. Barbara intended to travel, and the residence, which had a reliable concierge service, was easy to lock up and leave at a moment's notice. Since Barbara realized that she would never be comfortable living totally alone, she invited her older sister to live with her. Barbara's designer, then, needed to anticipate the needs of both women as they aged in place. It was necessary to include in the design two master suites and communal areas that will support both Barbara's and her sister's individual preferences and make the best use of selected existing furnishings.

Richard and Laura's difficult personal circumstances escalated in the four months subsequent to Bill's diagnosis as his health deteriorated quickly, and he required round-the-clock care sooner than originally anticipated. The family's designer helped them develop a graduated approach to their situation. To keep Richard and Laura's personal and professional lives as balanced as possible and to keep Bill in his own home—a familiar environment for him—the family arranged for a reverse mortgage to finance alterations to Bill's residence. The designer's plan called for converting an existing den and adjacent main bath into a bed-and-bath suite for a full-time, live-in caregiver, as well as for a number of short-term adjustments to the home.

But before any remodeling work began in earnest at Bill's residence, medical tests revealed that Richard has a 50/50 chance of developing FAD himself. The couple realized that they also could be facing a situation similar to Bill's in a few years. Richard's concerns about this prospect and its implications for Laura's future led them to rethink their plans for Bill and for themselves. They asked their designer to now plan strategically for their own residence. The resulting proposal called for the couple to build a separate 600-square-foot, two-bedroom guest cottage at the rear of their property, replete with universal design features, for Bill and a caregiver.

To maximize the justification for its construction, the new structure was designed to be flexible and adaptable to a number of uses: a retreat for their teenage children, a guest area for visitors or returning adult children, and even a future office for Laura. Should Richard be stricken with FAD in the future, the guest cottage could be an onsite residence for a caregiver.

DESIGN PROFESSIONALS CAN HELP WITH IMPORTANT DECISIONS BEYOND DESIGN

There is little doubt that the "designs for aging-in-place" movement will rise to meet demand. With 76 million Americans who will need one day to live in

11.10 All spaces can be accessible and adaptable, but hearing is often a problem in homes with larger volumes of interior space. Chairs that can be moved and people grouped closer together is one solution. Textured walls and a light tray lowered from the ceiling combined with textured rugs and wicker weave accents will break up a lot of background noise often found with tall ceilings. Creating environments that facilitate audible social activities keeps baby boomers, parents, family, and friends engaged in conversation.

11.11 Residential design for aging in place is planning a project with and for the client to achieve design goals and include the supportive, user-friendly details transparent by their nature and planned by design until the right time arrives when they will be called into service.

a secure and safe environment—one of their own choosing—there is much more work to be done. Interior designers, architects, and homebuilders can take the lead.

Designers will design better living environments. Architects will create places with this segment of the population in their vision. Builders will provide housing solutions to give support, safety, and security for an elder population. Clearly clients, residents, and end users will benefit by the opportunities to retain an independent lifestyle to which they have grown accustomed.

But interior designers, homebuilders, and architects have yet to realize how vital their contributions as aging-in-place advocates might be for this vast number of people. Design professionals can be enormously important as the "aging-in-place coach" when called upon to assemble an interdisciplinary network of related professionals—including design/build contractors, sustainable design and technology consultants, healthcare professionals, physical therapists, and social service agents. The team of professionals might also include financial, insurance, real estate, and investment experts that can fully assemble a clear set of options.

Collected together and viewed over time, these endeavors create sound evidence of the value of design well beyond aesthetics. Appropriate design decisions that are based on collective assessments and evaluations, performance expectations, research, and strategic planning will result in a demonstrated improvement to client satisfaction, safety, and security.

References

1. Steuteville, Robert, "The New Urbanism: An Alternative to Modern, Automobile-Oriented Planning and Development," *New Urban News*, www.newurbannews.com/AboutNewUrbanism.html (accessed October 8, 2007).
2. *The Palm Beach Post*, Palm Beach, FL, September 29, 2007.
3. U.S. Census Bureau, *American Housing Survey (2005)* www.census.gov/hhes/www/housing/ahs/new.html (accessed October 8, 2007).
4. Franklin D. Roosevelt Presidential Library and Museum, *Franklin D. Roosevelt Biography*, www.fdrlibrary.marist.edu/educat33.html (accessed October 8, 2007).
5. Ibid.
6. Waite, John C., *The President as Architect: Franklin D. Roosevelt's Top Cottage*, Mount Ida Press: Albany, NY (2001).
7. Ibid.
8. Ward, Geoffrey C., *Closest Companion: The Unknown Story of the Intimate Friendship Between Franklin Roosevelt and Margaret Suckley*, Wilderstein Preservation: Rhinebeck, NY (1995).
9. Waite, John C., *The President as Architect: Franklin D. Roosevelt's Top Cottage*, Mount Ida Press: Albany, NY (2001).
10. Ibid.
11. American Society of Interior Designers, *Aging in Place: Aging and the Impact of Interior Design*, Washington, DC (2001).
12. Karasik, Sherry, *Futureproof Your Home*, http://www2.newhomesource.com/newhomeguide/articles.aspx?pid=2&passage=futureproofing, (accessed August 3, 2007).

Appendix A

Building Professional Alliances

Professional design organizations, groups, and associations create beneficial networks among their members and industry partnerships that build opportunities for knowledge and resource sharing, education, and advocacy. But when design professionals move out and away from their normal circles to build alliances with related professionals, an expanded wealth of information and trends can have a positive effect on the design and overall outcome for the client.

As examples, architects, interior designers, and homebuilders in the practice of design for aging in place can benefit from networking together and with those in the healthcare profession to garner a deeper understanding of the process of aging. Each profession has much to learn from each other. Each has information to share. Each can be educated to further the depth of understanding of the challenges everyone will face as a result of the aging process.

Networks can be built outside the normal design community, too. As an example, having knowledge of alternate methods of financing a remodeling project can be gleaned from those in the reverse mortgage industry. Understanding the skills a physical therapist brings to the client to help with mobility and transfers can give the design professional a different view in creating accessibility.

Following are a number of professional associations, organizations, and research groups that can help design professionals understand the specific needs of the elder population to build better environments for aging in place. The list will also assist the design professional in assembling a team of advocates on behalf of the client.

- **AARP** www.aarp.org

  The leading organization representing the interests of people 50 and older in the United States. AARP offers a wealth of information and research findings on the 50+ population, including home, work, recreation, and other life and lifestyle trends and preferences.

- **Adaptive Environments** www.adaptenv.org

  This group promotes accessibility as well as universal design through education programs, technical assistance, training, consulting, and various publications.

- **Administration on Aging** www.aoa.dhhs.gov

  This is a government website sponsored by the U.S. Department of Health and Human Services. It provides information for researchers, students, caregivers, and health professionals.

- **Ageworks** www.ageworks.com

  This is a University of South California organization with the latest in information on education and aging.

- **American Association for Homes and Services for the Aging**   www.aahsa.org

This group provides information for family caregivers on choosing facilities and services for older adults. There is also information concerning Medicare education geared toward professionals so that they might educate their clients.

- **American Association of Geriatric Psychiatry**   www.aagpgpa.org

This healthcare group provides information for patients and caregivers with a focus on depression and dementia. It also provides a section for healthcare professionals that includes research, teaching, and training information.

- **American Geriatric Society**   www.americangeriatrics.org

This is a professional organization of healthcare providers whose purpose is to improve the health and well-being of older adults.

- **American Institute of Architects**   www.aia.org

This is the leading group representing the interests of the architectural community.

- **American Occupational Therapy Association, Inc.**   www.aota.org

This group represents the interests and concerns of occupational therapy practitioners to improve the quality of occupational therapy services.

- **American Physical Therapy Association**   www.apta.org

The goal of this group is to foster advancements in physical therapy practice, research, and education.

- **American Society of Interior Designers**   www.asid.org

This group is the largest organization representing the interests of the interior design profession and advocacy for the design community.

- **American Society on Aging**   www.asaging.org

The association provides resources, publications, and educational opportunities to enhance the knowledge and skills of people working with older adults and their families.

- **ADARA**   www.adara.org

This is a group of professionals networking for excellence in service delivery with individuals who are deaf or hard of hearing.

- **AdvantAge Initiative**   www.vnsny.org/advantage

This initiative helps communities facilitate aging in place through a comprehensive survey measuring how well older adults are faring in key areas including housing.

- **Archstone Foundation**   www.archstone.org

This is a private grantmaking organization, whose mission is to contribute toward the preparation of society in meeting the needs of an aging population.

- **Center for Aging Services Technology (CAST)**   www.agingtech.org

A program of AAHSA, CAST is a coalition of more than 400 organizations working on developing and deploying emerging technologies that can improve the aging experience.

- **Center for Healthy Aging   www.healthyagingprograms.org**

  This is a program of the National Council on Aging that promotes and assists communities in providing healthy living programs for older adults. It includes information on falls and other health topics.

- **Center for Universal Design   www.design.ncsu.edu/CUD**

  This is a national information, technical assistance, and research center that evaluates, develops, and promotes accessible and universal design in housing, commercial and public facilities, outdoor environments, and products.

- **Centers for Disease Control and Prevention   www.cdc.gov**

  This is a government agency for consumers and healthcare professionals that contains information on a wide variety of health topics.

- **Certified Aging-in-Place Specialist Program (CAPS)   www.nahb.org**

  The NAHB Remodelers Council, in collaboration with the AARP, NAHB Research Center, and NAHB Seniors Housing Council, developed this program to provide comprehensive, practical, market-specific information about working with older and maturing adults to remodel their homes for aging in place.

- **Concrete Change   www.concretechange.org**

  This is an organization advocating accessible, visitable home design for people with disabilities based in Atlanta.

- **Cystic Fibrosis Foundation   www.cff.org**

  This is an association that supports research to achieve a cure and control cystic fibrosis and to improve the quality of life for those with the disease.

- **Department of Health & Human Services   www.os.dhhs.gov**

  This website contains links to various health and human services agencies. It provides information on a wide variety of health topics and includes a news section.

- **Disability Information   www.disabilityinfo.gov**

  This is the most comprehensive federal website of disability-related government resources.

- **Easter Seals   www.easterseals.com**

  This group provides services to ensure that people living with autism and other disabilities have equal opportunities to live, learn, work, and play.

- **EasyLivingHome.org   www.easylivinghome.org**

  This is the premier site for information about a voluntary program that encourages easy access to homes for everyone.

- **Eldercare Locator   www.eldercare.gov**

  This site is a public service of the U.S. Administration on Aging. The Eldercare Locator connects older Americans and their caregivers with sources of information on senior services.

- **Elderweb   www.elderweb.com**

  This is an award-winning online eldercare directory with product resource links.

■ **Family Caregiver Alliance   www.caregiver.org**

This is a nationally recognized information center for caregivers. It provides information on grants, programs, and services and is also intended for use for people interested in developing programs and conducting research for caregivers.

■ **Gerontological Society of America   www.geron.org**

This group provides information and education for the improvement of quality of life as one ages.

■ **HealingHomes   www.healinghomes.com**

This site provides accessible home-based solutions to issues related to aging.

■ **Homemods.org   www.homemods.org**

This is the National Resource Center on Supportive Housing and Home Modifications.

■ **Lighthouse International   www.lighthouse.org**

This is a leading worldwide resource on vision impairment and vision rehabilitation.

■ **Living to 100 Life Expectancy Calculator   www.livingto100.com**

This site is designed to translate what we have learned from studies of centenarians and other longevity research into a practical and empowering tool for individuals to estimate their longevity potential.

■ **MetLife Foundation   www.metlife.org**

The Foundation funds programs that promote healthy aging and address issues of caregiving, intergenerational activities, mental fitness, and volunteerism. The Foundation also supports research on Alzheimer's disease through its Awards for Medical Research program.

■ **National Aging in Place Council   www.naipc.org**

NAIPC engages professionals from a wide range of disciplines—remodeling, architecture, elder law, interior design, finance, product design and manufacturing, urban planning, social services, health, and others—to work together to promote aging in place.

■ **National Council on Aging   www.ncoa.org**

Among many other services, NCOA provides information to seniors to help them remain in their homes as they age.

■ **National Association of Area Agencies on Aging   www.n4a.org**

This organization is for healthcare professionals and caregivers and contains links to Eldercare, a toll-free number used to locate support services throughout the country.

■ **National Association of Home Builders   www.nahb.org**

This is the largest association representing the interests of home contractors and builders, industry partners and advocacy groups.

■ **National Center for the Dissemination of Disability Research (NCDDR) www.ncddr.org**

This group provides dissemination and utilization of disability research.

- **National Center on Elder Abuse**   www.elderabusecenter.org

  This site was designed for the public and healthcare professionals and lists the steps for reporting elder abuse.

- **National Council on the Aging**   www.ncoa.org

  This is a group that supports and promotes dignity, self-determination, and the well-being of older adults through services and programs.

- **National Family Caregivers Association**   www.nfcacares.org

  This organization supports those who are caregivers. It provides information about projects and programs designed to educate, support, and validate caregivers and to raise public awareness for this population.

- **National Fire Protection Association**   www.nfpa.org

  This group publishes model codes and fire and building safety standards.

- **National Floor Safety Institute**   www.nfsi.org

  This group's mission is to aid in the prevention of slip-and-fall accidents through education, training, and research.

- **National Institute on Aging**   www.nia.gov

  This government website contains information about aging research and related issues.

- **National Kitchen and Bath Association**   www.nkba.org

  This group of designers, cabinet dealers, and industry professionals represents the kitchen and bath cabinet industry. Its books and research materials include accessibility standards for residential applications.

- **The National Rehabilitation Information Center**   www.naric.com

  This site is a library and information center focusing on disability and rehabilitation research.

- **National Resource Center on Supportive Housing/Home Modification**
  www.usc.edu/dept/gero/nrcshhm

  The Center promotes aging in place and independent living for the frail, elderly, and disabled, with home modification and supportive housing, for successful aging, long-term care, and elder-friendly communities.

- **National Reverse Mortgage Lenders Association**   www.nrmlaonline.org

  This group provides educational resources to educate consumers about the pros and cons of reverse mortgages and to train lenders to be sensitive to clients' needs.

- **Partners for Livable Communities**   www.livable.com

  The organization is developing a "Blueprint for Change" that would outline what an elder-friendly community might be—what it would look like; what services it would provide; how the elderly could be involved in its planning; what special educational, recreational, and cultural opportunities would be needed; how cross-generational contacts could be made; and what programs would make the elderly safe and secure.

- **Rebuilding Together   www.rebuildingtogether.org**

   Rebuilding Together preserves and revitalizes houses and communities, assuring that low-income homeowners, particularly those who are elderly and disabled and families with children, live in warmth, safety, and independence.

- **Retirement Research Foundation   www.rrf.org**

   This group supports efforts that enable older adults to live at home or in residential settings that facilitate independent living.

- **United States Access Board   www.access-board.gov**

   This is a federal agency committed to accessible design. It also provides links to additional information on universal design.

- **United States Department of Veterans Affairs   www.va.gov**

   This site contains information about services and rights provided to veterans including healthcare, education, and compensation and pension benefits.

- **Universal Design Network   www.universaldesign.net**

   This site is an archive of monthly online newsletters with links to international universal design resources.

- **Unlimited by Design   www.ap.buffalo.edu/idea/ubdweb**

   This is the University of Buffalo's research center on universal design.

Appendix B

From Civil Rights to Universal Design and Beyond

A HISTORY OF CIVIL RIGHTS

The concept, principles, and practice of universal design (UD) has but a half-century of history, but with its development, UD has and continues to be a significant influence on the independence of American society. Quite simply, *universal design* is defined as the design of products and the built environment to be usable by everyone, regardless of age, ability, or status in life.[1] The use of UD principles encourages accessibility in residential buildings, commercial, and public facilities and promotes an inclusive, user-friendly approach to the design of products regardless of one's ability.

Prior to 1960, there was no government regulation to protect the rights and independence of those individuals with disabilities to come and go as they chose with little physical restrictions or barriers. But beginning with the American Civil Rights Movement in the late 1950s, which encouraged civil rights, human rights, and social justice, the idea of accessibility as a right of all Americans was conceived. These ideas led to a number of laws that continue to provide equal rights (and accessibility) to all segments of the U.S. population regardless of race, economic status, or handicap.

In 1961, the Veterans Administration was the first government agency to focus on the development of accessible standards for government buildings. With the help of the National Easter Seals Society and the President's Committee on Employment of the Handicapped, guidelines for building access were developed.[2] The standard, titled "A117.1—Making Buildings Accessible To and Usable by the Physically Handicapped," was not enforceable unless adopted by state or local governments.

The first legislation that mandated free accessibility to public spaces, transportation, and education for anyone with a disability was the Architectural Barriers Act of 1968. It required that all federally funded buildings be designed, modified, remodeled, or constructed with no significant obstacles that would restrict a disabled person from living or working in a facility.

Many other pieces of legislation mandated broad civil rights and nondiscrimination including:

- Section 504 of the Rehabilitation Act of 1973, the first of its kind that made it illegal to discriminate on the basis of disability on any one or group receiving federal funding.

- The Individuals with Disabilities Education Act guarantees a free education for disabled children.

- The Fair Housing Amendments Act of 1988 expanded the Civil Rights Act of 1968 to include families and those with disabilities.

In signing the ADA, President George Bush stated, "We are keeping faith with the spirit of our ... forefathers who wrote ... 'We hold these truths to be self-evident, that all men are created equal, that they are endowed by their Creator with certain inalienable rights.' This Act is powerful in its simplicity. It will ensure that people with disabilities are given the basic guarantees ... (of) freedom of choice, control of their lives, the opportunity to blend fully and equally into the ... mosaic of the American mainstream."[3]

But it was the Americans with Disabilities Act that has had the largest impact on building accessibility creating a comprehensive, often complex law but one requiring equal opportunity for individuals with disabilities. President George Bush signed the Act into law in July, 1990. Under the primary enforcement and responsibility of the U.S. Department of Justice, the law and its numerous updates, agreements, and court tests of the law include the civil rights of employment, public accommodations, telecommunications, and access to transportation. It also requires state and local government programs that receive federal financial assistance to give equal opportunity to anyone with a disability.[4]

A HISTORY OF UNIVERSAL DESIGN

To be in compliance with the ADA, many architects, interior designers, contractors, industrial designers, and even those with disabilities struggled with ways to make the design of products and building accessibility supportive and functional while also reducing physical and attitudinal barriers between people with and without disabilities. It was challenging to define singular methods, principles, and practices to integrate people into the mainstream of American life.

Enter Ronald L. Mace, FAIA. Facing the personal and physical challenges of accessibility as a result of having polio, Mace knew too well how difficult it was to get about in a wheelchair. After receiving his degree in architecture from North Carolina State University (NCSU) in 1966, he realized the need for design and accessibility standards and helped to develop the first building code for accessibility. His efforts and contributions were important in the passage of the Fair Housing Amendments Act of 1988 and the ADA.

In 1989, the Center for Universal Design was founded by Mace and headquartered under the College of Design at NCSU. With his strong vision of a future that is "design for all," the Center created research, developed guidelines, and published documents on accessible design that encouraged innovative approaches to design, communication, finance, and management of adaptive housing and accessible buildings.

With funding from the National Institute on Disability and Rehabilitation Research, Mace and a group of architects, product designers, engineers, and environmental design researchers—each advocates of accessibility—gathered together to establish a set of standards to guide product development and building design. The results of their work established the Principles of Universal Design, which has been heralded as a backbone for accessibility around the world.[5]

PRINCIPLES OF UNIVERSAL DESIGN

◾ **PRINCIPLE ONE: Equitable Use**

This principle encourages designs that are functional with the same or equivalent means of use that appeals to a wide number of individuals.

◾ **PRINCIPLE TWO: Flexibility in Use**

Designs following this principle feature a choice in preferences and methods of use, including accommodating left- or right-handed operation while allowing for users' precision, accuracy, and pace of work.

◾ **PRINCIPLE THREE: Simple and Intuitive Use**

In this principle, design should be simple and consistent with the expectation and intuition of the user, with information presented based on its importance while accommodating a wide range of literacy and language skills. Designs should give prompting and feedback during and after each use.

◾ **PRINCIPLE FOUR: Perceptible Information**

This design principle provides that products give appropriate information to the user, using different modes of redundant presentation (pictorial, verbal, tactile) and regardless of ambient conditions or the user's sensory abilities.

◾ **PRINCIPLE FIVE: Tolerance for Error**

Designs in this principle should facilitate their safe use; be forgiving if errors are made and minimizing adverse and unintended consequences. This includes providing warning or error alerts or discouraging unconscious action in tasks that require close attention to the use.

◾ **PRINCIPLE SIX: Low Physical Effort**

This principle calls for designs that are effective, comfortable by their nature, and require little effort to use. Designs should allow the user to successfully operate without a lot of force and without twisting, turning, or repetitive action.

◾ **PRINCIPLE SEVEN: Size and Space for Approach and Use**

In this principle, spatial design should be created that is appropriate to its size, providing a clear line of sight, or making it comfortable to reach whether seated or standing regardless of a user's body size, posture, or mobility.

The Center for Universal Design continues as a national assistance center that provides research and technical information. The Center promotes its philosophy through its publications and instructional materials in the belief that all designs, both product and building environments, should be usable by any one individual without regard to age, ability, or circumstance.[6]

Appendix C

Products and Vendors

The following websites are not all specifically for the aging client or the physically challenged. However, we provide here a list of companies that have items in their line that could be attributed to aging in place and universal design, accessibility, and adaptability.

The authors make no recommendation of any of these resources—they are provided as a convenience for the reader.

RESOURCE LIBRARIES AND DIRECTORIES

DesignerEsources
www.designeresources.com An important Internet resource for the design community

Bellacorpro.com
www.bellacorpro.com Primarily a lighting resource but features many other additional products

Trade Only Design Library, Inc.
www.todl.com The industry's largest product research and specification database, online or in print

Accessibility Products

Abledata
http://www.abledata.com/abledata.cfm?pageid=19327&ksectionid=19327
Links to products providing assistance with daily living as well as products for the deaf and hard of hearing and the blind and those with low vision

ActiveForever
www.activeforever.com Offers independent living products and innovative items for everyday life

Adaptive Access
www.adaptiveaccess.com Lists adaptive equipment and accessibility products specialists throughout the United States; it also offers wheelchair-accessible home modifications, remodeling, and construction in Houston, Texas.

Alzheimer's Store
www.alzstore.com Offers products for those with Alzheimer's and their caregivers

Be Able To Do—Functional Solutions
http://www.beabletodo.com/StoreFront.bok North Coast Medical Functional Solutions Catalog offers products for use in the kitchen and bath as well as other parts of the house to help with daily tasks.

Beyond Barriers
www.beyondbarriers.com Offers a full line of accessible, barrier-free, and universally designed products and services to improve daily living conditions for people with disabilities

Can-we-talk—EM Enterprises
www.can-we-talk.com Features various voice recognition programs for homes and offices; also features many useful products for people with physical, visual, learning, and reading disabilities

Closet Carousel—White Home Products
http://closets.net/indexnof.htm Features an innovative product that allows physically challenged individuals to reach for their belongings

Comfort House
www.comforthouse.com The source for products that make your life easier

The Dispenser
www.dispenser.com Dispensers for shampoos, conditioners, soaps, and lotions that can be mounted in the shower

Gold Violin
www.goldviolin.com Offers a variety of products for making activities of daily living easier for the hearing impaired, the sight impaired, and the disabled

Grabit
www.grabitonline.com A portable grab bar manufacturer offering a new kind of grab bar that requires no drilling or stud, and it can be positioned anywhere you need.

Great Grips
www.greatgrips.com A very affordable alternative to lever hardware; can be fitted for round doorknobs and modified for faucets.

Harris Communication
www.harriscomm.com Company specializes in products for the hard of hearing but also has a "senior store" of products to make daily living easier

Hafele
http://www.hafele.com/us/ Offers a variety of accessories, hardware, and lighting

Life@Home, Inc.
www.lifehome.com An online store with many safety and convenience products available

Maddak, Inc. Ableware
http://service.maddak.com/about.asp Offers many special assistive devices for a variety of needs throughout the house

Max-Ability, Inc.
www.max-ability.com Provides solutions for a user-friendly, safe environment

MaxiAids
http://www.maxiaids.com/store/default.asp Offers a variety of products for better living

MOMS Home Healthcare Products
www.momscatalog.com Offers hard-to-find healthcare products and a variety of products for daily living

NanoPac, Inc.
http://www.nanopac.com/Cintex3.htm CINTEX3 is an environmental control system for use with voice recognition systems (such as DragonDictate, NaturallySpeaking) or any other keyboard replacement. There are three major components: telephone, appliance, and infrared. Bed controls and A/C controls are optional.

Ocutech
www.ocutech.com—Funded by the National Institute of Health, the company develops and manufactures VES® low-vision telescopic aids, including hands-free magnification.

Sammons' Preston
www.sammonspreston.com Offers rehabilitation equipment and a variety of products for daily living

Accessibility—Exterior

Beneficial Designs, Inc.
http://www.beneficialdesigns.com/rectech/rectech.html Uses recreational and leisure technologies to provide outdoor access to recreation for everyone

Designer Doors
www.designerdoors.com Provides wood garage and walk-through doors; overhead operation and custom or standard design

Gardener's Supply Company
www.gardeners.com Offers many gardening products, some of which particularly lend themselves to universal design

Gardenscape
www.gardenscapetools.com Offers children's gardening tools as well as tools for accessible gardening for all

Hill Hiker
www.hillhiker.com Manufactures lift systems for steep home sites, waterfront properties, and mountainous terrain

Marine Innovations
www.marineinnovations.com Manufactures incline tram systems to allow for the enjoyment of the pleasures of hilltop living; products include Hill Climbers, Lakeside Lifts, and Lake Lifts, Hill Lifts, and Hillside Trams

Playworld Systems
http://www.playworldsystems.com/prodset.html Offers play systems including accessible play equipment

Redd Team Manufacturing
www.reddteam.com Manufactures accessibility products for ramps including the Ramp Rider

SafDek
www.safdek.com Pathway Services, Inc. produces non-slip playground and pool equipment.

Scenery Solutions
http://www.vegherb.com/ Provides designs for raised gardens

Vertical Platform Lifts
www.vertical-platform-lifts.com Manufactures vertical platform lifts

Verti-Gro
www.vertigro.com Offers products for vertical planting

Accessories—General

Barrier Free Architecturals, Inc.
www.barrierfree.org Offers unique accessibility products

Control Products, Inc.
www.controlproductsinc.com Provides innovative technology in custom electronic design and manufacturing; includes the FreezeAlarm

Design Linc
www.designlinc.com Offers design resource information for products and services available to the physically challenged and their caregivers

Dynamic Living
www.dynamic-living.com Offers a variety of helpful products that promote a convenient, comfortable, and safe home environment for people of all ages

Elder Web
www.elderweb.com An award-winning long-term care and elder care directory with good articles, resources, and links; an excellent resource for helpful universal design accessory items from various companies

First Street
www.firststreetonline.com A leader in innovation and technology; offers a variety of innovative products

My One Remote
www.myoneremote.com A product that operates as a cordless phone and a remote for almost every other home entertainment device

Pik Stik
www.PikStik.com The original all-purpose tool to extend your reach

Planet Mobility
http://www.planetmobility.com/index.html Offers a number of products from which to choose for all areas inside and outside the home to help provide independence

QuietCare
www.quietcare.com Functions as a 24–hour-a-day, 7–day-a-week early detection and early warning system that lets caregivers and family members know that a loved one is safe. It recognizes emerging problems before they become emergencies.

Harmonic Environments
www.harmonicenvironments.com Offers architectural water elements, including indoor waterfalls.

Ultra Cane
http://www.soundforesight.co.uk/ultracane_demonstrator.htm Cane that alerts users to obstacles

Universal Mall—Path Lighter
http://www.universalc.com/cane.html A path lighter cane that illuminates paths, stairs, and so on as you use it

Accessories—Exterior

Abundant Earth
www.abundantearth.com Natural, organic, recycled, and health-inspiring products

Copper Forge
www.copperforge.com Features copper garden art, including sprinklers

Lunaform of Maine
www.lunaform.com Offers garden planters, urns, and so on that can withstand the harshest elements and are all hand turned

Rain Chains Direct
www.rainchainsdirect.com Supplier of rain chains and rain cups

Stone Forest
www.stoneforest.com Features hand-carved granite products: sculptures, fountains, lanterns, tableware, and so on.

Woodstock Chimes
www.chimes.com The source for musical items for the home and garden for 25 years; many of the chimes are tuned to scales or melodies from some of the world's most enduring musical cultures.

Appliances—General Home

DuoVac
http://www.duovac.com/pages/nous_joindre/coordonnees.aspx?lang=EN-US Offers DuoVac central vacuum systems

GE Appliances
http://www.geappliances.com/shop/prdct/wsh_dry/ Offers GE laundry equipment

Kenyon Custom
http://www.kenyonmarine.com/index.html Manufactures Kenyon Marine custom ceramic glass cooktops

Kohler Residential Power
http://www.kohlerpowersystems.com/residential.html Provides Kohler Power Systems back-up generators

M&S Systems
www.mssystems.com Provides M&S Systems central vacuums

Nutone
www.thinkvacuums.com/nutone/vacuums.htm Manufactures central vacuum systems

Salton
http://www.esalton.com/control/main Home of the Smart Appliances such as the Smart Microwave, Smart Coffeemaker, Icebox entertainment center, and so on.

Universal Appliance and Kitchen Center—Eurotech
http://www.universal-akb.com/eurwasdryerc.html Eurotech combination washer-dryer with no dryer vent needed

Vacuflo
www.vacuflo.com Manufactures central vacuum systems

Whirlpool Appliances
www.whirlpool.com Offers great variety of new laundry appliances

Automation

AD-AS
www.ad-as.com Furniture solutions for universal design including electronics to move cabinets up and down

Assis-Tech
www.assis-tech.com Offers a variety of products including adjustable sink and cooktop mechanisms and remote control devices

Home Automated Living (HAL)
www.automatedliving.com Offer a variety of products to create a "smart" home; HAL's vision is to provide consumers with the freedom to control their homes—and all the wonderful technology within—by voice or by Internet, from anywhere.

Auton Motorized Systems
www.auton.com Offers television lifts

Control 4
www.control4.com Manufacture home automation systems

HAI
www.homeauto.com Offer integrated security and automation products, providing comfort, convenience, and safety for homeowners and businesses around the world

i Command
www.i-command.com Home automation systems offering the latest in whole house systems control

Intellon
www.intellon.com A world leader in powerline technologies; creating instant networks

Lutron
www.lutron.com Specializes in technology for home automation—lighting, window treatments, etc.—for ease and safety

Master Voice

www.mastervoice.com Home environmental control system that responds to voice commands

Mecoshade

www.mechoshade.com Remote-controlled power window treatments

Smart Home

www.smarthome.com Offers wireless home automation products, lighting, and systems

S M Automatic

www.smautomatic.com Manufactures automated window treatments

Truth Hardware

www.truth.com Offers a power window (and door) operator

Universal Design Products

www.universal-design-products.com Accessible products for kitchens and baths, including height-adjustable cabinets, shelving, countertops, and so on.

Vantage Controls

www.vantagecontrols.com Manufactures home automation and lighting control equipment

Victor e-lok

www.victorelok.com High security digital locks with integrated burglar alarm

Bathroom Accessories

Atlanta Baths

http://www.atlantabaths.com/barrier_free_accessories.htm Offers a variety of barrier-free bath and shower products

Baci Mirrors—Remcraft Lighting Products, Inc.

www.bacimirrors.com Offers magnifying mirrors and lighting

Franklin Brass

www.franklinbrass.com Features decorative bathware as well as a complete selection of grab bars, tubs, showers, and toilet safety items to fit the needs of safety-conscious consumers

Hewi LifeSystem

http://www.hewi.com/produkte/produktuebersicht/barrierefrei/ A new generation of barrier-free sanitary products; all are flexible, adaptable, and expandable

Mobility, Inc.

www.mobilityinc.net Manufacture air lift toilets and other products

Otto Bock Health Care Products

www.ottobockus.com Leader in healthcare products; go to "products" and "rehabilitation/daily living" for bath aids

Planet Mobility
http://www.planetmobility.com/index.html Offers a number of products from which to choose for all areas inside and outside the home to help provide independence

Robern
www.robern.com Bathroom storage—can include lighting, mirror defoggers, interior electrical outlets, and so on.

Sani-Med Healthcare
www.sppi.com (Click on "Sani-Med Division") Markets healthcare and handicapped seating aids to consumers, hospitals, and nursing homes

Sunrise Medical
www.sunrisemedical.com Guardian padded transfer bench for bathing with commode opening

Bathroom—Grab Bars

Adaptive Access
http://www.adaptiveaccess.com/grabbar_handrail.php Grab bar installation

DiaDot Disability Solutions
http://www.diadot.com/catalog/ Offers a variety of grab bars

Franklin Brass
www.franklinbrass.com Features decorative bathware as well as a complete selection of grab bars, tubs, showers, and toilet safety items to fit the needs of safety-conscious consumers

Grabit
www.grabitonline.com A portable grab bar manufacturer offering a new kind of grab bar that requires no drilling or stud, and it can be positioned anywhere you need.

Great Grabz
www.greatgrabz.com Offers a line of grab bars that add style and beauty to the bath while providing safety for all ages

HEWI
www.hewi.com New U.S. website with terrific products and color selections for grab bars, folding seats, tilting mirrors, and more; all products designed for barrier-free use

Invisible Caregiver
www.invisiblecaregiver.com Maker of the OuttaBed and Off-The-Pot all-in-one grab bar products

Moen
www.moen.com Moen has incorporated a variety of "bath safety" products into their line, including grab bars and anchors.

WingIts
www.wingits.com Offers a patented grab bar fastening system, as well as shower and tub seats, curved shower rods, and other bathroom accessories

Bathroom—Miscellaneous

HygieniCare
www.hygienicare.com Features wheelchair-accessible disability bathrooms including all-in-one disability bath

Pressalit Care
http://www.acessinc.com/flexible_system.htm Provides easier access to Pressalit Care products and information than the Pressalit company website

Tubcut
www.tubcut.com Easily convert bathtub to shower with tub cutout

TubSafe
http://www.stopslipping.com/TubSafe.htm Offers slip-resistant surface treatment for tubs

Bathroom—Plumbing Fixtures

Alsons
www.alsons.com Manufactures hand showers, shower heads, palm showers, custom shower systems, and body sprays

American Standard
www.americanstandard-us.com Offers a variety of ADA-compliant products

American Whirlpool
www.americanwhirlpool.com Luxury hydrotherapy tubs—some with doors

Aquabath
www.aquabath.com Offers barrier-free showers and tubs/showers

Aquassure
www.aquassure.com New approach to "walk-in" tub; created a model with a sliding door designed to be installed at a height for the user to transfer to the floor of the tub and slide in; also offers grab bars and recessed tub flow.

Bathease
www.bathease.com Offers a bathtub/shower with a door

Best Bath Systems
www.best-bath.com Offers a variety of accessible bathing products, including walk-in tubs and ADA showers

Brizo
www.brizofaucet.com Premium faucet brand crafted by Delta

Brondell
www.brondell.com American company, developer of innovative, quality bathroom products, including their bidet toilet seat

Caroma
www.sustainablesolutions.com Caroma dual flush water-saving technology toilets—LEED product solutions—with 4-inch trap is the largest in the industry; particularly important for hotels and commercial projects.

Comfort Designs
http://www.comfortdesignsbathware.com/index.cfm A division of Praxis Industries developed to focus on their all-new line of user-friendly and code-compliant bathware

Delta Faucet
www.deltafaucet.com Both commercial and residential easy-use faucet

Dornbracht
www.dornbracht.com Variety of bathroom lavatory fixtures with single and double lever handles; also electronic bathroom faucet—kitchen plumbing fixtures with single lever mixers & sprays

Duravit
www.duravit.us/ International site for Duravit plumbing products, including Starck wall-mounted toilets

Gerberit
www.us.geberit.com Manufactures recessed wall-mounted toilet

Grohe
www.groheamerica.com Offers a variety of single-lever faucets, electronic faucets, showerheads, and other products

Hansgrohe
www.hansgrohe-usa.com Manufactures kitchen and bath faucets and shower systems

Hastings Bath
www.hastingstilebath.com Manufactures high-quality bath and tile products, including a number of wall-mounted sinks

Interbath-Ondine
http://www.interbath.com/ondine/ Manufactures innovative units with lighted showerheads, remote systems, hand-held showers, and shower organizational systems

Invacare Continuing Care
www.invacare.com Offers bath and shower products primarily for commercial use; some can be used in residential projects.

Jaclo
www.jaclo.com Manufactures hand-held showers and hoses; ADA compliant

Kohler
www.kohler.com Offers ADA-compliant products, Comfort Height toilets, and more

Lasco Bathware
www.lascobathware.com Offers a Freedomline product line of barrier-free products for the bathroom

Mustee
www.mustee.com Offers shower and bath walls and floors and plumbing products for a retrofit

Porcher

http://www.porcher-us.com/ Offers a variety of ADA-compliant products, including a number of wall-mounted sinks

Soft Bathtub

www.softbathtubs.com Offers Jacuzzi tubs, hydrotherapy tubs, deep and soft bathtubs, and spas

Toto

www.totousa.com Offers a wide selection of toilets, sinks, tubs, and other bathroom products

Bath—Ventilation

Broan-Nutone

www.broan-nutone.com Offers a variety of premium quality air filtration, ventilation, and household convenience products

Cabinets and Storage

Blum

www.blum.com Provides functional hardware for kitchen cabinet industry—main focus on lift systems, concealed hinges, and drawer runners; includes Servo-Drive™ touch control system and Blumotion™ for doors

Cabico

www.cabico.com One of North America's leading manufacturers of custom cabinetry for kitchens, bathrooms, or any other room in the home

Dura Supreme Cabinetry

www.durasupreme.com Cabinet manufacturer who meets ADA requirements

ezyfold

www.ezyfold.com Provides cabinet and closet hardware

Grass America

www.grassusa.com Offers functional cabinet hardware and organizational items, including Sensotronic™ touch control system with a brain

Hafele

http://www.hafele.com/us/index.htm Manufactures furniture, cabinet, closet, and architectural hardware—many of their products provide increased accessibility.

Knape & Vogt

www.kv.com Manufacturers a variety of functional hardware, storage-related components, and ergonomic products to help with organization and that make life easier

Kraftmaid Cabinetry

www.kraftmaid.com Cabinet manufacturer with Passport Line specifically designed for accessibility and convenience

Neff Kitchens

www.neffkitchens.com Cabinet manufacturer with a variety of accessories; select line of cabinetry for those who are chemical sensitive; virtually free of VOC emissions

Quality Cabinets

www.qualitycabinets.com Cabinets for the kitchen, bath, and other rooms in the house; also manufactures Woodstar Cabinets which meet ADA requirements

Rev-a-Shelf

www.rev-a-shelf.com Produce a variety of products to make life easier and more organized behind those cupboard doors and drawer fronts

Shelf Conversions

www.shelfconversions.com Custom designed storage solutions with glide out shelving

Soss

www.soss.com Ultralatch hardware to open doors with elbow as well as invisible hinges

Wellborn Cabinet, Inc.

www.wellborn.com Cabinet manufacturer who meets ADA requirements

Elevators, Lifts, Dumbwaiters

Acme Home Elevator

www.acmehomeelevator.com Manufactures elevators, incline lifts, dumbwaiters, and so on

Acorn Stairlifts

http://www.acornstairlifts.com/us/ Manufactures stairlifts

Accessibility Design Associates

www.adaproducts.com A family-owned and operated business specializing in meeting needs of the physically challenged; with first-hand experience in the field, they offer products, consulting, service, rentals, and more

Baronmead International Limited

www.baronmead.com English company carrying the Stairmatic, a battery-powered mobile stair climber as well as the Access Lift, Wheelchair Carrier, stairlifts, and more

Bruno

www.bruno.com Producer of mobility and accessibility products, including scooters, wheelchair lifts, and curved or straight stairlifts

Concord Elevator

www.concordelevator.com Leading designer and manufacturer of residential elevators, luxury home elevators, commercial elevators, and lifts for over 30 years

Powerlift Dumbwaiters, Corp.
www.dumbwaiters.com Manufacturers a variety of standard and custom dumbwaiters

Garaventa
www.garaventa.ca Canadian manufacturer of elevators, vertical lifts, and more

Handi-Lift
www.handilift.com Manufactures elevators, incline chair lifts, and attached and portable stair lifts, and more

Inclinator Company of America
www.inclinator.com Manufactures elevators, dumbwaiters, stair lifts, vertical lifts, and chair lifts

MAC's Lift Gate, Inc.
www.macslift.com Producers of simple, residential vertical platform lifts

KONE, Inc.
www.myecospace.com KONE EcoSpace™ is designed to fit in the hydraulic footprint and still deliver pure traction, machine-room-less performance. It's an ideal low-rise solution for residential, office, or public-access spaces.

Raydoor
www.raydoor.com Designs panels that can divide the space and cut down on noise, while not prohibiting light from passing through

Savara
www.savara.com Producers of simple, residential vertical platform lifts

Silver Cross
www.silvercross-elevators.com Home elevator guide's mandate is to provide free information to assist in the selection of residential home elevators in the United States, Canada, and England. Accessibility solutions provide freedom to access all parts of the home.

Pneumatic Vacuum Elevators, LLC.
www.vacuumelevators.com Developers of vacuum elevators

Waupaca Elevator
www.waupacaelevator.com Manufactures elevators, dumbwaiters, and more

Wheelovator
www.wheelovator.com Manufactures residential elevators

Fabrics

Crypton Fabric
www.cryptonfabric.com Choose from suedes, wovens, prints, twills, metro, chenille, and even velvets. All are extremely strong and durable, yet soft, breathable, and beautiful.

Sunbrella
www.sunbrella.com Fabrics available at many fabric showrooms; products stand up well to light

Toray Ultrasuede, Inc.
www.ultrasuede.com Used for upholstery, wall coverings, and so on; over 200,000 double-rubs; clean with soap and water; commercial fabric for use in residential spaces

Flooring

Amtico
www.amtico.com Vinyl flooring with many custom possibilities

Antron
http://www.antron.invista.com/content/toolbox/ant05.shtml Toolbox with environmental calculator, carpet mentor, and so on

Armstrong
www.armstrong.com Among other things, you can add flooring to uploaded photographs (and change other options)

Deltawarm
www.delta-warm.com Floor-warming and snow-melting products

Dodge-Regupol, Inc.
http://www.regupol.com/resident/corktile_frame.html Leaders in recycled products technology; Dodge Cork Tiles are nonlaminate, 100 percent cork tiles

Duro-Design
www.duro-design.com Bamboo and cork flooring

Infloor Heating Systems
www.infloor-heat.com Radiant flooring

FLOR
www.flor.com Interface environmentally friendly modular kitchen and bath flooring; impervious to moisture, easy to clean, and inexpensive to replace; "rug-in-a-box" or "room-in-a-box"

Halo Floors
www.halofloors.com Founded by the ex-CEO of Amtico USA, the company offers one of the widest ranges of luxury vinyl flooring in the industry for the commercial specifiers; also for residential use

Heatizon Systems
www.heatizon.com Offers floor-warming, radiant in-floor space heating, and snow-melting products

Natural Cork, Ltd. Company
www.naturalcork.com U.S. importer and supplier of cork flooring, wall covering, and underlayment

Nuheat
www.nuheat.com Electric floor heating system to warm ceramic tile and natural stone floors; $1/_8$ inch thick making it quick and easy to install directly between tile and subfloor with minimal increase in height of floor

Pawling Corporation
www.pawling.com Manufacturer of rubber mats; could be inserted into entry area for non-slip capabilities

Posi Grip
www.posigrip.com Provides Posi Grip non-slip finish for floors, tubs, and showers

Slip Grip
www.slipgrip.com ADA-compliant, wet-floor safety without destroying the finish of the floor; for polished stone, porcelain tiles, glazed ceramic tile, and more

Sponge-Cushion
www.sponge-cushion.com Rubber cushion recommended under carpet for radiant floors

SunTouch
www.suntouch.net SunTouch® electric radiant heat mats are designed to warm tile and stone floors in bathrooms, kitchens, entries, and sunrooms.

Teragren
www.teragren.com Bamboo flooring; expanded to include Teragren bamboo flooring in random lengths, wide planks, and floating applications as well as bamboo accessories and stair parts

TerraMai
www.terramai.com Reclaimed woods from around the corner and around the world

Thermosoft
www.thermosoftinternational.com Offers tile floor heaters, ThermoTile, and ThermoFloor as well as other products using patented technology

Warmboard
www.warmboard.com Offers radiant heating and subflooring in one

Warmly Yours
www.warmlyyours.com Offers radiant floor heating

Warm Tiles
www.warmtiles.com An electric floor-warming system

Warmup
www.warmup.com Offers radiant floor heating

Watts Radiant Heat
www.wattsradiant.com Offers floor-heating and snow-melting technologies

Weyerhaeuser Lyptus Flooring
http://www.weyerhaeuser.com/ourbusinesses/buildingproducts/building
materials/ourproducts/lyptus/ "Beautiful, practical, and eco-friendly high-
grade hardwood from Brazil"

WE Cork
www.wecork.com Manufacturer of cork flooring for more than 150 years

Wicanders
www.wicanders.com "Cork flooring since 1868" by Ipocork

Wilsonart
www.wilsonart.com Provides flooring, solid surfaces, counters, and more
with WilsonArt Laminate

Flooring—Outdoor; Decking and Railing

Cable Rail
www.cablerail.com Light, open railings that let you see through to the
view, yet remain strong, durable, and virtually maintenance free

CorrectDeck
http://www.correctdeck.com/products/cx/default.htm CX with Safeguard;
an anti-microbial composite decking; resistant to mold, mildew, stains, and
color fading

Eon
www.eonoutdoor.com A complete alternative decking system composed of
100 percent plastic with a wood grain finish

Everwood
www.ipe-wood.com Distributor of Ipe and other rare wood products

FiberTech Polymers, Inc.
www.fibertechpolymers.com Composite manufacturer with the industry's
first composite privacy fencing product; privacy without maintenance; also
supplies benderboard and other products

Finyl Vinyl
www.finylvinylbp.com Provides fencing, railings, and decks

GeoDeck
www.geodeck.com Manufacturer of composite decks and railings; claims it
is fade-resistant

Global Decking
www.globaldecking.com Vinyl waterproof systems and decking that also
offers an aluminum railing system available in pickets or glass

Nexwood
www.nexwood.com Composite building product used for decks, fences,
docks, and railings

Rubberific Mulch
http://www.rubberificmulch.com/index.asp Recycled tires used for mulch and play areas

Rubber Sidewalks
http://www.rubbersidewalks.com/default.asp Recycled tires used for sidewalks

Tendura
www.tendura.com Offers composite porch flooring in two sizes: the traditional 1 × 4 inch tongue-and-groove planks, and the larger classic 1 × 6 inch tongue-and-groove planks

Timbertech.
www.timbertech.com Composite decking that has a skid-free, splinter-free surface that doesn't need painting, staining, or sealing; patented process uses a variety of cellulose materials, wood flour, and virgin polyethylene

Trex
www.trex.com Provides decking and railing products made from a combination of reclaimed wood and plastic

Furniture—Beds

Electropedic Beds
www.electropedicbeds.com Carry a variety of adjustable beds, including the high-low models

Ergo
www.ergobeds.com Adjustable power beds, Tempur-Pedic mattresses, Sleep on Air, and more

Golden Rest Adjustable Beds
www.goldenrest-adjustable-beds.com Carry a variety of adjustable beds, including the high-low models

Royal-Pedic
www.royal-pedic.com Manufactures a variety of mattresses, including custom mattresses and adjustable beds

Select Comfort
www.selectcomfort.com Manufactures mattresses with individual controls

Transfermaster
www.transfermaster.com Manufacturer of Hi-Low bed, which combines the functions of a medical bed with the look of a residential bed

Zoom Room
www.zoom-room.com Wireless retractable bed—even better than Murphy bed

Furniture—General

Arcadia Chair
www.arcadiachair.com Commercial furniture with some very good reception furniture for residential use

Bernhardt Design
www.bernhardtdesign.com Transitional and contemporary commercial furniture that can be used for residential design as well

Hooker Furniture
www.hookerfurniture.com Primarily office and home entertainment furniture

KI
www.ki.com/healthcare Several "sleep" chairs that could be advantageous for someone who is trying to use their current recliner for sleeping, as well as single sleepers for use by caregivers

Loewenstein
www.loewensteininc.com Offers commercial furniture with residential possibilities

St. Timothy
www.sttimothychair.com Contract manufacturer with healthcare products for aging population and universal design

Styker Medical
http://www.strykerbertec.ca/eng/products/furniture/tables.asp Offers the Tru-Fit Overbed Table

Furniture—Home Office

Health Postures
www.healthpostures.com or www.anglechair.com Offers a great adjustable computer chair, keyboard, monitor, and more for functional comfort, proper back alignment, and wrist and lumbar support

Brayton International
www.brayton.com Offers commercial furniture with applicable use for aging; also a healthcare division

Brueton
www.brueton.com Commercial line of furniture; mostly with residential application

Campbell Contract
www.campbellcontract.com Leading commercial manufacturers of commercial seating and occasional tables, many of which are applicable to residential design

Davis
www.davisfurniture.com Commercial line of furniture with some applicable to residential; new COMpod offered for working at home with beneficial flexibility

Harden Contract
www.hardencontract.com Commercial furniture, much of which will work well for the home

Haworth
www.haworth.com Office furniture that can meet the needs of the home office

Herman Miller
www.hermanmiller.com Furniture for the office that can work in the home

Neutral Posture, Inc.
www.igoergo.com Texas-based manufacturer of ergonomic office seating products and accessories

Nova Solutions, Inc.
www.novadesk.com Technology solutions for e-environments

Steelcase
www.steelcase.com Furniture for the office that can work in the home

Furniture—Motion

All Liftchairs
www.all-lift-chairs.com Offers a variety of lift chairs, toilet seat lifts, bath lifts, seat lifts, table lifts, and more; also distributes Pride Mobility and Golden Lift chairs

Berkline
www.berkline.com Offers a variety of recliners, sofa recliners, and theater seating designs

Med-Lift & Mobility, Inc.
www.medlift.com Offers lift chairs and recliners

Pride Mobility Products Corp.
http://www.pridemobility.com/products/lift_chair/lift_chair.html Offers a variety of lift chairs, including one that reclines far enough for sleeping

Furniture—Outdoor

Barlow Tyrie
http://www.teak.com/index.cfm Offers teak furniture including benches for resting while enjoying the garden

Dayva
www.dayvacontract.com Offers a variety of outdoor furnishings including umbrellas, umbrella lighting, protective coverings, patio heaters, and mobile serving units; also have remote-controlled market umbrella

Flower to the People
www.flower2people.com Offers landscape design and Pamalex—outdoor furniture of Ipe wood; also art and "custom views"

Giati Furniture
www.giati.com Offers furniture for indoors and out, including a number of outdoor dining chairs with arms

Gloster
www.gloster.com Offers outdoor furniture, for contract and residential use, including benches and arm chairs to help all ages enjoy the garden

Kingsley Bate
www.kingsleybate.com Offers teak outdoor furnishings for pools and patios, including benches and armchairs for all to enjoy the garden

Landscape Forms
www.landscapeforms.com Provides commercial outdoor furnishings, including waste receptacles; many products can work well for residential use as well

O.W. Lee
www.owlee.com Provides handcrafted outdoor furniture and accessories, including chairs and benches for all ages to enjoy outdoor living

Steel Living
www.steelliving.com Offers handcrafted home and garden décor, including raised planters

Suncoast Furniture
www.suncoastfurniture.com Manufactures aluminum outdoor furniture, many pieces with arms for added support for the user

Sutherland
www.sutherlandteak.com Offers furniture for indoors and outdoors

Terra Furniture
www.terrafurniture.com Offers outdoor furniture and lighting systems

Tropitone
www.tropitone.com Offers outdoor furnishings for residential and hospitality use

Veneman Collections
www.venemangroup.com Offers outdoor furniture, including aluminum frames with wood trim and Sunbrella fabrics

Walters Wicker
www.walterswicker.com Provides indoor and outdoor furniture in a variety of materials

Whitecraft
www.whitecraft.net Offers wicker furniture for indoor and outdoor use

Wood Classics
www.woodclassics.com Provides teak garden furniture

Woodard Furniture
www.woodard-furniture.com Provides outdoor furniture for commercial and residential use

Lighting

Acrilex Inc.
http://www.acrilex.com/lightinghome.cfm Acriglo Photoluminescent to provide illumination without back-up power sources during a power outage, or to extend the period of illumination once battery back-up fails

Concealite
www.concealite.com Offers a unique line of emergency lighting fixtures to meet all existing egress codes

Lite Touch, Inc.
www.litetouch.com Provides solutions for lighting control and automation

Lutron
http://www.lutron.com/eh/ Provides lighting and window treatment control systems, including HomeWorks® whole-home lighting control systems as well as RadioRA® and AuroRa® for all budgets; extends beyond lighting control to window treatments, security, and more

Ozonelite
www.ozonelite.com Provides a bacteria-zapping light–air purification system that creates a photo-catalytic reaction that destroys microbes

SentryLight
www.sentrylight.com During loss of utility power recessed lamp housing automatically emerges from a wall or ceiling and illuminates the area, providing more than 90 minutes of emergency egress lighting.

Solatube International, Inc.
http://www.solatube.com/residential/res_ideabook.php Manufactures a Solatube Daylighting System—a tubular, new 21–inch square model for residential or commercial use; captures sunlight and diffuses in the room

Vulux America
www.veluxusa.com Designs skylights and the Sun Tunnel light tube

Kitchen—Appliances

American Range
http://www.americanrange.com/residential/30walloven.html Manufactures a 30-inch French door oven

Asko
www.askousa.com Manufactures dishwashers that can be installed under 34-inch counters; other appliances also available

Caldera
www.calderacorp.com Manufacturer of cooktops with unusual shapes; allow installation in small spaces with a variety of operation possibilities

Dacor
www.dacor.com Offer a variety of appliances, including 30-inch-wide dishwashers, electric glide control cooktops, microwave drawers, and appliances for outdoor entertaining

Fisher & Paykel
usa.fisherpaykel.com Offers dish drawer dishwasher, among other items including the DCS brand cooking appliances

Frigidaire
www.frigidaire.com Offers oven with side-hinged door as well as other appliances

Gaggenau
www.gaggenau.com Offers ovens with side-hinged doors as well as other appliances

GE Appliances
www.geappliances.com Offers a variety of "aging client-friendly" appliances

Haier
www.haieramerica.com Offers both standard and custom small and large appliances

Inside Advantage
www.insideadvantage.com Listing of Whirlpool appliances with links to Amana, JennAir, Kitchenaid, and Maytag

Kenmore
www.kenmore.com Offers a variety of appliances including the triple-door side-by-side refrigerator

Kenyon Appliances
http://www.kenyonappliances.com/custom/customhome.html Manufacturer of marine cooktops now designing them for homes that are "aging-client friendly"

LG Appliances
http://us.lge.com/index.jhtml Offers bottom-mount refrigerators, narrow refrigerators, Internet refrigerators, microwaves, combination microwave/toaster, laundry, and air conditioners

Miele
www.miele.com Offers appliances, including convection steam ovens, 24-inch ovens for easier access, and appliances that are simple and intuitive in directions to use

Smeg
http://www.smeg.it/international/menu.htm Italian company that produces cooktops, dishwashers, refrigerators, and other appliances

Sub-Zero and Wolfe
www.subzero.com Offers built-in refrigerators and other appliances

Viking Range
http://www.vikingrange.com/consumer/index.jsp Offers Viking Range cooktops, ovens, ranges, microwaves, and portable induction cooktops good for flexible cooking

Kitchens—Compact and Smaller Appliances

Dwyer Kitchens
http://www.dwyerkitchens.com/cervitorDefault.aspx Cervitor compact kitchens—some with pull-out surfaces and open under sink areas

Danby
http://www.danby.com/index.asp? Offers a variety of appliances, particularly specialty appliances and appliances for small spaces

Equator Appliance
www.equatorappliance.com Offers a variety of space-saving appliances

FiveStar
www.fivestarrange.com Offers apartment-size professional ranges

Marvel Industries
www.marvelindustries.com Manufactures under-counter refrigerators in ADA-accessible styles

Kitchens—Plumbing Fixtures

Elkay
www.elkay.com Offers pull-out faucets, lever handles, and more

Grohe
www.groheamerica.com Offers a variety of faucets

Kohler
www.kohler.com "Assures" kitchen sink, as well as other products for the kitchen and bath, meets ADA standards

KWC
www.kwcfaucets.com Offers pull-out faucets, lever handles, and water station, which can be used for island installations to offer flexibility in food preparation

Price Pfister
www.pricepfister.com Offers faucets with single control/lever

Sterling
www.sterlingplumbing.com Manufactures ADA-accessible sinks; a division of Kohler

Kitchen—Miscellaneous

Dycem
www.dycem-ns.com Offers a variety of non-slip products

TRUEBRO
www.truebro.com Offers under-sink protective devices and enclosures

White Home Products
www.closets.net Manufactures a kitchen carousel

Miscellaneous

Air2Water
www.air2water.net Offers a water-generating machine designed to draw moisture from the air and purify it

BJ Industries, Inc.
www.bjindustries.com Manufactures the Adjust-a-Sink System—a patented telescoping drain designed to provide universal access for the able-bodied and the physically challenged

Ramps

AlumiRamp, Inc.
www.alumiramp.com "Bridges the gap" with modular ramping systems

Bayport Healthcare
www.bayporthealthcare.com Represented in the United States in Kansas; the company manufactures home medical equipment in a variety of very useful products including portable ramps

National Ramp
www.nationalramp.com Manufactures a low-cost modular ramp system that is easy to use and quickly installed; can be purchased or rented

Prairie View Industries, Inc.
www.pviramps.com Offers a variety of folding ramps that fold up and can be carried like a suitcase

Rehab Designs, Inc.
www.rehabdesigns.com Provides wheelchair and scooter ramps

Windows and Doors

Door Butler/RA Products Co., Inc.
www.doorbutler.com Provides a non-electric screen door opener and closer

Gentleman Door Automatic Door Openers
www.gentlemandoor.com Provides low-profile units with remote or palm buttons to operate

Henselstone Window & Door Systems
http://www.henselstone.com/default.asp?P=1 Offers a variety of windows and doors, including those designed with the aging client in mind

Lutron
http://www.lutron.com/eh Provides window shading control systems as well as lighting designs

Mechoshade
http://www.mechoshade.com/site/home.cfm Provides commercial and residential manual and motorized shades

Medeco High Security Locks
www.medeco.com Designs security systems, including a Captive Thumb-turn Deadbolt, for easy exits in emergencies

Open Sesame
www.opensesamedoor.com Manufactures remote-controlled door opening systems

NanoPac, Inc.
http://www.nanopac.com/Open%20Sesame.htm Offers Open Sesame Un-locks, which opens and closes a door by voice command (with one of NanoPac's ECU units) or a wink of the eye or a touch of a remote-controlled switch

Power Access Corporation
www.power-access.com Manufacturer of an automatic door opener that was designed to assist the handicapped through side-hinged doors

Private Door
www.privatedoor.com Offers automatic door openers

Somfy
www.somfysystems.com Largest manufacturer of specialized tubular mo-tors for rolling shutters, retractable awnings, solar screens, shades and blinds, projection screens, and more

Van Duerr Industries
www.vanduerr.com SafePath™ Products' EZ Edge™ Transition Ramp or ElegantTransition™ Ramps remove all vertical-rise barriers at step en-trances and door thresholds; made out of recycled tires

Vista Window Film
www.vista-films.com Manufactures a window film that helps reduce or cut glare

ADDITIONAL RESOURCES

Design Science
www.dscience.com A consulting firm dedicated to one mission: tailoring products to the needs of their users

Healing Landscapes
http://www.healinglandscapes.org/ Therapeutic Landscapes Database

Healing Landscapes
www.healinglandscapes.org Provides links to many other helpful sites

J.L. Mueller, Inc.
www.jlmueller.com A site about universal design

Louis Tenenbaum
www.louistenenbaum.com Louis Tenenbaum is an "independent living strategist" who focuses on developing and implementing strategies and de-signs for successful aging

MIT Age Lab
http://web.mit.edu/agelab/index.shtml Develop new ideas and technology to improve the quality of life for older adults and those who care for them

National Center on Accessibility
www.ncaonline.org Links to accessible products for recreation (playground equipment, fishing, hunting, sailing, and so on)

Savvy Senior
www.savvysenior.org Nationally syndicated newspaper column that channels useful information and resources to seniors and their families; also provides tips and information through a resource book, a weekly radio show, and regular television features

Senior Resource
www.seniorresource.com The "E-cyclopedia" of housing options and information for retirement, finance, insurance, and care

The Enabler Website
www.enabler.nu Provides tools for professional assessments of accessibility problems in the environment

Toolbases Services
www.toolbase.org The homebuilding industry's technical information resource

Transgenerational Design
www.transgenerational.org Discusses the practice of making products and environments compatible with aging

Universal Design Alliance
http://www.universaldesign.org/about.asp Organization founded to create awareness and expand the public's knowledge of universal design, which is design for all ages, sizes, and abilities

Appendix D
Common Diseases and Disabilities

DOES DISEASE AND DISABILITY AFFECT DESIGN?

Disease and disability cripple lives, families, and home life all across the country, often bringing to light the barriers that exist in a residence that, until something in life occurs that brings them out in the spotlight, go unnoticed. Understanding how lives are disrupted as a result of afflictions is an important step in creating designs that support and secure a peaceful home life in the residence.

A *disease* is an abnormal condition of the human body that impairs the bodily functions—more often biological processes that alter the organs in some fashion and prevent them from making their contributions to a healthy body.

A *disability* is generally a condition that impairs or limits one's ability to function in an activity of daily living (ADL) relative to the ADLs of another individual or group. Disabilities come in all types, from physical to mental disorders, and can range from the temporary to the permanent and from the simplest forms such as the need to wear glasses to other chronic and severe forms of disability like arthritis, muscular dystrophy, and dementia.

With an expanding population of seniors living longer, the likelihood that some form of disability will affect people during at least a part of life will expand in significant numbers. In fact, studies show that a 20-year-old worker has a three in ten chance of becoming disabled by the time he or she reaches the traditional age of retirement.[1]

The design professional should have an understanding of the complexities associated with various forms of disabilities—developmental, physical, mental, and acquired—so as to design appropriate solutions to accommodate current and future needs of the client.

COMMON DISABILITIES DEFINED

■ **Alzheimer's Disease**

"Alzheimer's disease (AD) is the most common form of dementia among older people. Dementia is a brain disorder that seriously affects a person's ability to carry out daily activities."[2] It is a progressive, incurable condition that gradually causes the loss of intellectual abilities, such as memory, and causes extreme changes in personality and behaviors.[3] Familial Alzheimer's Disease (FAD) identifies families that have more than one member with AD, usually multiple members. Early-onset Alzheimer's affects people who are under 65, often during their 40s to 50s.[4]

227

■ **Amyotrophic Lateral Sclerosis (ALS)**

Also known as Lou Gehrig's disease, ALS is the degeneration of the motor neurons, the nerve cells that control the movement of voluntary muscles. As the nerve cells die, the muscles are paralyzed.[5]

■ **Arthritis**

Common to 46 million Americans, arthritis is the leading cause of disability in the United States, fully limiting the activities of 19 million adults.[6] It is the inflammation of a joint often accompanied by pain, swelling, and limiting mobility.

■ **Blindness**

Blindness is the degree of loss, the limitations in the fields of vision, or the absence of the ability to perceive visual images and can be caused by disease, genetic defects, abnormalities, or injury.[7]

■ **Cancer**

Cancer develops when cells in a part of the body begin to grow abnormally and replace normal tissues, then frequently travel to other parts of the body, a process called metastasis.[8]

■ **Cerebral Palsy**

Cerebral palsy (CP) is the general term for a group of permanent brain injuries that result in limited motor skills, speech difficulties, and learning disabilities. There are some 750,000 individuals who are afflicted with some form of CP.[9]

■ **Deafness**

Deafness is the partial or complete loss of hearing. Age-related hearing loss affects 30 to 35 percent of those between 65 and 75 and 40 percent of those over 74 years of age.[10]

■ **Depression**

This is a mental health condition in which individuals experience sadness and lack of interest in everyday activities and events and feel a sense of worthlessness.[11]

■ **Epilepsy**

Repeated, often intermittent seizures in the brain caused by random yet powerful electrical impulses are referred to as epilepsy. While there is no known cause in the majority of cases, medications help control seizures.

■ **Essential Tremor**

Essential tremor is a visible tremor of hands and forearms and is the most common movement disorder worldwide, with the prevalence often increasing in persons over 60 years. Essential tremor develops subtly and progresses slowly. Onset peaks both in teenagers and with those in their 50s. The tremors usually start in a single limb but over time will expand to the other side of the body and most often involve wrist movements. Tremors may be amplified with stress, fatigue, and certain medications and may increase with certain voluntary activities such as holding a fork or cup.[12]

■ **Heart Disease**

Heart disease is a number of conditions that affect the heart and blood vessels in the heart, including heart arrhythmias, heart failure, and the most common type, coronary artery disease (CAD), the leading cause of heart attacks.[13]

■ **Huntington's Disease**

Huntington's disease results from the genetically programmed degeneration of brain cells (neurons) in certain areas of the brain. The degeneration causes uncontrolled movements, loss of intellectual faculties, and emotional disturbance. It is passed from parent to child, and each child has a 50/50 chance of getting it. If the child does not get it, they will not pass it on to their children.[14] The average age of onset of Huntington's disease is between 30 and 50 years.[15]

■ **Multiple Sclerosis**

Multiple Sclerosis (MS) is a chronic degenerative disease of the central nervous system that results in the weakness of the muscle systems, loss of coordination and speech, and visual disabilities.[16]

■ **Muscular Dystrophy**

Muscular Dystrophy (MD) is a genetic disorder of the muscles that causes the muscle systems to break down and over time be replaced with fatty deposits resulting in physical weakness.[17]

■ **Parkinson's Disease**

Parkinson's disease (PD) is a disorder of the central nervous system that is characterized by muscle rigidity, tremors, and a slowdown of physical movement. Advanced symptoms can include cognitive dysfunction and speech problems.[18]

■ **Pick's Disease**

Pick's disease is a form of dementia similar to Alzheimer's, characterized by a slowly progressive deterioration of social skills and changes in personality, along with impairment of intellect, memory, and language. Patients typically have atrophy of the frontal and temporal lobes with abnormalities in nerve cells. The cause is unknown. The average age of onset is 54.[19]

■ **Spinal Cord Injury (SCI)**

Trauma or damage to the spinal cord can result in a loss or partial impairment of mobility and can result in debilitating pain, paralysis, and sensory/touch disabilities.[20]

■ **Stroke**

A stroke occurs when a blood vessel bursts in the brain or is clogged by a mass that causes nerve cells in the brain to die within minutes without vital oxygen and nutrients delivered from the blood stream.[21]

References

1. U.S. Social Security Administration, *Disability Benefits, SSA Publication # 05-10029* (2006).
2. National Institute on Aging, *Alzheimer's Disease*, "Medline Plus," http://www.nlm.nih.gov/medlineplus/alzheimersdisease.html (last reviewed July 6, 2007).

3. Alzheimer's Association, www.alz.org/living_with_alzheimers_4521.asp (accessed October 14, 2007).

4. Alzheimer's Association, *Early-onset Alzheimer's: I'm too young to have Alzheimer's disease*, http://www.alz.org/national/documents/brochure_earlyonset.pdf, 2005.

5. Amyotrophic Lateral Sclerosis Association www.alsa.org/als/what.cfm?CFID 54843392&CFTOKEN522191651 (accessed October 14, 2007).

6. The Arthritis Foundation, www.arthritis.org/research.php (accessed October 14, 2007).

7. Foundation Fighting Blindness, www.blindness.org/content.asp?id=9 (accessed October 14, 2007).

8. American Cancer Society, www.cancer.org/docroot/home/index.asp (accessed October 14, 2007).

9. United Cerebral Palsy, www.ucp.org/ucp_channelsub.cfm/1/16/10527 (accessed October 14, 2007).

10. National Association of the Deaf, www.nad.org/site/pp.asp?c5foINKQMBF&b 591587 (accessed October 14, 2007).

11. Depression and Bipolar Support Alliance, www.ndmda.org (accessed October 14, 2007).

12. Smaga, Sharon, M.D., Southern Illinois University School of Medicine, Carbondale, Illinois, *Tremor*, "American Family Physician," American Academy of Family Physicians, October 15, 2003.

13. American Heart Association, www.americanheart.org/presenter.jhtml?identifier =1200002 (accessed October 14, 2007).

14. National Institute of Neurological Disorders and Stroke, *NINDS Huntington's Disease Information Page*, http://www.ninds.nih.gov/disorders/huntington/huntington.htm (accessed March 1, 2007).

15. Huntington's Outreach Project for Education at Stanford, *The Inheritance of HD*, http://www.stanford.edu/group/hopes/causes/inherit/c7.html (accessed March 1, 2007).

16. Multiple Sclerosis Association of America, www.msassociation.org/about_multiple_ sclerosis/whatisms/ (accessed October 14, 2007).

17. Muscular Dystrophy Association, www.mdausa.org/research/ (accessed October 14, 2007).

18. American Parkinson Disease Association, www.apdaparkinson.org/user/AboutParkinson. asp (accessed October 14, 2007).

19. National Institute of Health, *Pick's Disease*, "Medline Plus Medical Dictionary," http://www.nlm.nih.gov/medlineplus/ency/article/000744.htm (accessed October 1, 2007).

20. National Spinal Cord Injury Association, www.spinalcord.org/html/injury.php (accessed October 14, 2007).

21. American Stroke Association, www.strokeassociation.org/presenter.jhtml?identifier =3030066 (accessed October 14, 2007).

Index